Financial Innovation and Technology

Series Editor

The book series 'Financial Innovation and Technology' features scholarly research on the latest developments in the world of finance such as AI, FinTech startups, Big Data, Cryptocurrencies, Robo-Advisors, Machine Learning, and Blockchain applications among others. The book series explores the main trends and technologies that will transform the finance industry in the years to come. The series presents essential insights into the financial technology revolution, and the disruption, innovation, and opportunity it entails. The books in this series will be of value to both academics and those working in the finance industry.

Sami Basly
Editor

Decentralized Finance

The Impact of Blockchain-Based Financial Innovations on Entrepreneurship

Springer

Editor
Sami Basly
University of Paris Nanterre
Nanterre, France

ISSN 2730-9681 ISSN 2730-969X (electronic)
Financial Innovation and Technology
ISBN 978-3-031-49514-4 ISBN 978-3-031-49515-1 (eBook)
https://doi.org/10.1007/978-3-031-49515-1

This Springer imprint is published by the registered company Springer Nature Switzerland AG
The registered company address is: Gewerbestrasse 11, 6330 Cham, Switzerland

Paper in this product is recyclable

Reviewers

Khoula Al Harthy, Acting Asst. HoD,
Middle East College, Sultanate of Oman

Jitesh Aggarwal, Blockchain and ML Engineer
Block Convey, USA

Emmanuel Ajike, Associate Professor
Babcock University, Nijeria

Stefano de Nichilo, Lecturer
University of Cagliari, Italy

Elisa Facciotti, Finance Expert
e-Campus University, Italy

Samet Gunay, Associate Professor of Finance
Corvinus University, Hungary

Vijaya Hake, Associate Professor
Vishwakarma University, India

Abubakar Jamilu Baita, PhD Scholar
Universitas Islam Internasional, Indonesia

Shadrek Matindike, Post-doctoral Fellow
Nelson Mandela University, South Africa

Samuel Musungwini, Lecturer
Midlands State University, Zimbabwe

Nishant Sapra, Research Scholar
MDI Gurgaon, India

G.V. Satya Sekhar, Associate Professor
GITAM, India.

Acknowledgements

The making of this book was a collaborative effort, and I owe a debt of gratitude to many. I'm deeply appreciative of the contributors for their expertise, commitment, and enthusiasm. I extend my thanks to the reviewers whose insights were indispensable to this project.

Special thanks to Springer's editor, Rocio Torregrosa, as well as to Poongothai Chockalingam and Sneha Arunagiri for their consistent backing and significant feedback during the book's preparation and writing.

Lastly, I cannot express enough gratitude to my family for their understanding and kindness.

Contents

Editor and Contributors

About the Editor

Sami Basly holds a Ph.D. in Management Sciences (University of Bordeaux) and is authorized to supervise Doctoral research (University Paris Nanterre). Before joining the University Paris Nanterre, he was a lecturer at the University of Bordeaux. He is interested in family businesses, digital entrepreneurship, and digital technologies. He has conducted research on family businesses, internationalization, and digital transformation and has published his research in many national and international journals (Management International, Review of Entrepreneurship, Journal of Entrepreneurship, etc.).

Contributors

Khoula Al Harthy Middle East College, Seeb, Oman

A. Agarwal Middle East College, Seeb, Oman

J. Aggarwal Vellore Institute of Technology, Vellore, India

A. J. Baita Faculty of Economics and Business, Universitas Islam Internasional Indonesia, Depok, Indonesia

Department of Economics, Yusuf Maitama Sule University Kano, Kano, Nigeria

S. Basly University of Paris Nanterre, Paris, France

S. Behdad Environmental Engineering Sciences, University of Florida, Gainesville, FL, USA

V. Dzenopoljac Zayed University, College of Interdisciplinary Studies, Dubai, UAE

B. Esmaeilian Andrew F. Brimmer College of Business and Information Sciences, Tuskegee University, Tuskegee, AL, USA

E. Facciotti e-Campus University, Novedrate (Como), Italy

D. Federico e-Campus University, Novedrate (Como), Italy

S. Gunay College of Business Administration, American University of the Middle East, Egaila, Kuwait

S. Muhammed College of Business Administration, American University of the Middle East, Egaila, Kuwait

D. Kirimhan Department of Economics and Finance, University of Texas at El Paso, Woody L. Hunt College of Business, El Paso, TX, USA

S. Lukito Faculty of Economics and Business, Indonesia International Islamic University, Depok, Indonesia

A. Notte e-Campus University, Novedrate (Como), Italy

P. -L. Saunier University of Paris Nanterre, Paris, France

Abbreviations

$ISLM	Islamic Coins
ADF-GLS	Augmented Dickey-Fuller Generalized Least Squares
AML	Anti-Money Laundering
AMMs	Automated market makers
ATM	Automated Teller Machine
BTC	Bitcoin
CBDC	Central Bank Digital Currency
CeFi	Centralized Finance
Cex	Centralized Exchange
DAO	Decentralized Autonomous Organization
DeFi	Decentralized Finance
Dex	Decentralized exchange
DLT MTF	Multilateral trading facility DLT
DLT SS	Settlement system DLT
DLT TSS	Trading and settlement system DLT
DLT	Distributed Ledger Technology
DORA	Digital Operational Resilience
DoS	Denial of Service
DRs	Delivery robots
DVC	Decentralized Venture Capital
EC	European Community
EHMIs	External Human–Machine Interfaces
EMIR	European Market Infrastructure Regulation
ERC	Ethereum request for comment
ERC-20	Ethereum Request of Comment
ESG	Environmental Social and Governance
ESMA	European Securities and Markets Authority
ETH	Ethereum
EU	European Union
EVM	Ethereum Virtual Machine
FinSer	Financial Services

FinTech	Financial Technology
GDP	Gross Domestic Product
GFEVD	Generalized Forecast Error Variance Decomposition
HNWIs	High Net Worth Individuals
HRI	Human–Robot Interaction
ICO	Initial Coin Offering
ICT	Information and Communication Technology
IT	Information Technology
ID	Identity Document
IFRS	International Financial Reporting Standards
IMF	International Monetary Funds
Insur	Insurance Sector
InvSer	Investment Services
JB	Jarque-Bera
KYC	Know Your Customer
LTC	Litecoin
MiCA	Markets in Crypto Assets Regulation
MiFID	Markets in Financial Instruments Directive
MSME	Micro Small and Medium Enterprises
MTF	Multilateral Trading Facility
NFT	Non-Fungible Token
NRZ	National Railways of Zimbabwe
P2P	Peer-to-Peer
QVAR	Quantile Vector Autoregression
RPA	Robotic Process Automation
SDGs	Sustainable Development Goals
SME	Small and Medium Enterprise
SSA	Sub-Saharan Africa
Std. Dev.	Standard Deviation
TAM	Technology Adoption Model
TVL	Total Value Locked
TradFi	Traditional Finance
USD	United States dollar
USDC	US Dollar Coin
USDT	US Dollar Tether
VC	Venture Capital
ZISCO	Zimbabwe Iron and Steel Company

Introduction: Blockchain, Decentralized Finance, and Entrepreneurship

Sami Basly

The internet has made it possible for individuals to connect, communicate, and transact without the need for intermediaries. Similarly, blockchain technology has the potential to revolutionize how we live our lives by removing unnecessary middlemen from transactions and making information more accessible for all to see. A blockchain is essentially a digital ledger of transactions, agreements, contracts, and records. This ledger can be distributed across many different computers, with no centralized record of who owns what. This technology offers a new way to trade and transact online and has the potential to disrupt many industries and create a lot of opportunities for entrepreneurs. Blockchains also help improve the business operations by providing a reliable, secure, and decentralized way of building trust between parties. Blockchain technology also introduces the idea of smart contracts, which are computer protocols intended to digitally facilitate, verify, or enforce the negotiation or performance of a contract. These are agreements which are written in computer code as opposed to legal prose, which are then automatically executed by a computing system without any human intervention (Buterin, 2014).

Blockchain emerged as the backbone of Bitcoin, but it has now evolved beyond digital currencies and is changing the way firms and entrepreneurs do business (Hughes et al., 2019). Blockchain technology is particularly changing the finance industry (Harvey et al., 2020). Banks and other financial institutions are adopting this disruptive technology to improve their services. This new technology has the potential to change the world of finance as we know it, making it more transparent and efficient. Through decentralization and increased transparency, blockchains allow for creating peer-to-peer lending platforms, which enable borrowers and lenders to interact directly without the need for third parties like banks. In the world of insurance, blockchains may offer greater transparency and security. Through smart

S. Basly (✉)
University of Paris Nanterre, Paris, France
e-mail: sbasly@parisnanterre.fr

S. Basly (ed.), *Decentralized Finance*, Financial Innovation and Technology,
https://doi.org/10.1007/978-3-031-49515-1_1

contracts, they have the potential to change the way that insurance professionals work by allowing them to transact in a faster and more secure manner which will result in an increase of trust from customers.

These are just a few examples of the financial innovations that make up what is now referred to as decentralized finance (DeFi). DeFi is a system for exchanging value without centralized intermediaries. It relies heavily on peer-to-peer lending and borrowing, decentralized exchanges (DEX), and trustless systems (Harvey et al., 2020; Schär, 2021). DeFi is seen as a disruptive technology that could replace traditional banking systems in the future due to its advantages of being inclusive, non-discriminatory, resilient to risk management failures, cost-effective for lenders and borrowers to access the system, and more efficient in terms of financial intermediation through automated trustless systems (Larios-Hernández, 2017; Ahluwalia et al., 2020; Harvey et al., 2020; Schär, 2021).

Blockchain and decentralized finance are not just about the future, but they are now providing a revolutionary addition to the world of finance. With these emerging technologies, financial markets will become more efficient and secure. Beyond finance, these technologies are transforming many different industries (Frizzo-Barker et al., 2020) such as healthcare (Hölbl et al., 2018), insurance (Kar & Navin, 2021), supply chains (Queiroz et al., 2020), or the music industry (Chalmers et al., 2019). These technologies create new ecosystems for business growth, as well as new opportunities for collaboration between organizations. They are also enabling entrepreneurs to explore new business model opportunities in various industries (Morkunas et al., 2019). Blockchain technology can reduce transaction costs, generate distributed trust, and empower decentralized platforms, potentially becoming a new foundation for decentralized business models (Chen & Bellavitis, 2020). Through tokenization, blockchain technology has also sparked a new wave of innovation, which started to revolutionize entrepreneurship and innovation (Chen, 2018). Importantly, the opportunities provided by DeFi in terms of lower costs, almost-immediate transactions, and global reach play a crucial role for entrepreneurs in developing their businesses. This is because DeFi has the potential to drastically change the financing and investment processes for entrepreneurship and innovation.

This book aims at providing a comprehensive overview of the rapidly expanding field of DeFi and showing how entrepreneurs can leverage it in their entrepreneurial ventures and business activities. Overall, DeFi offers entrepreneurs new opportunities for innovation, funding, global reach, financial inclusion, and experimentation. It empowers them to create and scale businesses in a decentralized financial landscape, showcasing the potential of decentralization as a foundation for new business models.

DeFi aims to democratize finance by replacing legacy, centralized institutions with peer-to-peer relationships that can provide a full spectrum of financial services, from everyday banking, loans, and mortgages to complicated contractual relationships and asset trading. It eliminates intermediaries by allowing people, merchants, and businesses to conduct financial transactions through the emerging technology of blockchains. In a DeFi system, users have direct control over their assets and can participate in financial activities such as lending, borrowing, and trading without the need for a centralized authority. Four key characteristics of DeFi are commonly highlighted (Chen, 2018; Chen & Bellavitis, 2020; Harvey et al., 2020):

- Decentralization: DeFi systems are decentralized, meaning they operate on a blockchain network that is not controlled by a single entity.
- Transparency: Transactions on a DeFi network are transparent and publicly visible on the blockchain.
- Openness: DeFi networks are open to anyone with an internet connection, and users can participate in financial activities without the need for a bank account or credit check.
- Interoperability: Different DeFi applications can work together and share data, allowing for more complex financial activities.

DeFi is a growing field that has gained increasing popularity in the financial world. It has managed billions of dollars in assets, with a total value locked (TVL) exceeding 100 billion USD (Santos et al., 2022). According to DeFi Pulse, a website that tracks the total value locked (TVL) in DeFi protocols, the TVL in DeFi was $38 billion as of August 18, 2023. The DeFi ecosystem is rapidly evolving, and new applications and use cases continue to emerge as the technology matures. However, the main applications of decentralized finance (DeFi) are:

1. Decentralized lending and borrowing: DeFi platforms enable individuals and businesses to lend and borrow funds directly from other users without the need for traditional intermediaries. Examples of DeFi lending platforms include Aave, Compound, and MakerDAO.
2. Decentralized exchanges: DeFi has revolutionized the concept of exchanges by introducing decentralized exchanges (DEXs) that allow users to trade cryptocurrencies directly from their wallets without the need for a centralized exchange. Examples of DEXs are Uniswap, SushiSwap, and PancakeSwap.
3. Stablecoins: Stablecoins are cryptocurrencies designed to maintain a stable value by pegging them to a reserve asset, such as a fiat currency or a basket of assets. Stablecoins provide stability and can be used for various DeFi applications, including lending, trading, and remittances. Examples include Tether (USDT), USD Coin (USDC), and Dai.
4. Decentralized asset management: DeFi platforms offer decentralized asset management solutions, allowing users to manage and invest their digital assets. These platforms provide features such as yield farming, liquidity mining, and automated portfolio management. Yearn Finance, Balancer, and Curve Finance are examples of these platforms.
5. Decentralized insurance: DeFi has also introduced decentralized insurance platforms that leverage smart contracts to provide coverage against risks. These platforms enable users to purchase insurance policies and receive payouts automatically based on predefined conditions. Examples include Nexus Mutual and Cover Protocol.

6. Decentralized prediction markets: DeFi has facilitated the development of decentralized prediction markets, where users can bet on the outcome of future events. These markets provide a decentralized and transparent way to speculate on various outcomes, such as election results or sports events. Examples include Augur and Gnosis.
7. Decentralized identity and reputation: DeFi applications are exploring decentralized identity solutions that allow users to maintain control over their personal data and establish reputation scores. These identity systems can be used for various purposes, including accessing financial services and participating in decentralized governance. Examples include uPort and Sovryn.

Traditional financial systems, with banks and financial institutions at their core, operate in centralized models. These entities act as intermediaries between consumers and financial services, ensuring trust and legitimacy in transactions. While these systems have facilitated economies globally for centuries, they also carry limitations such as exclusivity, limited accessibility, and sometimes opaque fee structures. DeFi's value proposition lies in its elimination of intermediaries and its promise to provide open financial systems to anyone with an internet connection. Indeed, traditional finance involves intermediaries such as banks, brokerages, and exchanges, which act as middlemen in financial transactions. DeFi, on the other hand, eliminates intermediaries by using blockchain technology and smart contracts to automate transactions and remove the need for trusted third parties (Chen, 2018; Harvey et al., 2020). Therefore, while traditional financial services rely on trust in centralized institutions, DeFi applications leverage the security and trustlessness of blockchain technology, where transactions are verified and executed through a consensus mechanism. This reduces the reliance on trust in centralized entities (Hughes et al., 2019; Harvey et al., 2020). Correspondingly, intermediation implies a control power vested in the intermediary. In traditional finance, users have to trust third parties such as banks with their money and personal information. Particularly, banks have control over who can open an account, how money can be spent, and when access to money is granted. In contrast, DeFi gives full control to the users over their funds and information. Users also interact with smart contracts directly, reducing the need to share personal information.

DeFi and traditional financial differ also regarding access and inclusion. Traditional financial institutions can restrict access based on geographical location, credit history, and wealth. Today, more than 1.7 billion adults worldwide are unbanked, without an account at a financial institution or through a mobile money provider (Demirgüç-Kunt et al., 2018). DeFi can bridge this gap, offering financial services to those excluded from the traditional system, with just a smartphone and internet connectivity (Larios-Hernández, 2017). It allows individuals from around the world to participate in financial activities without the need for a traditional bank account (Chen & Bellavitis, 2019a, 2019b). DeFi transactions are processed on public blockchains, primarily Ethereum, which enables faster, and more efficient transactions compared to traditional finance. Traditional finance often involves manual processes, paperwork, and delays, whereas DeFi transactions can be settled quickly and automatically through smart contracts. DeFi transactions are also transparent and visible to all participants on the blockchain, as everyone involved can see the full set of transactions, providing a level of transparency that is not typically found in traditional finance. This transparency can help build trust and reduce the risk of fraud. Finally, while traditional finance is heavily regulated, providing consumer protection but also limiting innovation and inclusion, DeFi currently operates in a regulatory grey area, allowing for rapid innovation but also posing risks due to the lack of regulatory oversight. In short, traditional finance offers stability, regulatory protection, and familiarity, while DeFi provides innovation, accessibility, and control.

DeFi is a rapidly evolving field that encourages innovation and experimentation. The open-source nature of DeFi allows developers to build and iterate on existing protocols, leading to the creation of new financial services and business models (Chen, 2018; Chen & Bellavitis, 2020; Chalmers et al., 2019; Schueffel, 2021). For example, beyond basic financial services, DeFi platforms offer innovative mechanisms like liquidity mining and yield farming. These processes allow users to provide liquidity or participate in platform-specific activities to earn rewards, thereby giving users more avenues for financial growth. DeFi provides entrepreneurs with the ability to develop and offer decentralized financial services that are more innovative, interoperable, borderless, and transparent compared to traditional finance (Chen & Bellavitis, 2019a, 2019b). This opens up avenues for them to create new types of financial products and services that cater to specific market needs. Further, DeFi allows for permissionless innovation, meaning that entrepreneurs can build and deploy financial applications on the blockchain without seeking approval from centralized authorities (Chen & Bellavitis, 2019a, 2019b; Chen & Bellavitis, 2020). Permissionless innovation lowers the barriers to entry for entrepreneurs, fostering a more inclusive and competitive environment. DeFi platforms also offer alternative funding sources for entrepreneurs, as decentralized lending platforms and crowdfunding mechanisms enable entrepreneurs to borrow funds or raise capital without relying solely on traditional funding channels (Lingelbach, 2022). Importantly, DeFi applications are accessible to anyone with an internet connection, allowing entrepreneurs to tap into a global user base and expand their business beyond geographical boundaries (Chen & Bellavitis, 2020; Schueffel, 2021). This global reach opens up opportunities for entrepreneurs to reach a larger audience and scale their businesses. Furthermore, as DeFi has the potential to broaden financial inclusion by providing access to financial services to individuals who are unbanked or underbanked (Chen & Bellavitis, 2019a, 2019b; European Commission, 2022), entrepreneurs can develop DeFi applications that cater to underserved populations, enabling them to participate in the global financial system. Last but not least, DeFi encourages innovation and experimentation by providing a fertile ground for entrepreneurs to explore new business models and revenue streams within the decentralized ecosystem (Chen & Bellavitis, 2020, as entrepreneurs can leverage the programmability and interoperability of DeFi protocols to create unique and innovative solutions.

For the past few years, the scholarly community has been increasingly focusing on the topic of DeFi since it presents a radically different approach to traditional finance bypassing centralized institutions and intermediaries and offering peer-to-peer financial systems. There is a growing interest in studying and understanding the various aspects of decentralized finance within academic research, as DeFi is a significant departure from traditional centralized banking and finance structures, making it a fascinating area of study. DeFi protocols are largely governed by algorithms and smart contracts, often involving intricate economic mechanisms and incentives. This opens up avenues for research in game theory, finance, and behavioral economics. The rise of DeFi also raises questions about societal power structures, wealth distribution, and the role of traditional institutions. These are of interest to sociologists, anthropologists, and political scientists. A number of academic debates about decentralized finance (DeFi) are ongoing and cover a range of topics:

1. Decentralization vs. centralization: One of the key debates in DeFi is whether it can truly be decentralized or if it will inevitably become centralized over time. Some argue that DeFi protocols are still reliant on centralized entities, such as exchanges and liquidity providers, and that true decentralization may not be possible (Sun et al., 2022).
2. Regulatory challenges: DeFi operates in a largely unregulated space, which can pose challenges for both users and developers. There is ongoing debate about how DeFi should be regulated, and whether existing regulations are sufficient to address the unique challenges posed by DeFi (Alamsyah & Syahrir, 2023).
3. Risk management: DeFi protocols are still relatively new and untested, and there are concerns about the potential risks associated with using them. Some argue that DeFi protocols are inherently risky due to their decentralized nature, while others believe that proper risk management strategies can mitigate these risks (Santos et al., 2022).
4. Interoperability: DeFi protocols are often siloed, meaning that they operate independently of one another. Current research is focusing on enhancing the interoperability among various DeFi protocols, a development that could facilitate more complex financial transaction activities (Alamsyah & Syahrir, 2023).
5. Role of intermediaries: While DeFi aims to eliminate intermediaries, some argue that intermediaries may still have a role to play in the DeFi ecosystem. For example, intermediaries could provide liquidity or help manage risk (Grassi et al., 2022).

These debates highlight the complex and evolving nature of the DeFi ecosystem, and the challenges that must be addressed as it continues to grow and mature.

This edited volume seeks to enrich both theoretical and empirical discussions by providing detailed insights into these matters. In Jitesh Aggarwal's chapter, the author paper elaborates on methods for funding entrepreneurial ventures through decentralized blockchain networks. The chapter explores the practice of asset tokenization into NFTs (non-fungible tokens) for these ventures and discusses how these NFTs can be traded on decentralized exchanges in return for cryptocurrencies like stablecoins.

The chapter by Samet Gunay, Shahnawaz Muhammed, Destan Kirimhan, and Vladimir Dzenopoljac investigates the relationship between traditional finance

(TradFi) and DeFi. Drawing evidence from four sectors—banking, financial services, investment services, and insurance—they aim to determine the depth of this connection. Their findings highlight significant net spillovers from the traditional finance sectors to the DeFi index, particularly noticeable in extreme quantiles, implying higher connectivity during volatile times. They attribute this to DeFi's early stages and advise both investors and entrepreneurs to keep an eye on traditional market trends.

In the context of Zimbabwe, Samuel Musungwini and Samuel Simbarashe Furusa propose a decentralized finance model to enhance financial inclusion for financially excluded marginalized communities. Their research includes a thorough literature review and a case study in Zimbabwe consisting of 10 in-depth interviews and a 12-member focus group. The chapter presents a comprehensive six-point framework for adopting decentralized finance in developing countries.

Abubakar Jamilu Baita and Shellvy Lukito's chapter examines sharia-compliant digital coins, specifically focusing on the Islamic Coin from the Haqq Blockchain. Through an analysis of primary and secondary data, they detail its origin, community-building endeavors, and its funding approach to bolster entrepreneurs. They underscore the ethical screening differentiating Islamic Coin from conventional cryptocurrencies and call for broader awareness campaigns about digital currency's potential in facilitating payments and entrepreneurship.

In their contribution, Sami Basly and Paul-Laurent Saunier present the preliminary results of an exploratory research study examining the receptivity of French accounting and auditing professionals to blockchain technology. While the study confirms initial conjectures regarding the technology's emergent status and the attendant lack of familiarity among some professionals in these fields, it also reveals a significant level of interest within the professional community toward blockchain technology. Despite barriers to its widespread deployment and its yet limited penetration in France's accounting sector, professionals exhibit a prevailing sense of optimism about the technology's future applicability in their disciplines.

Elisa Facciotti, Domenica Federico, and Antonella Notte's chapter reviews the development of alternative financial markets like multilateral trading facilities (MTFs). They discuss their functionality, their synergy with distributed ledger technology, and emphasize the Pilot Regime introduced by the European Commission's "Digital Finance Strategy". The study illustrates the opportunities digital technologies present for economic agents, especially concerning fundraising through DLT MTFs.

The aim of the study carried out by Behzad Esmaeilian and Sara Behdad is to examine the potential of integrating blockchain technology with last-mile delivery robots to elevate operational effectiveness and tailor services to individual needs. After presenting the results of a survey made to glean insights into marketing tactics and supplementary services that could augment the adoption of delivery robots, the authors explain how a blockchain-enabled robotic platform could expedite the realization of these ascertained marketing initiatives.

Khoula Al Harthy and Aparna Agarwal address DeFi's cybersecurity vulnerabilities. They elaborate on both the technical and non-technical risks and their implications for entrepreneurship. Highlighting concerns like fraud prevention and data privacy, they discuss the increased encryption measures undertaken to secure DeFi data. The chapter contends that despite its advantages, DeFi has its share of risks akin to traditional financial services.

The aim of final chapter contributed by Sami Basly is to delve into the prospective uses of Artificial Intelligence (AI) in decentralized finance, illustrating how this technology could help DeFi attain its desired goals of speed, operational efficiency, and inclusivity. According to the author, AI can bring about paradigm shifts in multiple facets of DeFi, from augmenting efficiency and security to enhancing risk evaluation and user engagement. Nevertheless, the successful combination of AI into DeFi requires meticulous planning, rigorous testing, and ongoing surveillance to ensure its efficacy, reliability, and conformity to legal standards.

The editor and the contributing authors hope that these insights will enrich readers, be they scholars, professionals, or policymakers, keen on deepening their understanding of decentralized finance and entrepreneurship.

References

Ahluwalia, S., Mahto, R. V., & Guerrero, M. (2020). Blockchain technology and startup financing: A transaction cost economics perspective. *Technological Forecasting and Social Change, 151*(January), 119854. https://doi.org/10.1016/j.techfore.2019.119854

Alamsyah, A., & Syahrir, S. (2023). The taxonomy of Blockchain-based Technology in the Financial Industry. *F1000Research, 12*, 457.

Chalmers, D., Matthews, R., & Hyslop, A. (2019). Blockchain as an external enabler of new venture ideas: Digital entrepreneurs and the disintermediation of the global music industry. *Journal of Business Research, 125*, 577. https://doi.org/10.1016/j.jbusres.2019.09.002

Buterin, V. (2014). A next-generation smart contract and decentralized application platform. *White Paper, 3*(37), 2–1.

Chen, Y. (2018). Blockchain tokens and the potential democratization of entrepreneurship and innovation. *Business Horizons, 61*(4), 567–575. https://doi.org/10.1016/j.bushor.2018.03.006

Chen, Y., & Bellavitis, C. (2019a). *Decentralized finance: Blockchain technology and the quest for an open financial system*. Stevens Institute of Technology–School of Business Research Paper Series.

Chen, Y., & Bellavitis, C. (2019b). *Blockchain disruption and decentralized finance: The rise of decentralized business models*. Stevens Institute of Technology–School of Business Research Paper Series.

Chen, Y., & Bellavitis, C. (2020). Blockchain disruption and decentralized finance: The rise of decentralized business models. *Journal of Business Venturing Insights, 13*(October 2019), e00151. https://doi.org/10.1016/j.jbvi.2019.e00151

Demirgüç-Kunt, A., Klapper, L., Singer, D., Ansar, S., & Hess, J. (2018). Opportunities for expanding financial inclusion through digital technology.

European Commission. (2022). *Directorate-general for financial stability, financial services and capital markets union, decentralized finance: Information frictions and public policies: Approaching the regulation and supervision of decentralized finance*. Publications Office of the European Union. https://data.europa.eu/doi/10.2874/444494

Frizzo-Barker, J., Chow-White, P. A., Adams, P. R., Mentanko, J., Ha, D., & Green, S. (2020). Blockchain as a disruptive technology for business: A systematic review. *International Journal of Information Management, 51*, 102029.

Grassi, L., Lanfranchi, D., Faes, A., & Renga, F. (2022). Do we still need financial intermediation? The case of decentralized finance–DeFi. *Qualitative Research in Accounting & Management., 19*(3), 323–347.

Harvey, C. R., Ramachandran, A., & Santoro, J. (2020). DeFi and the future of finance. *SSRN Electronic Journal.* https://doi.org/10.2139/ssrn.3711777

Hölbl, M., Kompara, M., Kamišalić, A., & Nemec, Z. L. (2018). A systematic review of the use of Blockchain in healthcare. *Symmetry, 10*(10), 470. https://doi.org/10.3390/sym10100470

Hughes, A., Park, A., Kietzmann, J., & Archer-Brown, C. (2019). Beyond bitcoin: What blockchain and distributed ledger technologies mean for firms. *Business Horizons, 62*(3), 273–281. https://doi.org/10.1016/j.bushor.2019.01.002

Kar, A. K., & Navin, L. (2021). Diffusion of blockchain in insurance industry : An analysis through the review of academic and trade literature. *Telematics and Informatics, 58*, 101532. https://doi.org/10.1016/j.tele.2020.101532

Larios-Hernández, G. J. (2017). Blockchain entrepreneurship opportunity in the practices of the unbanked. *Business Horizons, 60*(6), 865–874. https://doi.org/10.1016/j.bushor.2017.07.012

Lingelbach, D. C. (2022). *De Gruyter handbook of entrepreneurial finance*. De Gruyter handbook of entrepreneurial finance.

Morkunas, V. J., Paschen, J., & Boon, E. (2019). How blockchain technologies impact your business model. *Business Horizons, 62*(3), 295–306. https://doi.org/10.1016/j.bushor.2019.01.009

Queiroz, M. M., Telles, R., & Bonilla, S. H. (2020). Blockchain and supply chain management integration: A systematic review of the literature. *Supply Chain Management, 25*(2), 241–254. https://doi.org/10.1108/SCM-03-2018-0143

Santos, S. D., Singh, J., Thulasiram, R. K., Kamali, S., Sirico, L. A., & Loud, L. (2022). A new era of Blockchain-powered decentralized finance (DeFi)–a review. In *2022 IEEE 46th Annual Computers, Software, and Applications Conference (COMPSAC)* (pp. 1286–1292).

Schär, F. (2021). Decentralized finance: On blockchain-and smart contract-based financial markets. *Federal Reserve Bank of St. Louis Review, 103*(2), 153–174. https://doi.org/10.20955/r.103.153-74

Schueffel, P. (2021). DeFi: Decentralized finance-an introduction and overview. *Journal of Innovation Management, 9*(3), I-XI.

Sun, X., Stasinakis, C., & Sermpinis, G. (2022). Decentralization illusion in decentralized finance: Evidence from tokenized voting in MakerDAO polls. *arXiv preprint arXiv:2203.16612.*

Sami Basly holds a Ph.D. in Management Sciences (University of Bordeaux) and is authorized to supervise Doctoral research (University Paris Nanterre). Before joining the University Paris Nanterre, he was a lecturer at the University of Bordeaux. He is interested in family businesses, digital entrepreneurship, and digital technologies. He has conducted research on family businesses, internationalization, and digital transformation, and has published his findings in many national and international journals (Management International, Review of Entrepreneurship, Journal of Entrepreneurship, etc.).

DeFi and Investing in Entrepreneurial Ventures

Jitesh Aggarwal

1 Introduction

In today's digital era, trust is scarce within the realm of the internet, and the concentration of power in centralized organizations has resulted in their dominance over the market. However, blockchain technology has emerged as a solution to restore trust by embracing decentralization.

The concept of blockchain was initially introduced by Satoshi Nakamoto in his seminal white paper. It outlined a distributed and open network that incorporates an immutable and transparent ledger in this network known as blockchain nodes that are interconnected and receive updates. Whenever a valid change occurs at any specific node, each transaction within the blockchain is encrypted using advanced techniques, and the ledger maintains that unalterable record nodes can add new valid blocks to the ledger, but they cannot modify or delete any past transactions stored within it.

1.1 Blockchain Mining in a Nutshell

After the completion of a transaction, it is appended to the mempool where all resting and ready-to-mine transactions reside. Miners are the individuals who add these transactions from the mempool to the block because these miners must provide proof of work consensus or answer a mathematical issue (Zheng et al., 2017). The valid nonce number is initially determined by miners who then share the resulting

J. Aggarwal (✉)
Vellore Institute of Technology, Vellore, Tamil Nadu, India
e-mail: jitesh.aggarwal2020@vitstudent.ac.in

S. Basly (ed.), *Decentralized Finance*, Financial Innovation and Technology,
https://doi.org/10.1007/978-3-031-49515-1_2

block with other nodes for verification. Following verification, this block is added to each node blockchain and updated in the ledger.

1.2 Distributed Peer-to-Peer Network

Whenever a valid node in the network mines a block of transactions adjacent nodes have to verify this recently mined block and upon successful verification add this block to the chain but in the case of tampering with logs by an attacker, this peer-to-peer network runs a general round of verification at every specific time to check whether all nodes have the same chain or not in the case of any tampering where a particular node gets corrupted the chain of the node is deleted and exchanged with a copy of the verified chain from another node (Bachmann et al., 2011).

To establish a DeFi system utilizing a secure distributed peer-to-peer blockchain network, it becomes essential to introduce a cryptographic token that enables transactions involving venture assets such as shares and equity. Additionally, the implementation of this token as an NFT is required to establish ownership of specific assets. However, despite the necessity of NFTs for proving ownership, their nonfungible nature prevents their use in actual transactions (Vujičić et al., 2018).

2 Decentralized Finance

DeFi has emerged as a groundbreaking movement that utilizes blockchain to revolutionize conventional financial systems, granting individuals greater control over their assets such as money and property. It offers an inclusive, transparent, and permissionless alternative to centralized finance, which is governed by governments and banks.

Unlike centralized financial institutions that exert control over invested funds through taxes and fees, DeFi operates on the principles of community-trusted and monitored codes known as intelligent contracts by leveraging cryptography blockchain technology and smart contracts DeFi ensures user anonymity and protection while also enabling secure transactions blockchain technology decentralizes finance among a network of trusted nodes on a specific chain.An essential aspect of DeFi is its commitment to financial inclusivity. Anyone with an internet connection and a compatible digital wallet can participate in the DeFi ecosystem. This inclusivity allows individuals worldwide, including the unbanked and underbanked populations, to access a wide range of financial services without relying on traditional banks or intermediaries. DeFi applications provide functionalities similar to traditional financial services, such as decentralized exchanges for peer-to-peer trading of digital assets, lending and borrowing platforms that facilitate loans without traditional lenders, stablecoins that offer price stability and represent fiat currencies and yield farming protocols that enable individuals to earn passive income by providing liquidity to DeFi platforms (Chohan, 2021).

Transparency is a fundamental characteristic of DeFi. All transactions and operations within the DeFi ecosystem are recorded on the blockchain, creating an immutable and auditable ledger of financial activities. This transparency allows users to verify and audit the system's integrity, ensuring that transactions are executed as intended without manipulation or fraudulent behavior. Additionally, DeFi emphasizes user control and ownership of assets. Unlike traditional financial systems that require individuals to trust centralized intermediaries, DeFi allows users to retain control of their assets through digital wallets and private keys. This reduces the risk of censorship, confiscation, or misappropriation of funds by third parties. However, it is important to note that DeFi is still in its early stages and faces challenges such as scalability limitations, regulatory considerations, and the risk of vulnerabilities in smart contracts. As the DeFi ecosystem continues to evolve, participants should exercise caution, conduct due diligence, and assess the risks associated with different DeFi platforms and protocols.

Despite these challenges, DeFi has immense potential to reshape the financial landscape. By eliminating intermediaries, lowering barriers to entry, and creating new economic opportunities, DeFi can promote financial inclusion, drive innovation, and empower individuals to take control of their financial lives. As technology advances and more people embrace decentralized finance, we can anticipate further growth, adoption, and transformation in the global financial ecosystem (Multazam, 2021).

3 Stablecoins

Stablecoins have become a vital part of the cryptocurrency ecosystem, serving to stabilize digital assets and mitigate their volatility. These digital currencies are specifically designed to maintain a steady value by pegging their price to a specific underlying asset, such as a fiat currency or a commodity.

When stablecoins are backed by real-world assets such as the USD, they bridge the gap between the advantages of blockchain technology and the stability offered by traditional fiat currencies. The issuance and withdrawal of 1 stablecoin correspond to the purchase and sale of 1 USD, ensuring stability. By providing price stability, stablecoins enable individuals and businesses to engage in transactions involving digital assets while minimizing the risk of value fluctuations.

There are different types of stablecoins, each utilizing various mechanisms to uphold their stability. Fiat-collateralized stablecoins are backed by reserves of fiat currency, such as the US dollar, held in bank accounts. Each stable coin represents a specific amount of the underlying fiat currency, aiming to maintain a one-to-one peg with its value. On the other hand, crypto-collateralized stable coins are supported by reserves of other cryptocurrencies. Users lock up a certain amount of cryptocurrency as collateral, and stablecoins are minted against this collateral. The value of the collateral exceeds the value of the stablecoins issued, ensuring stability even during volatile market conditions. Algorithmic stablecoins do not rely on collateral. Instead, their stability is maintained through algorithmic mechanisms that adjust the supply of stablecoins based on demand. These algorithms aim to keep the stablecoin price stable by expanding or contracting the supply according to market conditions.

Stablecoins offer several advantages. In contrast to conventional banking systems, they enable cross-border transactions that are both faster and more cost-effective. Stablecoins can be easily transferred globally and provide financial access to individuals in areas with limited banking infrastructure. They also enable seamless value transfers between different cryptocurrency exchanges and decentralized applications.

Additionally, stablecoins can serve as a reliable store of value, allowing users to hedge against volatility in the cryptocurrency market. Traders and investors often use stable coins as a temporary refuge during periods of market turbulence, preserving their value and enabling them to reenter the market at opportune moments. However, it is important to consider the risks associated with stablecoins. Regulatory scrutiny and compliance are crucial, especially for fiat-collateralized stablecoins. The reliability and transparency of the underlying assets and reserve management are essential factors in maintaining coin stability (Catalini et al., 2022).

Stablecoins have gained significant traction in recent years and have become an integral part of the broader cryptocurrency ecosystem. They offer stability, liquidity, and enhanced accessibility to digital assets, thereby contributing to the growth and adoption of blockchain technology. As the demand for stablecoins continues to rise, ongoing innovation and regulatory developments are expected to shape the future of these crucial digital assets.

4 Decentralized Exchanges

Generally, known as DEX, decentralized exchanges are more fun and secure than centralized exchanges. In centralized exchanges, there is no central person or authority that regulates the rules and regulations for the exchange of tokens or currency; rather, there is a piece of code called a "smart contract."

Smart contracts are similar to legal agreements between two parties who are going to do a financial exchange of tokens or services, where each party has to agree upon the smart contract, and if either of them denies it, the smart contract will not work. In decentralized exchanges, the catch is that the trade or exchange between the tokens can only be done within the same blockchain. Some benefits of decentralized exchanges over centralized exchanges are that decentralized exchanges are anonymous exchange platforms where the user does not have to submit their information, which can later be linked to their personal information, such as fingerprints, a profile picture, or an identity number.

Decentralized exchanges are faster than centralized exchanges, as they work on smart contracts, which are faster than human beings. Smart contracts are pieces of code that are trusted and reliable because they are open source to all the developers working on them, and only after their approval does the code work. Decentralized exchanges are much cheaper than centralized exchanges. Traditional centralized exchanges use the order book method, and this method can also be used in decentralized exchanges. If a person wants to buy something, it simply picks a price and then gives the order to a third party, either on the stock market exchange or through a smart contract (Platt et al., 2020).

This third-party vendor makes the person wait until it finds someone who wants to perform the exact trade and match the offering, then swaps the two and gives the person what it wants. The same goes with the scenario where the person wants to sell something on an exchange where the selling price is listed and recorded by the third party or in a smart contract, and then a buyer is searched, the order value and terms and conditions are matched, and then the exchange is done (Tsepeleva & Korkhov, 2022).

A big downside of this is that one has to wait around for some transactions. Another modern-day algorithm used is the automated market maker method. It removes the disadvantage of the previous method, where the seller did not have to wait until the buyer met the price.

This automated algorithm is designed such that the price of the pool of funds increases gradually when people intend to buy that particular token, and the price of the pool of funds decreases gradually when people intend to sell that particular token. These pools of funds are called liquidity pools. Modern-day decentralized exchanges commonly use this automated market-maker method (Wang, 2022).

5 Yield Farming

Yield farming has become one of the most popular and dynamic trends in the realm of decentralized finance. It is a strategy that allows cryptocurrency holders to put their assets to work and generate passive income by leveraging various DeFi protocols and liquidity pools. At its core, yield farming involves lending or staking digital assets into DeFi protocols in exchange for rewards, typically in the form of additional tokens. These rewards are earned for providing liquidity to the decentralized ecosystem, enabling other users to trade or access these assets.

Yield farmers essentially act as liquidity providers, facilitating the smooth operation of DeFi platforms. The process of yield farming begins by selecting a suitable DeFi platform or protocol. These platforms often operate on blockchain networks such as Ethereum, Binance Smart Chain, or others. Once a platform is chosen, users deposit their cryptocurrencies into smart contracts or liquidity pools, locking them for a specified period.

In return for their locked assets, farmers receive yield tokens, which represent their share of the platform's overall liquidity pool. These tokens can be staked or further utilized in other protocols to compound the earnings. The specific rewards and yields can vary significantly depending on the platform, the amount of liquidity provided, and the duration of the farming process. Yield farming offers several benefits to participants.

First, it provides an opportunity to earn additional tokens on top of the initial investment, effectively increasing the overall holdings. This can be particularly lucrative in scenarios where the value of the rewarded tokens appreciates significantly over time.

Second, yield farming allows investors to diversify their cryptocurrency holdings and explore different DeFi projects. By participating in multiple liquidity pools, farmers can spread their risk and potentially benefit from the success of various platforms and protocols (Andrew Balmford et al., 2018). However, it is important to note that yield farming carries certain risks.

The cryptocurrency market is inherently volatile, and the value of the rewarded tokens can fluctuate dramatically. Additionally, there are risks associated with smart contract vulnerabilities, potential hacks, or platform failures. Participants must conduct thorough research, assess the security measures in place, and exercise caution when engaging in yield farming activities.

Yield farming has significantly contributed to the growth and innovation in the DeFi space. It incentivizes liquidity provision, fosters decentralization, and enables the development of new financial products and services. As the DeFi ecosystem continues to evolve, yield farming is expected to remain a key element, attracting more participants and driving further experimentation and advancement in the realm of decentralized finance.

6 Decentralized Insurance

Decentralized insurance, also known as decentralized or blockchain-based insurance, is a revolutionary concept that has emerged with the advent of blockchain technology. It represents a significant shift from traditional insurance models, offering a more transparent, secure, and inclusive approach to risk management. In a decentralized insurance system, power is redistributed among participants rather than concentrated in the hands of a central authority.

Blockchain technology serves as the underlying infrastructure, providing a distributed ledger that records and verifies transactions in a transparent and immutable manner. This decentralization eliminates the need for intermediaries, such as insurance companies, and enables peer-to-peer interactions between individuals or entities seeking insurance coverage and those willing to underwrite or provide it.

One of the key advantages of decentralized insurance is its transparency. Every transaction and policy agreement are recorded on the blockchain, and visible to all participants. This transparency reduces information asymmetry and promotes trust between policyholders and insurers.

Additionally, it allows for efficient claim processing, as the entire claim history is easily accessible and verifiable on the blockchain. This transparency fosters accountability, as participants can hold each other accountable for their actions and ensure that the insurance process is fair and equitable.

Furthermore, decentralization enhances security in insurance. The blockchain's distributed nature makes it highly resistant to tampering and fraud. Transactions and policies stored on the blockchain are cryptographically secured, protecting them from unauthorized modifications.

Smart contracts, self-executing agreements encoded on the blockchain, automate the insurance process, ensuring that policy terms are followed, and claims are paid out promptly. This reduces the risk of human error or manipulation and increases the efficiency and reliability of insurance operations.

Decentralized insurance also promotes inclusivity and accessibility. Traditional insurance models often exclude certain demographics or regions due to various factors, such as high administrative costs, a lack of trust, or limited access to financial services. With decentralized insurance, anyone with an internet connection can participate, eliminating geographical boundaries and allowing individuals from underserved communities to access affordable and tailored insurance coverage.

Smart contracts can also facilitate micro insurance, enabling the provision of coverage for small-scale risks at lower costs. Despite its many advantages, decentralized insurance is still in the early stages of development. Challenges such as regulatory frameworks, scalability, and integration with the traditional insurance ecosystem need to be addressed. However, as blockchain technology continues to evolve and more innovative solutions emerge, decentralized insurance has the potential to transform the insurance industry, making it more efficient, inclusive, and customer-centric.

As this concept evolves and matures, it has the potential to reshape the industry, empowering individuals and communities to manage risks more effectively while fostering trust and accountability among participants.

7 NFTs (Non-Fungible Tokens)

Non-fungible tokens have taken the digital world by storm, revolutionizing the concept of ownership and uniqueness in the realm of digital assets. NFTs differ from cryptocurrencies in that they embody unique and indivisible digital assets, unlike fungible and interchangeable tokens. These NFTs can be purchased, sold, and owned. At their core, NFTs are built on blockchain technology, most commonly on Ethereum.

Each NFT is a unique token that is verifiably scarce, provably authentic, and immutably recorded on the blockchain. This provides a transparent and tamper-proof record of ownership and transaction history, ensuring the integrity and provenance of the digital asset.

NFTs can represent a wide range of digital or digitized assets, including digital art, music, videos, collectibles, virtual real estate, and even virtual experiences. They enable creators to tokenize and sell their work directly to collectors, bypassing traditional intermediaries.

This has opened up new opportunities for artists, musicians, and content creators to monetize their creations in the digital space. One of the key features of NFTs is their ability to establish provenance and authenticity. Each NFT contains metadata that details the unique characteristics and attributes of the digital asset it represents. This metadata can include information such as the creator's identity and any additional details that enhance the value and uniqueness of the asset. NFTs have also introduced a new level of ownership and value transferability (Wang et al., 2021).

When someone purchases an NFT, they acquire a digital certificate of ownership that is stored on the blockchain. This certificate verifies their exclusive ownership of the asset and enables them to transfer or sell it to others. The transparency and security of blockchain technology ensure that ownership rights are securely transferred and maintained. The explosion of NFTs has led to a vibrant and dynamic marketplace where collectors can buy, sell, and trade these digital assets.

Online platforms and marketplaces dedicated to NFTs have emerged, providing a space for creators and collectors to connect. These platforms utilize smart contracts to facilitate the seamless exchange of NFTs, ensuring that ownership rights and payment settlements are executed automatically and transparently.

While NFTs have garnered immense popularity and generated significant attention, it is important to note that they also come with challenges and considerations. Critics argue that the environmental impact of blockchain networks, particularly in the case of Ethereum, is a concern (Bao & Roubaud, 2022).

Additionally, questions regarding the long-term value and sustainability of the NFT market remain. Nevertheless, NFTs have undoubtedly sparked a new era in the digital economy, revolutionizing how we perceive and exchange digital assets. They have empowered creators, artists, and collectors, granting them new possibilities for expression, monetization, and engagement. As the NFT ecosystem continues to evolve and mature, it holds the potential to reshape industries, foster creativity, and redefine the notion of ownership in the digital age.

8 Different Approaches to Invest Through DeFi

Investing in entrepreneurial ventures has long been recognized as a rewarding opportunity. It involves supporting the vision and passion of innovative individuals who dare to transform ideas into reality. By allocating capital to these ventures, investors not only seek financial returns but also actively participate in shaping the future of industries and economies. Investing in entrepreneurial projects entails discovering interesting ideas and the people behind them and evaluating their feasibility, potential, and the entrepreneur's competencies. Investing in entrepreneurial ventures fosters economic growth and job creation. Startups and small businesses are often the engines of innovation and employment in many economies. By supporting these ventures, investors not only contribute to job creation but also promote economic resilience and diversification. Intending to replicate traditional financial services, such as lending, borrowing, trading, and investing in a decentralized and permission-less manner, decentralized finance was gaining significant traction in the world of cryptocurrency and blockchain technology.

Investing in entrepreneurship ventures through DeFi involves utilizing various DeFi protocols and platforms to fund startups and entrepreneurial initiatives. Some aspects to consider while building decentralized models are as follows:

- *Decentralized Crowdfunding Platforms*: DeFi platforms can facilitate decentralized crowdfunding for startups, allowing them to raise capital directly from a global pool of investors without the need for intermediaries (Gebert, 2017).
- *Liquidity Provision for Startup Tokens*: In DeFi, liquidity provision involves adding funds to a liquidity pool, often in exchange for token rewards. Startups can incentivize liquidity providers with tokens, which might be appreciated if the project succeeds.
- *Decentralized Lending and Borrowing for Entrepreneurs*: DeFi lending platforms allow entrepreneurs to borrow funds against their crypto assets without the need for traditional collateral.
- *Tokenization of Startup Equity*: Some DeFi platforms are exploring the tokenization of traditional assets, including equity in startups. This could revolutionize how ownership in startups is represented and traded.
- *Yield Farming and Staking for Startups*: Startups could engage with DeFi protocols to offer yield farming opportunities, where investors stake their tokens in exchange for rewards. Understanding the mechanisms and potential returns for both startups and investors is important.
- *Case Studies*: Analyzing real-world case studies of startups that have successfully utilized DeFi for funding and growth can provide insights into the challenges and benefits of this approach (Momtaz, 2022).

Some possible decentralized models that can be proposed to bring investment for entrepreneurial ventures while keeping all aspects in mind are as follows:

- Token Sales
- Venture Capital Funds
- Prediction Markets

8.1 Token Sales

DEX token sales leverage the power of decentralized networks to offer individuals from various backgrounds, regardless of their geographical location, an opportunity to participate and invest in the growth and development of these ventures. This can potentially attract a larger pool of investors, increase the chances of fundraising success, and allow a global audience to participate and invest in the growth and development of these ventures.

Unlike traditional centralized exchanges, decentralized exchanges operate on blockchain networks, enabling peer-to-peer trading without the need for intermediaries.

DEX token sales often involve community engagement, where participants can typically acquire tokens at a predetermined price. The acquisition of a certain amount of tokens gives benefits such as reduced fees, voting rights, or access to exclusive features. Investors who have equity in a venture and own a good amount of tokens can actively participate in decision-making processes concerning protocol changes. This can create a sense of ownership and loyalty among community members, which may lead to increased project visibility and support (Nagel & Kranz, 2022).

The evolution of a decentralized exchange provides liquidity, value appreciation, and exposure to the token. This can enable participants to trade the token and potentially generate profits, attracting more interest in the project.

Token sales conducted on DEX platforms that provide transparency and trust can benefit by potentially increasing trust among investors who can verify transactions and token allocations on the blockchain. Regulatory compliance can play a crucial role in the success and effectiveness of DEX token sales. Compliance with KYC and AML requirements is essential to ensuring investor protection and regulatory compliance (Romero-Castro et al., 2022).

Human sentiments do affect token sales, as they can significantly impact the effectiveness of DEX token sales. Bullish market trends and positive sentiment can contribute to higher participation and fundraising success.

8.2 Decentralized Venture Capital Funds

Decentralized VC funds have emerged as an innovative alternative to traditional, centrally managed venture capital models. Decentralized VC funds can tap into a global pool of investors, enabling access to a diverse range of perspectives, expertise, and capital to contribute capital to promising startups.

This democratization of decentralized VC funds brings great inclusivity and potential for retail investors through tokenized investment mechanisms. Decentralized VC funds, built on blockchain technology, offer unmatched transparency, accountability, and trust. Transaction records and investment decisions can be recorded on the blockchain, providing verifiability and trust for investors. Decentralized VC funds eliminate the need for intermediaries, reducing costs and enhancing the efficiency of the investment process. Instead, smart contracts automate and enforce investment terms, fund distributions, and governance mechanisms (Yadav & Sarasvathi, 2020).

Decentralized VC funds incorporate tokenization, issuing tokens that represent ownership in the fund. These tokens can provide benefits to investors. The tokenization of investments can potentially provide enhanced liquidity options for investors. This liquidity aspect can be attractive for investors seeking to exit or rebalance their investment positions. Decentralized VC funds need to adhere to regulatory compliance, such as securities laws, which impact the fund's operations and investor confidence.

Overall, blockchain market conditions significantly influence the effectiveness of decentralized VC funds. Successful projects and positive sentiment can contribute to increased investor interest and fund performance.

8.3 Prediction Markets

Prediction markets enable users to hedge and speculate on the success or failure of entrepreneurial ventures. By accurately predicting outcomes, investors can earn profits. Participants can make predictions on various events and outcomes with wisdom. When a large number of participants with diverse knowledge and perspectives are involved, the aggregated predictions have the potential to be more accurate than individual predictions.

Because of blockchain technology, all transaction records are transparent and immutable. This transparency can help establish trust among participants, as they can verify the integrity of market operations and outcomes.

Smart contracts ensure market integrity by automatically executing transactions and distributing payments based on the outcome of events. Participants receive financial incentives by sharing accurate information. By rewarding those who make correct predictions, prediction markets encourage participants to provide their honest beliefs and knowledge. Keeping the prediction market liquidated helps enhance market efficiency and encourages active participation. Higher liquidity attracts more participants and allows for more precise pricing, leading to improved market efficiency and accuracy. Decentralized governance models are used to provide token holders with necessary rights (Buckley, 2022).

Adhering to relevant securities laws, KYC/AML regulations, and other legal frameworks ensures investor protection and builds trust in the platform. The effectiveness of prediction markets can be influenced by the liquidity and depth of the markets.

8.4 A Case Study: Aave

- *Startup:* Aave
- *Industry:* Decentralized Finance (DeFi)
- *Founded:* 2017
- *Introduction:* Aave is a decentralized lending and borrowing platform built on the Ethereum blockchain. It allows users to lend and borrow a wide variety of

cryptocurrencies without intermediaries, using smart contracts to facilitate transactions. Aave's native token, AAVE, is used for governance and staking within the platform.

- *Utilizing DeFi for Funding and Growth:* Aave's journey showcases how DeFi protocols can utilize their platforms for fundraising and fueling growth:
  - *Initial Token Sale*: Aave's journey began with an Initial Coin Offering (ICO) in 2017, where they raised seed funding by selling LEND tokens, the precursor to AAVE. This allowed them to kickstart development and attract the attention of early DeFi enthusiasts.
  - *Transition to Decentralization*: As the DeFi ecosystem grew, Aave's team recognized the potential of their platform to support decentralized fundraising. They initiated a migration from the LEND token to the AAVE token, introducing key features such as staking, governance, and safety modules. This transition allowed users to participate in the platform's growth by staking AAVE tokens.
  - *Flash Loan Innovation*: Aave's introduction of flash loans revolutionized the DeFi space by enabling users to borrow assets without collateral, as long as the borrowed amount is returned within the same transaction. This innovation attracted developers and traders to the platform, driving adoption and liquidity.
  - *Protocol Resilience and Growth*: Aave's focus on security and constant improvement led to its growth as one of the leading DeFi platforms. Their bug bounty program and open-sourced code allowed security researchers to identify vulnerabilities and contribute to the platform's safety.

9 Flowcharts and Performance Metrics

9.1 Token Sale Model Flowchart

As shown in Fig. 1, Venture's lead project team develops a concept, a business plan, and a white paper outlining the project's goals, technology, token utility, and token distribution details.

The project team designs the token economics, including token supply, distribution mechanism, and any utility or governance features, with the founders and management team. They then develop a smart contract on a blockchain platform, such as Ethereum, to create and manage the token. The main public token sale, often referred to as the crowd sale or public offering, is conducted to allow a broader audience to purchase the tokens.

The sale may have a predetermined price or a dynamic pricing mechanism. Participants usually buy the project's tokens in exchange for crypto coins or stablecoins.

The project team works toward getting the tokens listed on cryptocurrency exchanges to provide liquidity and facilitate trading.

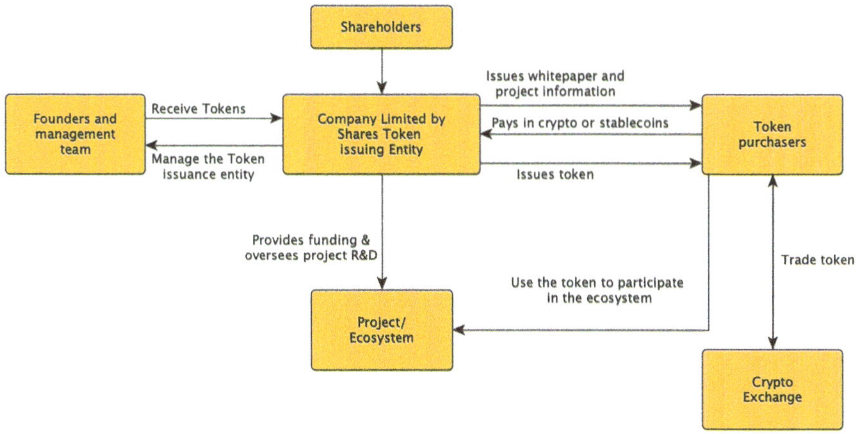

Fig. 1 Flowchart for the token sale model (Author)

Once the tokens are distributed, the project team integrates them into their platform or ecosystem. This may involve enabling token usage for accessing services, including governance. To maintain transparency and engage with token holders, the project team regularly communicates updates, progress reports, and plans. They may also involve the community in the decision-making process.

9.2 Token Sale Model Performance Metrics

This is a fictional example for explanation purposes.

- *Project Name:* DexTrade
- *Description:* DexTrade is a decentralized exchange platform built on the Ethereum blockchain. It aims to provide a secure and efficient trading environment for users to trade various cryptocurrencies without the need for intermediaries.
- *Token Name:* DEX Token
- *Token Sale Details:*
  - Token Type: ERC-20
  - Total Supply: 100,000,000 DEX Tokens
  - Token Price: 0.001 ETH per DEX Token
  - Soft Cap: 5000 ETH
  - Hard Cap: 20,000 ETH
  - Accepted Cryptocurrencies: ETH, BTC, and LTC
- *Token Distribution:*
  - Token Sale: 50%

  - Team and Advisors: 20%
  - Reserve: 20%
  - Marketing and Partnerships: 5%
  - Community Development: 5%

- *Token Sale Timeline:*
  - Presale Start Date: July 1, 2023
  - Presale End Date: July 15, 2023
  - Public Sale Start Date: August 1, 2023
  - Public Sale End Date: August 31, 2023

- *Token Sale Bonuses:*
  - Presale: Participants receive a 20% bonus on their token purchase.
  - Public Sale Week 1: Participants receive a 10% bonus on their token purchase.
  - Public Sale Week 2: No bonus offered.

- *Token Allocation and Use of Funds:*
  - Development and Platform Enhancements: 40% • Marketing and Promotion: 25%
  - Operations and Administration: 15%
  - Legal and Compliance: 10%
  - Reserve: 10%

9.3 Decentralized VC Fund Model Flowchart

The decentralized VC fund is created as a smart contract on a blockchain platform. The fund's structure, investment strategy, governance mechanisms, and economics of tokens are defined and encoded within the smart contract.

As shown in Fig. 2, the fund issues its native tokens through a token generation event. These tokens may represent ownership rights, governance rights, or access to the fund's services and benefits.

Capital is raised in the form of cryptocurrency and stablecoins in exchange for the fund's tokens. The fund's token holders can submit investment proposals.

Once an investment proposal is approved through the voting process, the fund's smart contract executes the investment and provides the necessary funding to the selected project or startup. The decentralized VC fund actively manages its portfolio of investments.

As the portfolio companies generate returns or exit through acquisitions, the decentralized VC fund receives proceeds. These profits are typically distributed to token holders based on their proportional ownership.

The decentralized VC fund's tokens can be traded on secondary markets, allowing token holders to buy and sell their holdings. This liquidity provides flexibility

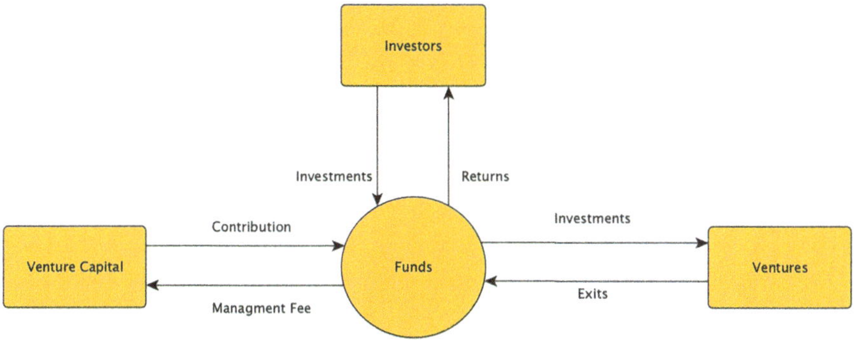

Fig. 2 Flowchart for the decentralized VC fund model (Author)

for investors to enter or exit their positions before the fund's investments reach maturity.

9.4 *Decentralized VC Fund Model Performance Metrics*

This is a fictional example for explanation purposes.

- *Project Name:* DecentralVenture
- *Description:* DecentralVenture is a decentralized venture capital fund that aims to support early-stage blockchain and cryptocurrency projects. It operates on a decentralized platform, allowing for transparent investment decisions and community participation.
- *Token Name:* DVC Token
- *Token Sale Details:*
  - Token Type: ERC-20
  - Total Supply: 100,000,000 DVC tokens
  - Token Price: 0.01 ETH per DVC Token
  - Soft Cap: 5000 ETH
  - Hard Cap: 20,000 ETH
  - Accepted Cryptocurrencies: ETH, BTC, and LTC
- *Token Distribution:*
  - Token Sale: 50%
  - Reserve: 20%
  - Team and Advisors: 15%
  - Marketing and Partnerships: 10%
  - Community Development: 5%

- *Token Sale Timeline:*
  - Presale Start Date: September 1, 2023
  - Presale End Date: September 15, 2023
  - Public Sale Start Date: October 1, 2023
  - Public Sale End Date: October 31, 2023
- *Token Sale Bonuses:*
  - Presale: Participants receive a 20% bonus on their token purchase.
  - Public Sale Week 1: Participants receive a 10% bonus on their token purchase.
  - Public Sale Week 2: No bonus offered.
- *Token Allocation and Use of Funds:*
  - Investment in Blockchain Projects: 70%
  - Operations and Administration: 15%
  - Marketing and Promotion: 10%
  - Legal and Compliance: 5%
- *Governance and Decision-Making:* Token holders have voting rights proportional to their token holdings, allowing them to participate in investment decisions, fund management, and other governance matters.
- *Profit Distribution:* The fund's profits generated from successful investments will be distributed to token holders through regular dividends or token buybacks.

9.5 Prediction Market Model Flowchart

A prediction market serves as a tool of collective intelligence in several ways; it offers valuable insights to major corporations and policymakers regarding public opinions and expectations for future events. These markets gather information from diverse sources as traders employ various decision-making approaches. While efforts are made to enhance the accuracy of these methods, it is important to acknowledge the presence of several human biases.

As shown in Fig. 3, the prices of contracts in a prediction market are subject to fluctuations based on prevailing beliefs. For instance, if a contract indicating the occurrence of outcome a is traded at 65 cents, it signifies that the market perceives a 65 probability of that outcome; conversely, if a contract suggesting the occurrence of outcome b is traded at 35 cents, it reflects a market belief of a 35 likelihood for that outcome.

Many prediction markets provide traders with the option to sell their contracts before their expiration; when a participant acquires a contract supporting the correct outcome, they will receive 1 upon contract expiration; conversely, they will receive 0 if they choose the incorrect outcome. However, it is worth noting that contract prices may fluctuate over time (Conitzer, 2012).

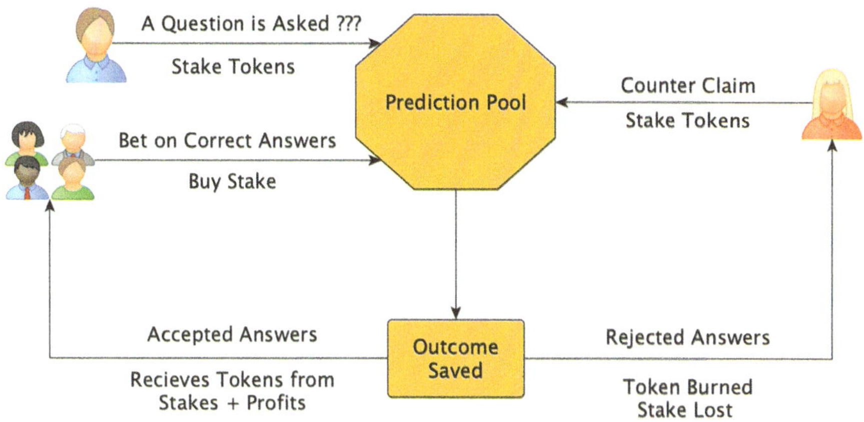

Fig. 3 Flowchart for the prediction market model (Author)

9.6 Prediction Market Model Performance Metrics

This is a fictional example for explanation purposes.

- *Project Name:* DeFiPredict
- *Description:* DeFiPredict is a decentralized prediction market platform built on the Ethereum blockchain. It allows users to make predictions on various events and outcomes, leveraging the wisdom of the crowd. Participants can buy and trade prediction tokens based on their beliefs, and the market prices reflect the aggregated predictions of the participants.
- *Token Name:* PRED Token
- *Market Creation Process:*
  - Any user can create a new prediction market by submitting a proposal with the event or outcome they want to predict.
  - The proposal goes through a voting process, where token holders can vote on whether the market should be created.
  - If the proposal receives enough votes, the market is created, and users can start trading prediction tokens related to the event.
- *Token Usage:*
  - PRED Tokens: Users need to hold PRED tokens to participate in the creation of prediction markets and trade prediction tokens.
  - Prediction Tokens: These are specific tokens created for each prediction market. Users can buy, sell, and trade these tokens based on their predictions.
- *Market Mechanics:*
  - Users can submit their predictions by buying and holding prediction tokens related to the outcome they believe will occur.

- The market prices of prediction tokens fluctuate based on supply and demand dynamics and the aggregated predictions of participants.
- At the end of the event or outcome, the final market price of the winning prediction token is determined.
- Users holding winning prediction tokens receive payouts based on their holdings and the final market price.

• *Token Distribution:*

- Token Sale: 50%
- Team and Advisors: 15%
- Reserve: 20%
- Marketing and Partnerships: 10%
- Community Development: 5%

• *Governance and Decision-Making:* PRED token holders have voting rights proportional to their token holdings. They can participate in decision-making processes such as proposal voting, platform upgrades, and market resolution.

10 Discussion and Conclusion

DeFi on blockchain technology offers decentralized and transparent financial services that are accessible to anyone with an internet connection. It enables individuals to engage in various financial activities such as lending, borrowing, trading, and earning interest without relying on traditional intermediaries such as banks. DeFi platforms have gained considerable traction due to their potential for high returns, low fees, and improved financial inclusivity.

Investing in entrepreneurial ventures requires capital to invest in early-stage businesses in exchange for a share of ownership. This form of investment can yield substantial rewards but also carries significant risks.

When considering DeFi and investing in entrepreneurial ventures, it is crucial to take certain factors into account. First and foremost, thorough research and due diligence are imperative before committing any capital. Understanding the market, industry, and potential risks associated with investment is essential for making well-informed decisions.

Second, diversification plays a vital role in risk management. Both DeFi investments and entrepreneurial ventures inherently carry risks, so spreading investments across multiple projects or startups can help mitigate potential losses.

Furthermore, staying informed about the latest trends, regulations, and developments in the DeFi and entrepreneurial landscapes is crucial. The industry is constantly evolving, and being aware of new opportunities, potential challenges, and regulatory changes can empower investors and entrepreneurs to navigate the market effectively.

In conclusion, DeFi and investing in entrepreneurial endeavors offer enticing prospects for individuals seeking financial growth and innovation support. However, it is crucial to approach these endeavors with caution by conducting thorough research, diversifying investments, and staying informed about market conditions. With the right knowledge and careful decision-making, individuals can participate in these domains and potentially achieve significant rewards while contributing to the advancement of innovative ideas and technologies.

References

Bachmann, A., Becker, A., Buerckner, D., Hilker, M., Kock, F., Lehmann, M., et al. (2011). Online peer-to-peer lending-a literature review. *Journal of Internet Banking and Commerce, 16*(2), 1.

Balmford, A., Amano, T., Bartlett, H., Chadwick, D., Collins, A., Edwards, D., et al. (2018). The environmental costs and benefits of high-yield farming. *Nature Sustainability, 1*(9), 477–485.

Bao, H., & Roubaud, D. (2022). Non-fungible token: A systematic review and research agenda. *Journal of Risk and Financial Management, 15*(5), 215.

Buckley, P. (2022). *Blockchain based prediction markets.*

Catalini, C., de Gortari, A., & Shah, N. (2022). Some simple economics of stablecoins. *Annual Review of Financial Economics, 14*, 117–135.

Chohan, U. W. (2021). *Decentralized finance (DeFi): An emergent alternative financial architecture.* Critical Blockchain Research Initiative (CBRI) Working Papers.

Conitzer, V. (2012). Prediction markets, mechanism design, and cooperative game theory. *arXiv preprint arXiv:1205.2654.*

Gebert, M. (2017). Application of blockchain technology in crowdfunding. *New European, 18.*

Momtaz, P. P. (2022). Decentralized finance (defi) markets for startups: Search frictions, intermediation, and efficiency. *Intermediation, and Efficiency (January 28, 2022).*

Multazam, M. T. (2021). Unleashing the potential of DeFi: A comprehensive guide to maximizing rewards while mitigating risks. *Ganaya: Jurnal Ilmu Sosial Dan Humaniora, 4*(2), 906–918.

Nagel, E., & Kranz, J. (2022). Revisiting Blockchain token sales: How crypto companies raise (D) money. In *Blockchains and the token economy: Theory and practice* (pp. 261–285). Springer International Publishing.

Platt, M., Pierangeli, F., Livan, G., & Righi, S. (2020, September). Facilitating the decentralised exchange of cryptocurrencies in an order-driven market. In *2020 2nd Conference on Blockchain Research & Applications for Innovative Networks and Services (BRAINS)* (pp. 30–34). IEEE.

Romero-Castro, N., Pérez-Pico, A. M., & Ulrich, K. (2022). ICOs, IEOs and STOs: Token sales as innovative formulas for financing start-ups. In *Financing startups: Understanding strategic risks, funding sources, and the impact of emerging technologies* (pp. 117–147). Springer International Publishing.

Tsepeleva, R., & Korkhov, V. (2022). Building DeFi applications using cross-blockchain interaction on the wish swap platform. *Computers, 11*(6), 99.

Vujičić, D., Jagodić, D., & Ranđić, S. (2018, March). Blockchain technology, bitcoin, and Ethereum: A brief overview. In *2018 17th international symposium infoteh-jahorina (infoteh)* (pp. 1–6). IEEE.

Wang, Q., Li, R., Wang, Q., & Chen, S. (2021). *Non-fungible token (NFT): Overview, evaluation, opportunities and challenges.* arXiv preprint arXiv:2105.07447.

Wang, Y. (2022, July). Prediction markets, automated market makers, and decentralized finance (DeFi). In *The International Conference on Mathematical Research for Blockchain Economy* (pp. 213–231). Springer International Publishing.

Yadav, N., & Sarasvathi, V. (2020, August). Venturing crowdfunding using smart contracts in blockchain. In *2020 Third International Conference on Smart Systems and Inventive Technology (ICSSIT)* (pp. 192–197). IEEE.

Zheng, Z., Xie, S., Dai, H., Chen, X., & Wang, H. (2017, June). An overview of blockchain technology: Architecture, consensus, and future trends. In *2017 IEEE international congress on big data (BigData congress)* (pp. 557–564). Ieee.

Jitesh Aggarwal was born and raised in Delhi, India. He completed his undergraduate degree in computer science from the Vellore Institute of Technology, Vellore. He was a five-time district-level basketball gold medalist during his years in school. With a keen interest in emerging technologies and being a certified AWS Cloud Practitioner, he has worked in various IT sectors in the past year to leverage his expertise in blockchain, cloud operations, and artificial intelligence. He has contributed to the International Journal of Engineering, Applied Sciences, and Technology with his research paper on predictive AI. His vision for writing this book's chapter was to propose different approaches to investing in entrepreneurial ventures through DeFi.

Extreme Return Connectedness Between DeFi Tokens and Traditional Financial Markets: An Entrepreneurial Perspective

Samet Gunay, Shahnawaz Muhammed, Destan Kirimhan, and Vladimir Dzenopoljac

1 Introduction

The emergence of digital finance and its applications in both centralized finance (CeFi) and decentralized finance (DeFi) settings gives rise to debates about the optimal way of restructuring the current financial system. The development of emerging digital financial solutions offers opportunities for all financial system participants, investors, entrepreneurs, and governments. Entrepreneurs have a crucial role in this transformation process by virtue of their ability to make innovation and cutting-edge technologies accessible to the masses through various solutions, as exemplified by NFT projects (Gunay & Muhammed, 2022). More importantly, this transformation broadens the horizons to entrepreneurs and small businesses in the area of startup capital raising. Characteristics of the DeFi market, such as removing intermediaries that impose various fees on entrepreneurs, increased transparency, and easier access to funds (for instance, through cryptocurrencies), have the potential to significantly contribute to small business development and reduce the time-to-market for these ventures. Additionally, the new paradigm creates novel and

S. Gunay (✉)
Institute of Finance, Corvinus University of Budapest, Budapest, Hungary
e-mail: samet.gunay@uni-corvinus.hu

S. Muhammed
MIS Department, American University of the Middle East, Egaila, Kuwait
e-mail: shahnawaz.muhammed@aum.edu.kw

D. Kirimhan
Department of Finance, American University of Sharjah, Sharjah, UAE
e-mail: dkirimhan@aus.edu

V. Dzenopoljac
Zayed University, College of Interdisciplinary Studies, Dubai, UAE
e-mail: vladimir.dzenopoljac@zu.ac.ae

S. Basly (ed.), *Decentralized Finance*, Financial Innovation and Technology,
https://doi.org/10.1007/978-3-031-49515-1_3

more efficient investment opportunities for capital owners. In this regard, investors also play an essential role in this transformation by allocating and diverting much-needed capital to various projects. From a social welfare point of view as well, new financial technologies that bring greater accessibility and security would be of tremendous interest. These positive implications may bring about the necessary regulations and frameworks in a timely manner without stifling innovation.

However, an essential concern for all such actors is the risks endemic to the potentially transformative changes these emerging digital financial technologies could bring. As discussed by Shumba (2021), several industry experts suggest that cryptocurrencies, on which most emerging digital financial applications are being built, could replace or rival fiat money in the not-so-distant future. For example, in a recent study, Gunay et al. (2021) report that Bitcoin already shows significant interaction with fiat currency. An important aspect of evaluating such risk hinges on understanding the connectedness between existing financial systems and emerging solutions. This study evaluates the potential connectedness between traditional financial systems and emerging digital financial systems in which investors and entrepreneurs would be interested in having a quantitative perspective of the potential risks. We thus start by examining the role of entrepreneurship in furthering digital financial solutions before we discuss its connectedness with traditional financial markets.

Entrepreneurship as a field of scholarly research has emerged as vital, dynamic, and relevant in social sciences (Wiklund et al., 2011). This novelty has unfolded numerous approaches to entrepreneurship. For example, the behavioral approach puts forward the necessary conditions for entrepreneurship: opportunity recognition, opportunity creation, and opportunity exploitation (Sarasvanthy et al., 2003; Venkataraman, 1997). Conversely, the performance-based perspective focuses on innovation (Audretsch, 2012). The pioneer in this point of view is doubtlessly Schumpeter, with the creative destruction thesis stating that "the function of entrepreneurs is to reform or revolutionize the pattern of production by exploiting an invention, or more generally, an untried technological possibility for producing a new commodity or producing an old one in a new way" (Schumpeter, 1942, p. 13). In other words, the disruption of deep-rooted and long-established practices, assumptions, products, or services can bring about new innovative ways of exploiting economic resources leading to economic development. A newly emerged literature points out social entrepreneurship, where a social entrepreneur is activated by the idea of making a positive social contribution through new business opportunities along with profitability concerns (Audretsch, 2012).

In light of these perspectives, DeFi, via its different applications and use cases, disrupts the processes, products, and services of traditional financial (TradFi) markets. DeFi also claims to benefit its user base via numerous social opportunities, such as financial inclusivity, financial participation, democratization of finance, and self-sovereignty. Therefore, DeFi can serve as a very comprehensive financial entrepreneurship project with a social dimension while providing early-stage crowdfunding for startups with initial coin offerings (ICOs) via tokenization (Catalini & Gans, 2018). DeFi startups raised funds from investors worth nearly $91 billion from

October 2015 until the writing of this book chapter, whereas fund-raising for CeFi projects was slightly behind, amounting to nearly $84 billion since June 2014 (DeFiLlama, 2023). Furthermore, DeFi exhibits characteristics that naturally fit with the entrepreneurship philosophy and paradigm.

This new approach opens doors for new opportunities in terms of thriving entrepreneurship and innovation through the creation of new and decentralized business models. The concept of DeFi fits with the entrepreneurial venture concept by promoting decentralization, innovativeness, interoperability, borderlessness, and transparency. Blockchain technology has the potential to lead to the creation of new business models that could boost entrepreneurial behavior. These models mainly include decentralized currencies (Ether, Litecoin, Monero, and the like), decentralized payment services (Libra or Bitcoin Lightning Network), decentralized fund-raising (such as initial coin offering), and decentralized contracting (platforms such as Dharma, MakerDAO, and Compound) (Chen & Bellavitis, 2020). Creation of the mentioned business models under the new DeFi paradigm is possible mainly because blockchain technology reduces transactional costs, enables various decentralized platforms, and creates an environment of distributed trust in the market (Chen & Bellavitis, 2020). Another innovative approach to boost entrepreneurship and create more startups is through crypto funds, which serve as intermediaries between DeFi markets and initial coin offerings (Cumming et al., 2022). In this way, the development of new startups and new business models is enabled, and competition in the market is strengthened, which leads to "creative destruction".

DeFi disrupts TradFi with its underlying blockchain technology, which reshapes financial market processes, products, and services. It forms a database of records on a distributed ledger for all transactions that are executed among peers (Angelis & Ribeiro da Silva, 2019). Digital private keys that are not directly linked to real-world identities are utilized to authorize transactions. All transactions recorded on the ledger are verified by particular network nodes conforming to the blockchain's consensus protocol. Blockchain technology mitigates yet not completely eliminates the need for a central authority such as a bank, hedge fund, or other financial institution to ensure the validity of transactions, unlike TradFi (Tan et al., 2021). It redefines trust established in the TradFi either as a trustless paradigm or a mix of algorithmic-based trust (Lustig & Nardi, 2015) and organizational trust (Pirson & Malhotra, 2011). Moreover, it brings about financial solutions that offer time- and cost-efficiency by a near-instant settlement of transactions and low transaction costs due to the reduced frictions in financial markets. Blockchain 2.0 led to the emergence of programmable smart contracts, meaning that a network of distributed nodes executes transactions when predetermined conditions are met and verified. These qualities of DeFi provide its users with privacy, security, transparency, immutability, trustlessness, programmability, and decentralization. Recently, with Blockchain 3.0 and 4.0, decentralized applications and artificial intelligence have caused a decay of organizational boundaries and autonomous decision-making (Angelis & Ribeiro da Silva, 2019).

It is apparent that DeFi brings various innovations to TradFi with its different use cases in finance, ranging from digital currency payments to lending. While TradFi refers to the long-standing financial institutions that can undertake investment projects in digital assets, CeFi includes companies whose main operation focuses on offering digital assets, products, and services in a centralized fashion, such as centralized crypto exchanges, crypto lending, and digital currency payments (Lielacher, 2022). However, CeFi shows similarities with its execution and compliance with financial regulations to TradFi. For instance, while DeFi provides self-sovereignty and self-custodial or noncustodial digital wallets, CeFi offers custody by its own platform, such as TradFi. Similarly, CeFi platforms do not forfeit their authority to suspend accounts or financial transactions of their user base, while DeFi services are technically always accessible (Cointelegraph, 2023). Unlike CeFi, DeFi is transparent in its execution of transactions and state changes, as they have to be publicly verified. Another difference is that transactions in DeFi are atomic, meaning that a sequence of changes in the database is either fully executed or not executed at all. However, CeFi is not specifically designed to host atomic transactions. While centralized exchange platforms keep orders off-chain like TradFi, decentralized exchange platforms match the transacting peers with the help of automated market maker protocols, which mimic price formation through equalization of supply and demand in financial markets. Furthermore, CeFi platforms require users to comply with regulations such as Anti-money Laundering (AML) and Know Your Customer (KYC) before being onboarded like TradFi. However, DeFi is mainly permissionless, allowing everyone to connect to the network aside from its privacy. Therefore, DeFi optimizes CeFi services by virtue of the unique capabilities of its underlying blockchain technology (Cointelegraph, 2023).

Despite the differences between DeFi and CeFi, they share the same objective of better serving customers via offerings of high-caliber financial goods, services, and processes (Cointelegraph, 2023). Furthermore, DeFi has yet to evolve from its very early stages, and it incorporates risks such as cybersecurity attacks, smart contract bugs and vulnerabilities, illicit activities, risk spillovers, financial instability, insufficient investor protection, high leverage, liquidity mismatch, interconnectedness risk, lack of shock absorbers such as an intermediary or government subsidy, and absence of regulatory monitoring (Aramonte et al., 2021; Kirimhan, 2023; Ozili, 2022). Apart from these risks, DeFi tokens, the native currencies of blockchain-based applications, and cryptocurrencies contain volatility risks, which can spill over onto other DeFi tokens, cryptocurrencies, and traditional assets, such as precious metals, equities, and fiat currencies. Consequently, debates on the safe-haven properties of DeFi tokens and cryptocurrencies and their contribution to the optimal portfolio diversification strategies of investors are ongoing. A comprehensive review of the related literature is presented in the next section.

In addition to volatility risks and spillovers, there are synergies and reliance among DeFi, CeFi, and TradFi. For instance, stablecoin, as a digital asset in DeFi, is one of the digital assets whose price is set in terms of fiat currencies since its value is pegged to fiat monies. Another example is that lending platforms in CeFi connect TradFi and the digital assets market by supplying fiat currency-denominated funds to borrowers after securing their digital assets as collateral (Cointelegraph, 2023). Therefore, it is crucial to investigate the time-varying correlation and risk-return spillovers between DeFi and CeFi to better inform investors, policymakers, and regulators about potential consequences, challenges, and opportunities in building a multitiered financial system with TradFi, CeFi, and DeFi.

Considering these market developments, in this study, we provide evidence for the relationship between the established TradFi market and recently emerged decentralized financial markets. Providing timely evidence regarding the direction and strength of the interactions between these two markets might be beneficial for investors and entrepreneurs in two ways: portfolio diversification and the generation of new business models. For instance, the extent and direction of spillovers from one market to another may indicate the order of information flow and thus the transmission of risks and returns. Taking the right decisions and actions at the right time would offer an excellent opportunity for investors in a rapidly growing market. Moreover, there might be further opportunities in the presence of extreme market returns and losses. Such price developments might occur during Black Swans, namely, for less predictable events with significant implications. Black Swans may appear on both sides of return distributions, thus bringing about extreme negative and positive returns. Considering this fact, in this study, we also aim to present evidence in the lowest and highest return quantiles for the interactions. Ascertaining the anteriority in transmitting returns in such quantiles might be attributed to the sequence of information flow in these markets. Thus, our results might be useful for investors seeking the underlying factors in examining the direction of information flow. The evidence we offer might also be useful for entrepreneurs seeking opportunities in the future developments of financial systems and markets. As the DeFi system takes up a fair number of investments made in conventional financial operations, it also offers a great chance for entrepreneurs to catch the trend of restructuring the financial markets and systems.

2 Literature Review

Understanding the volatilities and risk-return spillovers among traditional financial and digital assets in CeFi and DeFi is of utmost importance. In this regard, past studies focus on the safe-haven and hedging properties of tokens and cryptocurrencies, especially during a major event or a crisis in financial markets, and optimal portfolio diversification strategies for investors with a comprehensive set of asset alternatives from TradFi, CeFi, and DeFi utilizing various methods. Within very diverse research clusters, a set of studies analyzes the relations between unconventional DeFi tokens, cryptocurrencies, and some traditional assets such as crude oil, stocks, fiat currencies, precious metals, and U.S. Treasuries. Some researchers show evidence of substantial diversification benefits of DeFi assets for investors (Alawadhi & Alshamali, 2022). DeFi tokens hedge for stock market volatility (Caferra & Vidal-Tomás, 2021; Piñeiro-Chousa et al., 2022), and their returns are not affected by the GSI crude oil index (Piñeiro-Chousa et al., 2022). Moreover, there are positive but low spillovers between DeFi lending and borrowing tokens and centralized commercial bank stocks (Yousaf et al., 2022a). Additionally, DeFi tokens exhibit very low correlations with cryptocurrencies (Alawadhi & Alshamali, 2022), and causal interconnections between DeFi tokens and major cryptocurrencies are only valid during bear markets (Corbet et al., 2022).

On the other hand, some studies suggest a very limited or null diversification benefit of DeFi assets and cryptocurrencies through some research findings (Karim et al., 2022; Gunay & Kaskaloglu, 2022). First, DeFi tokens and cryptocurrencies can exhibit significant and substantial within- and between-market return spillovers, unlike stocks and safe-haven assets such as gold, U.S. dollar (USD), and U.S. Treasury bills (Corbet et al., 2023; Ugolini et al., 2023). Second, volatility figures of DeFi tokens and cryptocurrencies display substantial nonlinear correlations, although there is a slight nonlinear correlation in traditional assets, such as gold, crude oil, and the S&P500 index (Chowdhury et al., 2023). Third, the intensified market risk for cryptocurrencies due to leveraged trading can lead to risk spillovers onto other asset classes (Reitalu & Bajārs, 2022). Another set of analyses investigates the safe-haven properties of different asset classes, reporting no correlation or a negative correlation with other asset classes in extreme market conditions (Kumar & Padakandla, 2022). DeFi tokens and cryptocurrencies can establish safe-haven asset properties for investors (Piñeiro-Chousa et al., 2022), especially the largest cryptocurrencies, such as Bitcoin and Ethereum, due to their negative correlation with S&P500 returns during COVID-19 (Corbet et al., 2020; Mariana et al., 2021). Additionally, cryptocurrencies can hedge against high economic policy uncertainty (Jiang et al., 2021). Furthermore, DeFi tokens constitute a separate asset class from conventional cryptocurrencies since bubbles in major cryptocurrencies do not lead to bubbles in DeFi tokens (Corbet et al., 2023). As a consequence, DeFi tokens should be incorporated in optimally diversified portfolios (Corbet et al., 2023).

However, depending on financial market conditions, no consensus is reached on their safe-haven properties. For instance, Bitcoin prices increased during COVID-19 (Goodell & Goutte, 2021), and Bitcoin displays mixed results according to Kumar and Padakandla (2022). Similarly, Disli et al. (2021) report that Bitcoin is not a safe-haven asset because of its heightened return spillover and interconnectedness with the equity market. The COVID-19 crisis can eradicate the success of cross-currency hedge strategies among fiat monies and cryptocurrencies due to the high co-movement between the coronavirus panic index and major fiat prices (Umar & Gubareva, 2020). Moreover, the rise in spillovers and interconnectedness between DeFi tokens and major fiat currencies at the onset of the pandemic questions the safe-haven features of DeFi tokens (Yousaf et al., 2022b). Additionally, extreme market conditions can increase the tail connectedness among DeFi lending and borrowing tokens and centralized commercial bank stocks, especially in the left tail (Yousaf et al., 2022a). Furthermore, cryptocurrency policy uncertainty serves as a return spillover transmitter to cryptocurrencies and gold (Elsayed et al., 2022). Finally, speculative bubbles in DeFi token prices aggravate uncertainty in cryptocurrencies (Wang et al., 2022).

Entrepreneurial finance has gained increased interest in finance literature, especially after the significant rise in the dollar value of various venture capital funds, predominantly in the United States. This is evidenced by the growth of small businesses and new ventures, which is considered one of the major drivers of economic growth and job creation. The United States venture capital markets experienced a growth of dollar commitment to venture capital funds from US$3.1 billion to US$87.3 billion in the years between 1992 and 2000. Additionally, there was significant growth observed in the value of initial public offerings from US$21 billion in 1992 to US$60.5 billion in 2000. When analyzing the trends in relative terms, 75% of venture capital financing was allocated to information technology and healthcare sectors, which were seen as the major growth drivers for the US economy at the time (Denis, 2004). These trends had a major impact on DeFi and its relation with new venture creation.

Investments in new technologies led to a change in the nature of entrepreneurial finance. One of the important trends in this regard is the decreasing level of intermediation in startup financing. The main idea behind this decrease in intermediation is to create additional economic surplus available to entrepreneurs and investors, which can be invested in generating additional value instead of being "lost" in the process of intermediation. These mediators include venture capitalists, who traditionally charge performance fees of approximately 20% and annual management fees between 1 and 2% (Momtaz, 2022). The two most significant entrepreneurial financial market segments are said to be crowdfunding and initial coin offering, and these are considered to be game changers in removing redundant mediators in the process of raising funds for contemporary new business ventures (Block et al., 2021; Lambert, 2022; Mochkabadi & Volkmann, 2020). Apart from these frameworks, fintech lending, which includes peer-to-peer lending, has also gained importance in the field of gathering funds for new venture creation. This approach initially focused on funding startups and small firms (Bollaert et al., 2021).

DeFi markets for startups represent the potential next step in the development of entrepreneurial finance. This segment has exhibited exponential growth, jumping from US$4 billion to US$104 billion in the period between 2019 and 2022, creating "a solely code-based, intermediary-independent financial system" (Meyer et al., 2022, p. 2). Unlike the traditional financial system that is characterized by centralization, not being transparent, and very often difficult to access by potential entrepreneurs, the DeFi market offers easy access via Internet connection. Additionally, the DeFi system of lending and borrowing allows its users to seemingly exchange cryptocurrencies that can have fixed or variable interest rates. Furthermore, the new system eliminates intermediaries, together with their costs, and allows users to access needed funds without the obligation of having extensive credit history verification (which has the potential to be a downside at the same time). Finally, the system is more transparent, and loans are granted mainly based on overcollateralization or some other forms of ensuring repayment (Alp et al., 2023).

A related concept of pooling investment funds, including crypto funds, is viewed as an intermediary between crowdfunding investors and various tokenized startups, which resembles the traditional venture capitalists and new business formation relationship. However, with the new concepts, it is currently offered in a digital, more streamlined, and efficient way (Momtaz, 2021). More specifically, in the DeFi markets for startups, the concept of crowdfunding is replaced with the notion of smart contracts, which enable the next level of efficiency in the process of raising necessary capital for a new venture. These smart contracts serve the purpose of minimizing intermediation and its related costs in entrepreneurial finance, thus enabling higher levels of value creation for startups (Colombo et al., 2022; Fisch, 2019). In addition to cost minimization, DeFi markets offer mitigation of recently increasing portfolio risks for startups (Metelski & Sobieraj, 2022). From the standpoint of fundraising, there is a trend of attracting investors to investments in the DeFi arena, such as initial coin offerings, through social media accounts of these cryptocurrencies (Gunay et al., 2022, Gunay & Muhammed, 2022). This further decentralizes the process of attracting investors and raising funds while at the same time decreasing the time-to-market lead times for new entrepreneurial ventures.

The DeFi market is not without its drawbacks and weaknesses for startups, which are primarily reflected in the DeFi market's ability to remove the issues associated with trust. In this regard, the DeFi market is built on the notion that new startups do not need to be concerned about trust in individuals, but rather that the participants in the DeFi market "potentially only have to trust computer code that is enforced by a decentralized network of computers" (Saengchote et al., 2022, p. 0). However, empirical results point to the conclusion that, in practice, smart contracts within DeFi markets still do not remove the need for trust in individuals since they are subject to run risk, which concludes that trust among individuals is still an important factor in this new setting (Saengchote et al., 2022).

3 Empirical Analysis

In the empirical section of the study, we investigate the connectedness between the DeFi and TradFi markets. Employment of smart contracts allows DeFi projects to reshape the structure and mechanism of the current financial system, which raises the following question: what is the current relation between these markets? This question is particularly important because it touches upon the desynchronization of developments in Internet services and financial systems. According to data from the World Bank Group, there are still approximately 1.7 billion people without access to financial services, who mainly lack access to bank accounts, whereas Internet services are more accessible at the global level (Abdulhakeem & Hu, 2021). This discrepancy between the accessibility of financial services and internet services complicates the process of raising necessary funding by entrepreneurs. While DeFi markets can facilitate the fundraising process, there is a need to understand the interactions of DeFi and TradFi markets.

Furthermore, new venture creators already face difficulties in regard to raising startup capital within the traditional financial system since they rarely have access to debt financing due to their lack of credit history and tangible assets (Denis, 2004). Therefore, they mainly rely on three sources of finance: venture capitalists, angel investors, and corporate investors. The difficulty of accessing startup capital is significantly high for certain types of entrepreneurs. For example, female entrepreneurs receive less venture capital than their male counterparts. This is a commonly observed situation even in developed economies such as Germany (Lins & Lutz, 2016); however, it is even more pronounced in developing countries such as Kenya (Manwari et al., 2017). Apart from the evident gender gap, it is noted in the literature that ethnic minority entrepreneurs are less likely to receive the requested funds for a new venture than nonminority entrepreneurs. Furthermore, this issue is intensified when ethnic minority entrepreneurs have a lower level of education (Bewaji et al., 2015). Another group of entrepreneurs that face obstacles in gaining startup funds is low-wealth entrepreneurs, or entrepreneurs with low net worth whose household financial value is perceived to be low. These entrepreneurs are also less likely to receive external funding (Frid et al., 2016). Along with these traditional sources of raising startup capital, entrepreneurs are offered additional avenues, such as accelerators and incubators, proof-of-concept centers, university-based seed funds, and crowdfunding platforms, which offer benefits but also carry certain risks (Bellavitis et al., 2017). They can also serve as funding opportunities to recently formed companies that are operating in different life cycle stages (Bellavitis et al., 2017). The DeFi market could potentially eliminate current obstacles for startup entrepreneurs when entering into new venture opportunities. For this reason, it is important to assess the differences between the traditional finance environment and the decentralized one. Providing robust empirical findings regarding the relations of these markets would shed light on their risk-return tradeoff and risk spillovers for investors and entrepreneurs to guide these stakeholders more effectively in optimally selecting their investments.

To capture DeFi market developments, we create a DeFi index for the largest market capitalization tokens, considering the data availability during the analysis period. The selected tokens are as follows: LINK, LUNC, MKR, MC, and SNX. To represent the TradFi market, we select four indices related to the financial sector. They include the S&P Dow Jones U.S. Banks Index (Banks), S&P Dow Jones U.S. Financial Services Index (FinSer), S&P Dow Jones U.S. Investment Services Index (InvSer), and S&P Dow Jones U.S. Insurance Index (Insur). By considering various industries from traditional financial markets, we investigate the interdependencies and spillovers between TradFi and DeFi markets.

The sample for this study covers the time period between November 20, 2019, and January 13, 2023. Data are obtained through the Refinitive Eikon database. Empirical analyses are conducted through quantile time-frequency connectedness analysis. To evaluate the connectedness between DeFi and TradFi markets, we base our analysis on the quantile connectedness approach proposed by Ando et al. (2018) and Chatziantoniou et al. (2021). This method is based on the original time domain connectedness approach of Diebold and Yilmaz (2012, 2014). In the quantile connectedness approach, the time domain connectedness approach of Diebold and Yilmaz (2012) is evaluated within each quantile, providing a more nuanced understanding of the connectedness between DeFi and TradFi markets within the quantiles of interest. We first estimate a quantile vector autoregression to calculate connectedness metrics, QVAR(p). Then, the H-step ahead generalized forecast error variance decomposition (GFEVD) of Koop et al. (1996) and Pesaran and Shin (1998) is calculated to examine the connectedness between the DeFi and TradFi indices. This provides information about the total directional connectedness of a variable "TO" and "FROM" others and thus the "NET" connectedness. Spectral graphs provide further information about the connectedness of index pairs across several quantiles.

Descriptive statistics for each index are presented in Table 1. The mean values of all indices center around zero, with the DeFi index mean being slightly negative and the investment services index being slightly positive but close to zero. The volatility of price developments reveals that DeFi has the largest price fluctuations, which may imply relatively rapid price changes in cryptocurrencies compared to other financial assets. Skewness and kurtosis statistics show that each index departs from the normal distribution. Negative skewness in the returns of all assets indicates that the frequency of above-mean returns is higher than the values below the mean. In addition, as the kurtosis statistics reveal, all variables have a return distribution with thick tails, referring to higher chances of extreme price developments. This situation suggests that connectedness in the extreme tails would be important for these indices. Significant Jarque-Bera test statistics confirm the presence of a non-Gaussian distribution. In testing the stationarity of variables, we employ the ADF-GLS test of Stock et al. (1996). According to the results, all variables are stationary with a constant mean and variance over time.

Figure 1 exhibits the price series of DeFi and all TradFi indices. All variables display a sudden dip in the prices observed in the first quarter of 2020, corresponding to the COVID-19 market crash that occurred in March 2020. Furthermore, all TradFi indices recovered beyond or close to the prepandemic levels at the beginning of 2023. However, the DeFi index seems to remain depressed, possibly reflecting the crypto winter, as discussed by Chohan (2022). While the DeFi index peaked in the second quarter of 2021, the TradFi indices appear to have peaked around the beginning of 2022, except for the insurance index (Insur). As an exception, the insurance index recovered more rapidly than the rest of the equity indices and is at its highest level as of the last period considered in the sample of this analysis. Meanwhile, the DeFi index is at its lowest level in the last period analyzed in this study.

Table 1 Descriptive statistics

	DeFi	Banks	FinSer	InvSer	Insur
Mean	−0.0020	0.0000	0.0000	0.0010	0.0000
Std. Dev.	0.110114	0.024431	0.020837	0.019292	0.019071
Skewness	−0.178	−0.193	−0.379	−0.765	−1.148
Kurtosis	15.614	8.516	10.589	11.703	12.885
JB	8049.742***	2397.897***	3719.030***	4596.690***	5652.618***
ADF-GLS	−10.087***	−12.682***	−12.624***	−11.693***	−8.779***

*** denotes significance at the 1% level, Std. Dev.- standard deviation, JB- Jarque-Bera test statistic, ADF-GLS augmented Dickey-Fuller generalized least squares

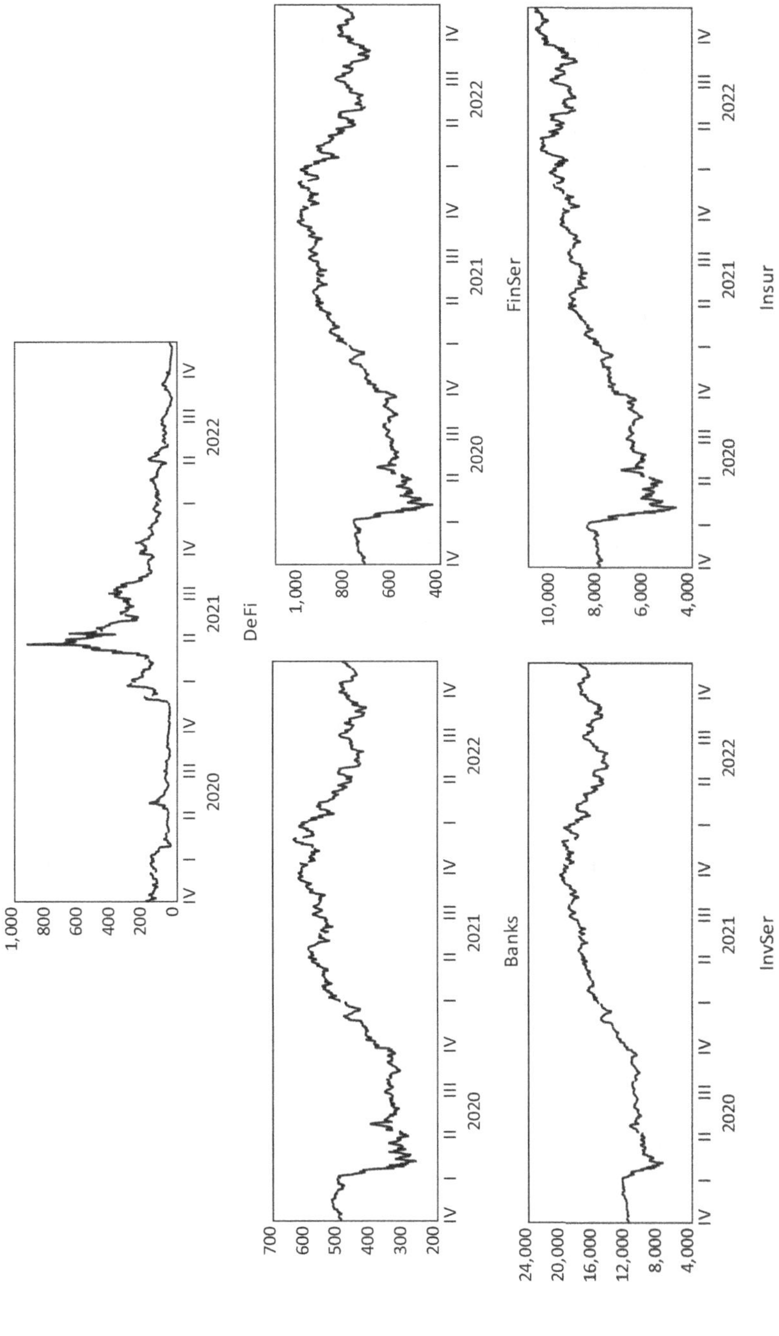

Fig. 1 Price Series of the DeFi and TradFi Indices

After evaluating the descriptive statistics, we examine the quantile return connectedness among DeFi and TradFi variable pairs. Connectedness is examined in the extreme tails and in the median quantile ($\tau = 0.50$). For extreme quantiles, both extreme lower quantiles ($\tau = 0.05$) and extreme upper quantiles ($\tau = 0.95$) are considered (Table 2).

The results indicate that DeFi is highly connected to all sectors of TradFi in the extreme lower and extreme upper quantiles, indicating strong extreme tail connectedness (between 31.92% and 37.48%). DeFi and TradFi sector connectedness is relatively weak in the median quantile (ranging from 1.01% to 4.44%) compared to the tails. The strongest connection is from FinServ to DeFi (37.48%) in the extreme upper quantile. The lowest own-variance share spillovers for DeFi range from 66.07% to 67.06% in the extreme upper quantile, from 62.52% to 64.2% in the extreme lower quantile, and from 95.56% to 98.01% in the median quantile. That is, the highest own-variance share spillovers for DeFi are in the median quantile. For extreme lower and upper quantiles, spillovers are in a similar range, with extreme upper quantiles having a slightly higher own-variance between the two.

Figure 2 displays the total net directional connectedness over all quantiles. While the left panel displays the net directional connectedness of traditional finance sector indices, which means spillovers from these indices to the DeFi index, the right panel illustrates the same connectedness in the opposite direction, namely, from DeFi to

Table 2 Results of connectedness analysis in various quantiles

	Extreme Lower Quantile ($\tau = 0.05$)			Median Quantile ($\tau = 0.50$)			Extreme Upper Quantile ($\tau = 0.95$)		
	DEFI	**Banks**	**FROM**	**DEFI**	**Banks**	**FROM**	**DEFI**	**Banks**	**FROM**
DEFI	67.06	32.94	32.94	97.69	2.31	2.31	63.66	36.34	36.34
Banks	31.92	68.08	31.92	2.36	97.64	2.36	33.69	66.31	33.69
TO	31.92	32.94	64.86	2.36	2.31	4.67	33.69	36.34	70.04
NET	−1.02	1.02		0.04	−0.04		−2.65	2.65	
	DEFI	**FinSer**	**FROM**	**DEFI**	**FinSer**	**FROM**	**DEFI**	**FinSer**	**FROM**
DEFI	66.92	33.08	33.08	95.56	4.44	4.44	62.52	37.48	37.48
FinSer	32.12	67.88	32.12	1.86	98.14	1.86	33.76	66.24	33.76
TO	32.12	33.08	65.2	1.86	4.44	6.3	33.76	37.48	71.23
NET	−0.95	0.95		−2.58	2.58		−3.72	3.72	
	DEFI	**InvSer**	**FROM**	**DEFI**	**InvSer**	**FROM**	**DEFI**	**InvSer**	**FROM**
DEFI	66.07	33.93	33.93	95.83	4.17	4.17	62.85	37.15	37.15
InvSer	32.87	67.13	32.87	2.79	97.21	2.79	33.27	66.73	33.27
TO	32.87	33.93	66.79	2.79	4.17	6.96	33.27	37.15	70.42
NET	−1.06	1.06		−1.38	1.38		−3.89	3.89	
	DEFI	**Insur**	**FROM**	**DEFI**	**Insur**	**FROM**	**DEFI**	**Insur**	**FROM**
DEFI	66.83	33.17	33.17	98.01	1.99	1.99	64.2	35.8	35.8
Insur	32.12	67.88	32.12	1.01	98.99	1.01	32.65	67.35	32.65
TO	32.12	33.17	65.29	1.01	1.99	3	32.65	35.8	68.45
NET	−1.04	1.04		−0.98	0.98		−3.15	3.15	

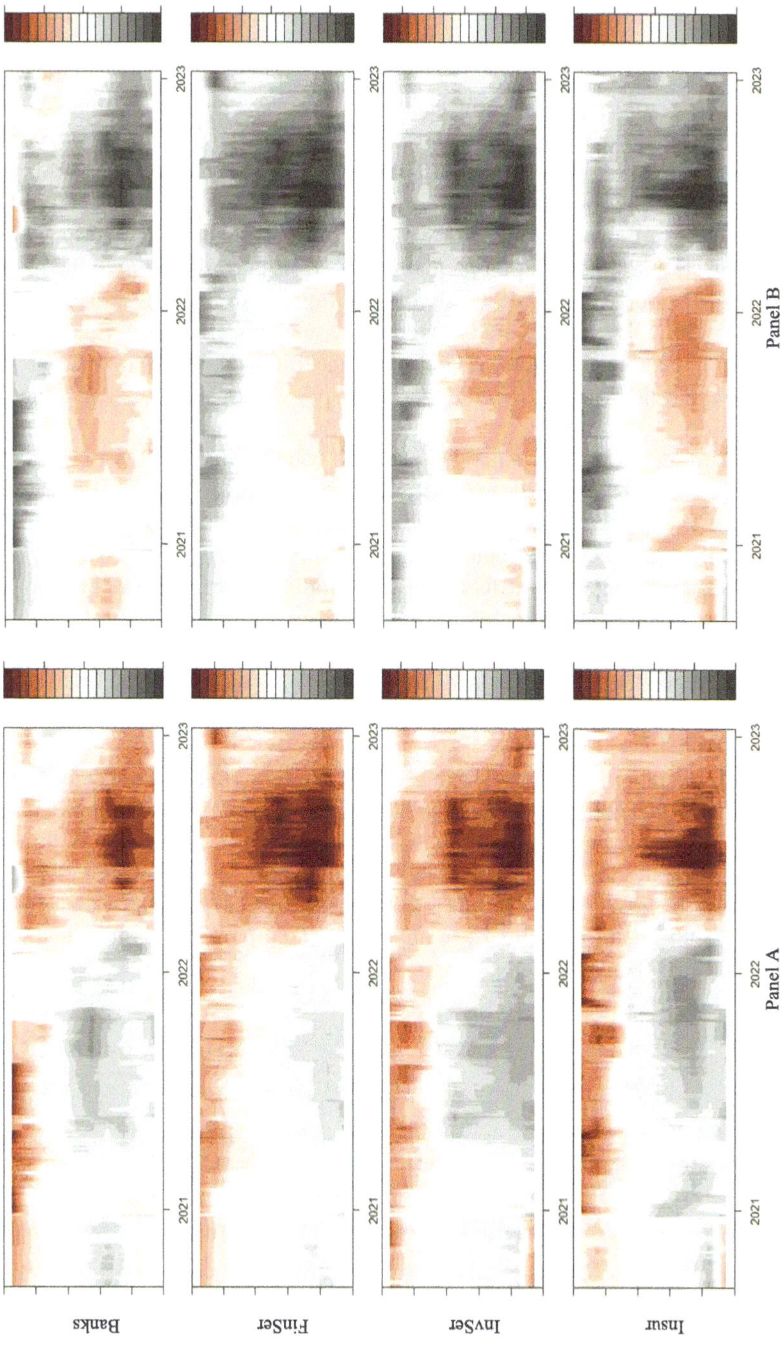

Fig. 2 Net total directional connectedness of TradFi sectors to DeFi (Panel A) and DeFi to TradFi sectors (Panel B)

traditional finance sector indices. The warmer shades on the spectral graph indicate higher connectedness. As noted, the extreme upper quantile displays a higher level of connectedness between DeFi and all TradFi sectors than other quantiles throughout the duration of the analysis.

Among the TradFi sectors, the investment services sector has the highest connectedness within the extreme upper quantile. In contrast, the banking sector has the weakest connectedness in this quantile and shows a sustained weakness from the last quarter of 2021 to the second quarter of 2022. This period corresponds to when equity markets were experiencing a downtrend from all-time highs starting in late 2021. However, during the first three quarters of 2021, corresponding to the recovery period of the post-COVID-19 crash, the banking sector acted as a strong transmitter of shocks to DeFi. This study extends the analysis of Yousaf et al. (2022a) that examines the connectedness of DeFi with specific bank stocks to an interconnectedness analysis with the overall banking index and other related financial sectors.

The spectral graph indicates that the strongest connectedness between DeFi and all sectors of TradFi is during the second and third quarters of 2022. The connectedness during this period is spread across all quantiles but is relatively stronger in the lower to median quantiles. The connectedness for this period is more broadly spread for the financial services index than for other TradFi sectors, followed by investment services, banking, and then the insurance index. Comparatively, transmission from the TradFi indices to the DeFi index seems to be diminishing beyond this period and especially during the last quarters of 2022 and early 2023. However, these effects are still stronger than the ones that were observed in earlier periods, especially in the lower quantiles.

Standard deviations of time-varying net total directional connectedness in Table 3 indicate that banks have the highest variation in the extreme upper quantile (3.8210) and the insurance sector has the lowest (2.9011) in this quantile. Within the median quantile, the investment services index has the highest variation (4.5620), and insurance has the lowest (2.3963). Investment services also have the highest variation (5.5388) in the extreme lower quantile, but within this quantile, the lowest variation is for the banking sector.

Table 3 Standard deviation of time-varying net total directional connectedness

	Banks	FinSer	InvSer	Insur
Extreme upper quantile ($\tau = 0.95$)	3.8210	3.1100	2.9505	2.9011
Median quantile ($\tau = 0.50$)	2.8395	4.0560	4.5620	2.3963
Extreme lower quantile ($\tau = 0.05$)	2.7954	3.6708	5.5388	2.9220

4 Conclusion

The future of money and financial services can be restructured by effectively combining the positive aspects of traditional and decentralized financial markets in a synergistic way. Blockchain technology underlying the DeFi markets offers several venues to democratize financial services and novel ways to facilitate fundraising and entrepreneurship by reducing transaction costs and increasing transparency. It also opens the doors to new ways in which new business ventures can access funding and generate novel business models. In this regard, it has the potential to mitigate the obstacles faced in traditional financial markets by female, ethnic minority, and low net worth entrepreneurs.

However, DeFi markets are not free from risks, which implies that the expected synergies between TradFi and DeFi assets may result in volatility spillovers onto each other. Therefore, it is important to examine the time-varying correlations and risk-return spillovers among various TradFi markets and DeFi markets. In this study, we analyze the interconnectedness between the DeFi market index and the indices of four different industries in TradFi, namely, banking, financial services, investment services, and insurance. Quantile connectedness analysis of the returns of DeFi tokens employed in this analysis and the returns of four different traditional financial sectors in the extreme tails indicate that overall traditional financial sectors continue to be a net transmitter to the DeFi sector. All four traditional financial sectors are net transmitters of return shocks received by the DeFi tokens except for the banking industry, which is marginally a net receiver from DeFi within the median quantile. The connectedness of TradFi with DeFi is highest in the extreme upper and lower quantiles, suggesting an increased influence of TradFi during extreme market conditions that are both positive and negative, indicating a certain degree of symmetry. Within the median quantile, both FROM and TO connectedness are minimal, suggesting that the DeFi returns are not greatly influenced by the developments in the traditional financial markets under those market conditions. However, the net directional connectedness is slightly lower in the extreme lower quantile, indicating a marginally weaker overall net effect than the median and extreme upper quantiles.

This study provides a considerably nuanced understanding of the connectedness between the specific sectors of the traditional financial markets and the emerging DeFi sector. The main lesson inferred from this analysis is that the DeFi market is still heavily affected by the traditional finance segment, especially in the extreme tails and during highly uncertain time periods. Therefore, entrepreneurs and investors interested in funding DeFi-related projects would better evaluate tradeoffs between certain benefits and risks offered by DeFi markets, such as spillover risks and diversification of investments. The dominance of traditional markets in relation to DeFi-focused initiatives can also provide an opportunity to forecast price changes and potential volatility in DeFi markets. As the direction of spillovers is from traditional markets to the DeFi market, the information that emerged in conventional markets and its dissemination to DeFi markets would provide an opportunity in terms of the lead-lag relationship and time to update the portfolio weights of investors and the investment strategies of entrepreneurs. From a social welfare point of view, this analysis has important implications for the effective allocation of financial resources.

References

Abdulhakeem, S. A., & Hu, Q. (2021). Powered by Blockchain technology, DeFi (decentralized finance) strives to increase financial inclusion of the unbanked by reshaping the world financial system. *Modern Economy, 12*(1), 1–16.

Alawadhi, K. M., & Alshamali, N. (2022). NFTs emergence in financial markets and their correlation with DeFis and cryptocurrencies. *Applied Economics and Finance, 9*(1), 108–120. https://doi.org/10.11114/aef.v9i1.5444

Alp, B. K., Vahit Ferhan, B., & Elcin, A. (2023). Decentralized finance and new lending protocols. *PressAcademia Procedia, 16*(1), 192–195. https://dergipark.org.tr/en/pub/pap/issue/75783/1247812

Ando, T., Greenwood-Nimmo, M., & Shin, Y. (2018). *Quantile connectedness: Modeling tail behavior in the topology of financial networks* (SSRN Working Paper No. 3164772).

Angelis, J., & Da Silva, E. R. (2019). Blockchain adoption: A value driver perspective. *Business Horizons, 62*(3), 307–314. https://doi.org/10.1016/j.bushor.2018.12.001

Aramonte, S., Huang, W., & Schrimpf, A. (2021). DeFi risks and the decentralization illusion. *BIS Quarterly Review*, 21–36.

Audretsch, D. (2012). Entrepreneurship research. *Management Decision, 50*(5), 755–764. https://doi.org/10.1108/00251741211227384

Bellavitis, C., Filatotchev, I., Kamuriwo, D. S., & Vanacker, T. (2017). Entrepreneurial finance: New frontiers of research and practice. *Venture Capital, 19*(1–2), 1–16.

Bewaji, T., Yang, Q., & Han, Y. (2015). Funding accessibility for minority entrepreneurs: An empirical analysis. *Journal of Small Business and Enterprise Development, 22*(4), 716–733. https://doi.org/10.1108/JSBED-08-2012-0099

Block, J. H., Groh, A., Hornuf, L., Vanacker, T., & Vismara, S. (2021). The entrepreneurial finance markets of the future: A comparison of crowdfunding and initial coin offerings. *Small Business Economics, 57*(2), 865–882. https://doi.org/10.1007/s11187-020-00330-2

Bollaert, H., Lopez-de-Silanes, F., & Schwienbacher, A. (2021). Fintech and access to finance. *Journal of Corporate Finance, 68*, 101941. https://doi.org/10.1016/j.jcorpfin.2021.101941

Caferra, R., & Vidal-Tomás, D. (2021). Who raised from the abyss? A comparison between cryptocurrency and stock market dynamics during the COVID-19 pandemic. *Finance Research Letters, 43*, 101954. https://doi.org/10.1016/j.frl.2021.101954

Catalini, C., & Gans, J. S. (2018, March). *Initial coin offerings and the value of crypto tokens* (NBER Working Paper No. 24418). https://www.nber.org/papers/w24418

Chatziantoniou, I., Gabauer, D., & Stenfors, A. (2021). Interest rate swaps and the transmission mechanism of monetary policy: A quantile connectedness approach. *Economics Letters, 204*, 109891.

Chen, Y., & Bellavitis, C. (2020). Blockchain disruption and decentralized finance: The rise of decentralized business models. *Journal of Business Venturing Insights, 13*, e00151. https://doi.org/10.1016/j.jbvi.2019.e00151

Chohan, U. W. (2022, June). *Crypto winters* (SSRN Working Paper). https://doi.org/10.2139/ssrn.4142885

Chowdhury, M. A. F., Abdullah, M., Alam, M., Abedin, M. Z., & Shi, B. (2023). NFTs, DeFi, and other assets efficiency and volatility dynamics: An asymmetric Multifractality analysis. *International Review of Financial Analysis, 87*, 102642.

Cointelegraph. (2023). *DeFi vs. CeFi: Comparing decentralized to centralized finance*. Accessed on January 14, 2023, from https://cointelegraph.com/defi-101/defi-vs-cefi-comparing-decentralized-to-centralized-finance

Colombo, M. G., Fisch, C., Momtaz, P. P., & Vismara, S. (2022). The CEO beauty premium: Founder CEO attractiveness and firm valuation in initial coin offerings. *Strategic Entrepreneurship Journal, 16*(3), 491–521.

Corbet, S., Goodell, J. W., Gunay, S., & Kaskaloglu, K. (2023). Are DeFi tokens a separate asset class from conventional cryptocurrencies? *Annals of Operations Research, 322*(2), 609–630.

Corbet, S., Goodell, J. W., & Gunay, S. (2022). What drives DeFi prices? Investigating the effects of investor attention. *Finance Research Letters, 48*, 102883. https://doi.org/10.1016/j.frl.2022.102883

Corbet, S., Hou, Y. G., Hu, Y., Larkin, C., & Oxley, L. (2020). Any port in a storm: Cryptocurrency safe-havens during the COVID-19 pandemic. *Economics Letters, 194*, 109377. https://doi.org/10.1016/j.econlet.2020.109377

Cumming, D. J., Dombrowski, N., Drobetz, W., & Momtaz, P. P. (2022, May). *Decentralized finance, crypto funds, and value creation in tokenized firms* (SSRN working paper). https://doi.org/10.2139/ssrn.4102295.

DefiLlama. (2023). *Raises*. Accessed on January 14, 2023, from https://defillama.com/raises

Denis, D. J. (2004). Entrepreneurial finance: An overview of the issues and evidence. *Journal of Corporate Finance, 10*(2), 301–326. https://doi.org/10.1016/S0929-1199(03)00059-2

Diebold, F. X., & Yılmaz, K. (2014). On the network topology of variance decompositions: Measuring the connectedness of financial firms. *Journal of Econometrics, 182*(1), 119–134.

Diebold, F. X., & Yilmaz, K. (2012). Better to give than to receive: Predictive directional measurement of volatility spillovers. *International Journal of Forecasting, 28*(1), 57–66.

Disli, M., Nagayev, R., Salim, K., Rizkiah, S. K., & Aysan, A. F. (2021). In search of safe haven assets during COVID-19 pandemic: An empirical analysis of different investor types. *Research in International Business and Finance, 58*, 101461. https://doi.org/10.1016/j.ribaf.2021.101461

Elsayed, A. H., Gozgor, G., & Yarovaya, L. (2022). Volatility and return connectedness of cryptocurrency, gold, and uncertainty: Evidence from the cryptocurrency uncertainty indices. *Finance Research Letters, 47*, 102732. https://doi.org/10.1016/j.frl.2022.102732

Fisch, C. (2019). Initial coin offerings (ICOs) to finance new ventures. *Journal of Business Venturing, 34*(1), 1–22. https://doi.org/10.1016/j.jbusvent.2018.09.007

Frid, C. J., Wyman, D. M., Gartner, W. B., & Hechavarria, D. H. (2016). Low-wealth entrepreneurs and access to external financing. *International Journal of Entrepreneurial Behavior & Research, 22*(4), 531–555. https://doi.org/10.1108/IJEBR-08-2015-0173

Goodell, J. W., & Goutte, S. (2021). Comovement of COVID-19 and bitcoin: Evidence from wavelet coherence analysis. *Finance Research Letters, 38*, 101625. https://doi.org/10.1016/j.frl.2020.101625

Gunay, S., Dženopoljac, V., & Bontis, N. (2022). Social media as a proxy for intellectual capital: Twitter posts in the cryptocurrency market. *International Journal of Web Based Communities, 18*(1), 1–20. https://doi.org/10.1504/IJWBC.2022.10044703

Gunay, S., & Kaskaloglu, K. (2022). Does utilizing smart contracts induce a financial connectedness between Ethereum and nonfungible tokens? *Research in International Business and Finance, 63*, 101773.

Gunay, S., Kaskaloglu, K., & Muhammed, S. (2021). Bitcoin and fiat currency interactions: Surprising results from Asian giants. *Mathematics, 9*(12), 1395.

Gunay, S., & Muhammed, S. (2022). *Identifying the role of investor sentiment proxies in NFT market: Comparisonof google trend, fear-greed index and VIX*. Fear-Greed Index and VIX (April 21, 2022). https://doi.org/10.2139/ssrn.4120176.

Jiang, Y., Wu, L., Tian, G., & Nie, H. (2021). Do cryptocurrencies hedge against EPU and the equity market volatility during COVID-19? New evidence from quantile coherency analysis. *Journal of International Financial Markets, Institutions and Money, 72*, 101324. https://doi.org/10.1016/j.intfin.2021.101324

Karim, S., Lucey, B. M., Naeem, M. A., & Uddin, G. S. (2022). Examining the interrelatedness of NFTs, DeFi tokens and cryptocurrencies. *Finance Research Letters, 47*, 102696. https://doi.org/10.1016/j.frl.2022.102696

Kirimhan, D. (2023). Importance of anti-money laundering regulations among prosumers for a cybersecure decentralized finance. *Journal of Business Research, 157*, 113558. https://doi.org/10.1016/j.jbusres.2022.113558

Koop, G., Pesaran, M. H., & Potter, S. M. (1996). Impulse response analysis in nonlinear multivariate models. *Journal of Econometrics, 74*(1), 119–147.

Kumar, A. S., & Padakandla, S. R. (2022). Testing the safe-haven properties of gold and bitcoin in the backdrop of COVID-19: A wavelet quantile correlation approach. *Finance Research Letters, 47*, 102707. https://doi.org/10.1016/j.frl.2022.102707

Lambert, T. (2022, February). *The rise of crowdfunding* (SSRN Working Paper). https://doi.org/10.2139/ssrn.4042613.

Lielacher A. (2022, October 29). *DeFi vs. CeFi: What's the difference between decentralized and centralized finance?* Cryptonews. https://cryptonews.com/exclusives/defi-*vs*-cefi-difference-between-decentralized-centralized-finance.htm

Lins, E., & Lutz, E. (2016). Bridging the gender funding gap: Do female entrepreneurs have equal access to venture capital? *International Journal of Entrepreneurship and Small Business, 27*(2–3), 347–365.

Lustig, C., & Nardi, B. (2015). Algorithmic authority: The case of bitcoin. In *2015 48th Hawaii International Conference on System Sciences* (pp. 743–752). IEEE. https://doi.org/10.1109/HICSS.2015.95

Manwari, L., Ngare, P., & Kipsang, R. (2017). Access to finance for women entrepreneurs in Kenya: Challenges and opportunities. *Journal of Emerging Trends in Economics and Management Sciences, 8*(1), 37–47.

Mariana, C. D., Ekaputra, I. A., & Husodo, Z. A. (2021). Are bitcoin and Ethereum safe-havens for stocks during the COVID-19 pandemic? *Finance Research Letters, 38*, 101798. https://doi.org/10.1016/j.frl.2020.101798

Metelski, D., & Sobieraj, J. (2022). Decentralized finance (DeFi) projects: A study of key performance indicators in terms of DeFi protocols' valuations. *International Journal of Financial Studies, 10*(4), 108.

Meyer, E., Welpe, I. M., & Sandner, P. G. (2022). *Decentralized finance—A systematic literature review and research directions* (SSRN Working Paper). https://doi.org/10.2139/ssrn.4016497.

Mochkabadi, K., & Volkmann, C. K. (2020). Equity crowdfunding: A systematic review of the literature. *Small Business Economics, 54*, 75–118.

Momtaz, P. P. (2022, January). *Decentralized finance (defi) markets for startups: Search frictions, intermediation, and efficiency* (SSRN Working Paper). https://doi.org/10.2139/ssrn.4020201.

Momtaz, P. P. (2021). *The economics of crypto funds* (SSRN Working Paper). https://doi.org/10.2139/ssrn.3865240.

Ozili, P. K. (2022). Decentralized finance research and developments around the world. *Journal of Banking and Financial Technology, 6*, 117–133. https://doi.org/10.1007/s42786-022-00044-x

Pesaran, H. H., & Shin, Y. (1998). Generalized impulse response analysis in linear multivariate models. *Economics Letters, 58*(1), 17–29.

Piñeiro-Chousa, J., López-Cabarcos, M. Á., Sevic, A., & González-López, I. (2022). A preliminary assessment of the performance of DeFi cryptocurrencies in relation to other financial assets, volatility, and user-generated content. *Technological Forecasting and Social Change, 181*, 121740. https://doi.org/10.1016/j.techfore.2022.121740

Pirson, M., & Malhotra, D. (2011). Foundations of organizational trust: What matters to different stakeholders? *Organization Science, 22*(4), 1087–1104. https://doi.org/10.1287/orsc.1100.0581

Reitalu, E., & Bajārs, R. (2022). *The asymmetric volatility of cryptocurrencies: What is the effect of leveraged trading?* (SSE Riga Student Research Papers No. 246). https://www.sseriga.edu/sites/default/files/2022-11/4Paper_Bajars_Reitalu.pdf

Saengchote, K., Putniņš, T., & Samphantharak, K. (2022, July). *Does DeFi remove the need for trust? Evidence from a natural experiment in stablecoin lending* (Working Paper). arXiv preprint arXiv:2207.06285.

Sarasvanthy, S., Nicholas, D., Ramakrishna, V., & Venkataraman, S. (2003). Three views of entrepreneurial opportunity. In Z. J. Acs & D. B. Audretsch (Eds.), *Handbook of entrepreneurship research* (pp. 141–160). Springer. https://doi.org/10.1007/0-387-24519-7_7

Schumpeter, J. A. (1942). *Capitalism, socialism and democracy*. Harper.

Shumba C. (2021). *Crypto assets could replace fiat currencies within as little as 5 years, financial execs tell*. Deloitte, Markets Insider. Accessed on January 30, 2023, from https://markets.businessinsider.com/news/currencies/crypto-to-replace-fiat-within-10-years-financial-execs-say-deloitte-2021-8

Stock, J., Elliott, G., & Rothenberg, T. (1996). Efficient tests for an autoregressive unit root. *Econometrica, 64*(4), 813–836. https://doi.org/10.3386/t0130

Tan, T. M., Salo, J., Ahokangas, P., Seppänen, V., & Sandner, P. (2021). Revealing the disintermediation concept of blockchain technology: How intermediaries gain from blockchain adoption in a new business model. In *Impact of globalization and advanced technologies on online business models* (pp. 88–102). IGI Global. https://doi.org/10.4018/978-1-7998-7603-8.ch006

Ugolini, A., Reboredo, J. C., & Mensi, W. (2023). Connectedness between DeFi, cryptocurrency, stock, and safe-haven assets. *Finance Research Letters, 53*, 103692.

Umar, Z., & Gubareva, M. (2020). A time–frequency analysis of the impact of the Covid-19 induced panic on the volatility of currency and cryptocurrency markets. *Journal of Behavioral and Experimental Finance, 28*, 100404. https://doi.org/10.1016/j.jbef.2020.100404

Venkataraman, S. (1997). The distinctive domain of entrepreneurship research. In J. A. Katz & R. Brockhaus (Eds.), *Advances in entrepreneurship, firm emergence and growth* (pp. 119–138). JAI Press.

Wang, Y., Horky, F., Baals, L. J., Lucey, B. M., & Vigne, S. A. (2022). Bubbles all the way down? Detecting and date-stamping bubble behaviors in NFT and DeFi markets. *Journal of Chinese Economic and Business Studies, 20*(4), 415–436. https://doi.org/10.1080/14765284.2022.2138161

Wiklund, J., Davidsson, P., Audretsch, D. B., & Karlsson, C. (2011). The future of entrepreneurship research. *Entrepreneurship Theory and Practice, 35*(1), 1–9. https://doi.org/10.1111/j.1540-6520.2010.00420.x

Yousaf, I., Jareño, F., & Esparcia, C. (2022a). Tail connectedness between lending/borrowing tokens and commercial bank stocks. *International Review of Financial Analysis, 84*, 102417. https://doi.org/10.1016/j.irfa.2022.102417

Yousaf, I., Nekhili, R., & Gubareva, M. (2022b). Linkages between DeFi assets and conventional currencies: Evidence from the COVID-19 pandemic. *International Review of Financial Analysis, 81*, 102082. https://doi.org/10.1016/j.irfa.2022.102082

Samet Gunay, Ph.D. holds the Associate Professor of Finance position at Corvinus University of Budapest, Hungary. Prior to this role, he served as an Associate Professor of Finance at the American University of the Middle East in Kuwait. His area of study is finance, and his research interest includes cryptocurrencies, modeling of volatility, and credit risk. Dr. Gunay received his Ph.D. from Istanbul University in 2013. He was a visiting scholar at Indiana State University in 2014 and was a visiting Ph.D. student at the National University of Singapore in 2013. Dr. Gunay published research articles in prestigious journals, including Energy Economics, Research in International Business and Finance, Annals of Operations Research, Journal of Cleaner Production, Resources Policy and Finance Research Letters.

Shahnawaz Muhammed, Ph.D. is a Professor of Information Systems and Operations Management at the College of Business Administration at the American University of the Middle East, Kuwait. His research interests include knowledge management, knowledge representation, supply chain management, and cryptocurrencies. He has several publications in leading journals in the field, such as the Journal of Knowledge Management, Journal of Cleaner Production, Journal of Innovation & Knowledge, Information Technology & People, Knowledge Management Research and Practice, Management Decision, and has presented at many international conferences. Prior to his current position, he taught at Fayetteville State University, USA and has held several senior-level administrative positions in his current institution. He is a Certified Supply Chain Professional (CSCP) by APICS and is a member of the Association for Information Systems (AIS).

Destan Kirimhan, Ph.D. is an Assistant Professor of Finance at the School of Business Administration at the American University of Sharjah (AUS) and research fellow at the Digital Euro Association. Prior to joining AUS, she worked at the Department of Economics and Finance at the University of Texas at El Paso. Dr. Kirimhan received her bachelor's degree in economics from TOBB University of Economics and Technology in Turkey, her M.A. in economics from Bilkent University in Turkey, and Ph.D. in finance from the University of South Carolina, USA. Dr. Kirimhan's research covers various dimensions of financial intermediation, financial regulation, financial technology (FinTech), and cybersecurity. Her research has been accepted or published by such outlets as the Journal of Business Research, Journal of Financial Research, and Journal of Hospitality and Tourism Management and has been presented at numerous prominent conferences worldwide.

Vladimir Dzenopoljac, Ph.D. is an Associate Professor of Business Transformation at the College of Interdisciplinary Studies, Zayed University, in Dubai. Previously, he served as the Associate Professor of Strategic Management at the College of Business and Economics, United Arab Emirates University in Al Ain. Before coming to the UAE, Vladimir was the Associate Professor, Director of the MBA program, and Business Consulting Center coordinator at the College of Business Administration, American University of the Middle East, Kuwait. He received his Ph.D. Degree from the University of Kragujevac, Serbia, in the field of impact of intellectual capital on value creation in contemporary enterprises, where he started his academic career in 2002. Alongside his academic career, Vladimir was providing business consultancy services in the fields of strategy development and execution, business planning, financial planning and analysis, and leadership. He is an active researcher in the areas of strategy, intellectual capital, knowledge management, leadership, and entrepreneurship.

A Framework for Implementation of Decentralized Finance for Financial Inclusion of Unbanked Populations in a Developing Context. A Case of Zimbabwe

Samuel Musungwini and Samuel Simbarashe Furusa

1 Introduction

The whole world is in the midst of a digital revolution (T. Qin et al., 2022), and this revolution is now straddling different socioeconomic sectors, such as agriculture (Musungwini, et al., 2022), tourism (Njerekai, 2020), health (Furusa & Coleman, 2018), education (Iglesias-Pradas & Prieto, 2021), and business (HSBC, 2018). In this revolution, the financial sector has not been spared, as reported by Kawasmi et al. (2019). These authors are convinced that the financial services sector is one area that is experiencing the greatest disruptive effect because of the evolution and revolution of information and communication technology (ICT) in that domain, ushering in new possibilities that resulted in the birth of fintech. One of the offshoots of this revolution is decentralized finance (DeFi), which is a rapidly growing area of finance that is transforming the way people access, store, and use their money, especially in the developed world. According to Abdulhakeem and Hu (2021), DeFi is a form of financial technology that uses blockchain technology to enable peer-to-peer transactions without the need for a centralized intermediary (Fig. 1). While this technology has been used in the developed world, it is vital to note that it has the potential to revolutionize the way people access financial services, especially in developing countries where access to traditional banking is limited (Mhlanga, 2021).

Zimbabwe is a developing country situated in sub-Saharan Africa (SSA) in the Global South. The country has a population of approximately 15 million people, and out of these, approximately 75% are unbanked, as asserted by Mujeyi and Sadomba (2019). As a result, the country faces a major challenge of financial

S. Musungwini (✉) · S. S. Furusa
Department of Information and Marketing Sciences, Faculty of Business Sciences, Midlands State University, Gweru, Zimbabwe
e-mail: musungwinis@staff.msu.ac.zw; furusass@staff.msu.ac.zw

S. Basly (ed.), *Decentralized Finance*, Financial Innovation and Technology,
https://doi.org/10.1007/978-3-031-49515-1_4

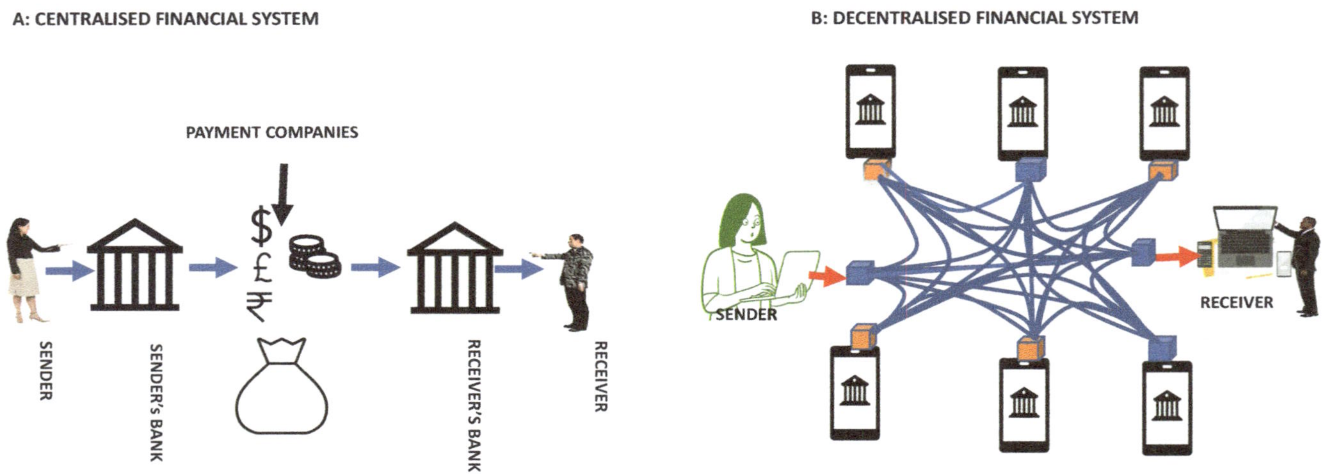

Fig. 1 Illustrating the difference between traditional and decentralized financial systems (Author's construction)

inclusion since the bulk of its populace is unbanked. The concept of financial inclusion is defined as the access and use of formal financial services by unbanked individuals and businesses (Boar et al., 2020). For people to access and use financial services, they must first have access to financial products and institutions. This access is often limited in developing countries due to a lack of infrastructure, poverty, and operational knowledge (Ozili, 2022). The implementation of DeFi for the financial inclusion of unbanked populations in a developing context has been a major challenge for many countries around the world, including SSA, and Zimbabwe is no exception. To situate this work in a developing context, we explore the Zimbabwean context. That is why this chapter explores the potential of DeFi to improve financial inclusion for unbanked populations in a developing context, with a particular focus on Zimbabwe. The authors looked at the current state of financial inclusion in Zimbabwe, the challenges and opportunities presented by DeFi, and proposed a framework for the implementation of DeFi for financial inclusion in the country. The chapter will also discuss the potential benefits of DeFi for financial inclusion, as well as the risks and challenges that must be addressed to ensure successful implementation. Finally, the chapter provides recommendations for how DeFi can be used to improve financial inclusion in Zimbabwe and the developing world in general.

2 Chapter Objectives

- To assess the current level of financial inclusion among the unbanked in Zimbabwe and pinpoint the difficulties encountered.
- To determine whether decentralized finance can bring financial inclusion to Zimbabwe's unbanked people.
- To examine how decentralized finance affects Zimbabwe's unbanked population's ability to access financial services.
- To assess how well the decentralized financial system is working to increase the financial inclusion of the unbanked in Zimbabwe.
- To create a framework for the deployment of decentralized finance to help Zimbabwe's unbanked communities become financially included.

3 Methodology

Our book chapter is guided by a qualitative research approach because this approach is used in exploratory research (Denzin & Lincoln, 2005). This is a systematic examination of social phenomena in unstructured environments, and these occurrences can encompass but are not restricted to how people perceive different aspects of their everyday lives, how these people behave individually or collectively, how businesses run, and how daily encounters affect relationships between individuals

(Astalin, 2013). In this approach, the researcher is the primary data-gathering tool. As a result, the researchers looked at the circumstances surrounding why things happen and what those things signify to the person or context under study. Because of this, our book chapter begins by exploring a literature review on the Zimbabwean context and then delves into disruptive technology, particularly the FinTech revolution, such as blockchain, cryptocurrency, decentralized finance, and financial inclusion. However, in carrying out the literature review on disruptive financial technology, primacy was given to the literature covering the developing world, especially sub-Saharan Africa (SSA) (Snyder, 2019). To add contextual significance to our work other than our views as the authors, we then carried out a 12-member focus group discussion and 10 in-depth interviews with 4 fintech experts in Zimbabwe and 6 individuals from marginalized communities in Zimbabwe.

4 Background and Context

Zimbabwe (Fig. 2) is a country with a population of over 15 million, and over 80% of the working-age population is unemployed, underemployed, or informally employed, which has resulted in the country seeing a rapid increase in poverty

Fig. 2 Map of Zimbabwe (UN Cartographic https://www.nationsonline.org/oneworld/map/zimbabwe_map2.htm)

levels and financial exclusion over the past two decades, as reported by Tipedze, Ngirazi, Mutenga, and Satande (2020). This has been largely due to a lack of access to basic financial services, such as banking and credit facilities. Despite the introduction of several government-led initiatives to increase financial inclusion, such as mobile banking and microfinance, financial inclusion challenges have remained in most marginalized communities, particularly rural unemployed masses. This is mainly because most of the old-fashioned initiatives have mostly been limited to urban areas and connected areas, leaving the bulk of the rural population largely unbanked. This is even though the second republic [as the new government of Zimbabwe calls itself] has been very vocal about the need to transform the country's fortunes and propel it toward an upper middle-income economy by 2030, which resonates well with the Sustainable Development Goals (SDGs) 2016–2030 development framework.

Zimbabwe attained independence in 1980, and the economy was a beacon. So good and sound was the state of the economy that one Zimbabwean dollar was equivalent to two United States dollars (Z$1:US$2). That is why the country was once regarded as the jewel of Africa. Since the attainment of independence, hundreds of businesses have folded or scaled down because of funding shortages and other problems. These encompass the mighty Zimbabwe Iron and Steel Company (ZISCO), the Shabanie and Mashaba Mines, and others, and this had a toll on the National Railway of Zimbabwe (NRZ) as the transportation of Cargo dwindled. The country has since been reduced to a supermarket economy considering the current status of the nation, and there is a need for a rapid turnaround. Some claim that the current state can be attributed to President Robert Mugabe and his government, mainly composed of combatants in the liberation war, as they apprenticed on the job of governing without any experience.

The closure of many industries resulted in rampant unemployment, which forced many people into informal economic activities such as artisanal mining, vending, and cross-border trading (Musungwini & Van Zyl, 2017). This also resulted in the sprouting of many micro, small, and medium enterprises (MSMEs). However, one of the challenges faced by many of these economic actors is access to finance to boost their economic activities. In light of this, in the new millennium, there have been calls for national financial inclusion strategies to be crafted and implemented, as they are increasingly being seen by many nations as necessary (Mashapure et al., 2022). That is why the introduction of national financial inclusion strategies by country governments was seen as providing an evidence-based approach that prioritizes better-resourced and more thorough ways to increase access to and usage of financial services by all citizens. As a result, the Zimbabwean government implemented its national financial inclusion plan with distinct aims and objectives to encourage cooperation between public and private sector partners and offer a framework for the implementation of financial inclusion laws and regulations in 2016 (RBZ, 2016). However, 6 years later, a study carried out in 2022 established that 94% of MSMEs in Zimbabwe are not registered, and 84% of them are informal (FinScope, 2022). Some of the reasons cited are that 37% of these indicated that they are too small to register, 17% do not have money to register, and some cited a lack of knowledge, among other reasons. As a result, these MSMEs, who constitute the bulk of economic actors in Zimbabwe, do not have access to the financial opportunities, if any, that are offered under the Zimbabwe national financial inclusion strategy 2016.

It is in this context that these researchers thought that DeFi offers an exciting opportunity to bridge the gap between the unbanked and the banking system. The authors believe that by leveraging the power of blockchain technology, DeFi can help facilitate access to financial services in a secure, transparent, and cost-effective manner for the unbanked populace in Zimbabwe and other developing countries. This is what inspired us to craft this book chapter, in which we provide an overview of the current state of financial inclusion in Zimbabwe and the potential of DeFi for improving access to financial services for the unbanked populace. Many adults historically banked through community clubs and Savings and Credit Cooperative Organizations in underdeveloped nations such as Zimbabwe, as reported by Kachingwe (1986) and echoed by Musungwini et al. (2014). These organizations do not require the lengthy documentation needed for traditional funding because they are built on trust. While offering easy access to funds, these organizations also demand exorbitant interest rates in some instances.

The literature has suggested that DeFi technology has the potential to revolutionize the banking operational landscape in Africa and provide a springboard for entrepreneurial activities that can subsequently make financial services more widely available to unbanked marginalized masses, offering easy access to affordable financial products, as suggested by HSBC (2018) and echoed by scholars such as Trivedi et al. (2021), di Prisco and Strangio (2021), and Kabanda (2021). That is why we believe that DeFi may also provide a lush area for blockchain-based smart contracts to prosper in decentralized finance, subsequently facilitating financial access for all, including underprivileged individuals in a developing context. While it is reported that some African nations are catching up and developing swiftly, the majority of them are still underdeveloped and hesitant to accept new technologies (Mavilia & Pisani, 2020). Many more people now have access to knowledge and jobs and are developing in different social spheres because smartphones are opening doors to the outside world thanks to the disruptive nature of technology (Musungwini & Van Zyl, 2017). However, DeFi is still in its infancy stages in Zimbabwe, as disruptive financial activities are looming on the horizon and a few projects are beginning to emerge. These projects are focused on providing financial services such as lending, borrowing, and trading, as well as other services such as payments and remittances, among other areas, as reported by di Prisco and Strangio (2021). These projects are still in the early stages of development and adoption, but they are beginning to gain a stranglehold on the country's financial landscape. However, we believe that there is a need for a guiding framework to be fashioned that can provide a guideline for the operationalization of DeFi and for reaping maximum positive vistas of development from the technology (Musungwini, et al., 2022).

5 Literature Review

5.1 Decentralized Finance

Decentralized finance is a rapidly evolving sector of the blockchain industry, and it can transform the financial services landscape, especially in the developing world, as asserted by Mavilia and Pisani (2020). DeFi is a financial technology that rides on blockchain technology to create a more efficient, transparent, and secure financial system (Abdulhakeem & Hu, 2021). Since it is centered on the principle of decentralization, it may function without the aid of a centralized administration or middleman (Fig. 3). Therefore, DeFi can give aspiring entrepreneurs and existing MSEMs access to financial services that are quicker, less expensive, and more dependable than conventional financial services by cutting out the intermediary (di Prisco & Strangio, 2021). That is why we believe that DeFi may have a major effect on entrepreneurship development in developing countries such as Zimbabwe, where the bulk of the population is unbanked mainly because they are either unemployed, underemployed, or working in the informal sector, as reported by Mujeyi and Sadomba (2019). As a result, DeFi can afford aspiring business owners to launch their business ventures more quickly and successfully by giving them access to financial services that are quicker, less expensive, and more dependable. This has the effect of lowering their operating expenses and boosting their revenue.

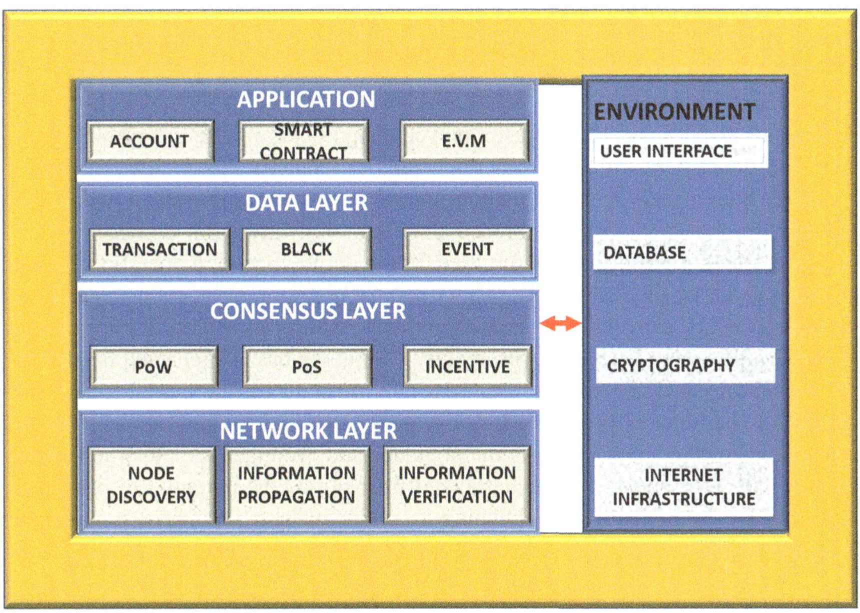

Fig. 3 Illustration of the operation of the DeFi network (Author's construction)

This means that DeFi has the potential to provide business owners with access to international markets and new funding opportunities, especially because of the growing diaspora population across the world (HSBC, 2018). These researchers believe that this can help entrepreneurs in Zimbabwe grow the businesses they operate and improve their chances of success. DeFi can further assist business owners in safeguarding their money and assets by enabling them to preserve their capital from fraud and theft by offering a safe and open platform for financial transactions. Instead of worrying about the safety of their money, DeFi can afford aspiring and existing business owners, especially those from marginalized communities, to concentrate on expanding their businesses (Kabanda, 2021). Therefore, DeFi can have a large impact on entrepreneurial activities and could change how financial services are delivered. This can be a boon to entrepreneurs in developing countries, as it can reduce the risk of their funds being misused or stolen. DeFi may assist aspiring entrepreneurs in launching their firms more quickly by allowing them to use quicker, less expensive, and more dependable financial services.

By giving individuals who are typically excluded from the conventional banking system the opportunity to use financial services using blockchain technology, DeFi might considerably enhance the quality of life for people in underdeveloped nations such as Zimbabwe while also promoting economic expansion and employment creation. DeFi can have a dual effect on entrepreneurship in a developing environment, as it can give people who otherwise would not be able to obtain credit or money access (Qureshi & Xiong, 2018). These include aspiring entrepreneurs and those who are just starting out and in need of access to finance to fund their businesses, and they may particularly benefit from this. Second, DeFi can offer access to financial services that are not offered by the conventional banking system, such as payments, remittances, multilateral netting, and lending. This can enable existing and aspiring entrepreneurs to conduct business more easily, as well as access global markets and customers.

Decentralized finance has already played a significant role in this growth trajectory, and given Africans numerous opportunities (Salami, 2020), African governments are increasingly realizing the promise of decentralized finance in Africa, even though they have not fully embraced the technology (Mavilia & Pisani, 2020). Africa presents a surfeit of opportunities for the deployment and operationalization of DeFi fueled by blockchain. The networks that are built on blockchain can lower barriers to using conventional financial systems and promote financial inclusion. However, like many African governments, Zimbabwe has also enacted harsh lending regulations that are making it increasingly difficult for the marginalized communities to be financially included. Additionally, there is a lack of financial literacy and a lackluster reputation among the populace and even the regulatory authorities. That is why we believe that decentralized finance has the potential to restore the power of the individual by establishing a system in which financial products are available to all.

5.2 Understanding the Need for Decentralized Finance in Developing Countries

Since there is a lack of financial resources and infrastructure, access to financial services is frequently restricted in developing nations, especially in SSA, as posited by Mazuruse (2023). That is why it is believed that by giving people an avenue that allows for access to financial products and services without depending on a centralized authority, DeFi could assist in bridging this gap (di Prisco & Strangio, 2021). Since the users of DeFi do not have to pay the fees associated with conventional banking institutions, this might result in a lowering of costs. In addition, DeFi can offer transactions that are more transparent and secure because all transactions are recorded on a public ledger, which makes it more difficult for fraud to occur (Aquilina et al., 2023). This DeFi can also assist in lowering the likelihood of corruption in emerging nations such as Zimbabwe, a country dogged by perennial government incompetence and corruption. The public ledger that records every transaction makes it considerably more difficult for corrupt people to take advantage of the system considering the revelations in the much-avowed documentary "Gold Maffia" by the Al Jazeera investigative unit https://www.aljazeera.com/news/2023/5/14/south-africa-to-investigate-gold-mafia-uncovered-by-al-jazeera. DeFi has the potential to boost financial services accessibility, which can aid in the reduction of income disparities and poverty in developing nations such as Zimbabwe. As a result, it can assist in lowering the financial strain on people and families, thereby enabling them to build up savings and reinvest more money by increasing access to financial services.

5.3 Examining the Benefits of Decentralized Finance for Financial Inclusion

Developing countries, especially SSA, have the largest number of marginalized people, and those people are naturally denied access to financial services by conventional banking systems owing to diverse factors. These factors encompass a lack of access to financial provisions, astronomical expenses, and a lack of confidence because of a very long time of being denied access, and these people may be able to do so through decentralized finance. This is because DeFi gives those who have been excluded from traditional banking systems access to financial services, which is one of its key advantages (Shinde, 2023). Hence, people who live in developing nations, where access to banking services is either very limited or nonexistent at all, will particularly benefit from this. In addition, DeFi offers access to financial services to people who are underbanked or unbanked, that is, those who have little or no access to conventional banking services (Wan et al., 2023). Those who reside in rural areas will particularly benefit from DeFi, as well as low-income earners. That is why we believe that this provides a springboard for countries such as Zimbabwe, whose bulk population is marginalized and resides in rural areas. Therefore, by presenting the possibility of using a variety of financial services, DeFi also promotes broader financial inclusion (Qin et al., 2021). This encompasses access to financial items, including loans, savings, investments, and insurance, as these are all encapsulated in the DeFi model. This makes financial goods available to those who might not otherwise have access to them, which is highly beneficial for those seeking to increase their wealth or safeguard their investments. DeFi also makes a variety of financial services available that are more reasonably priced and easily accessible than traditional banking services. Lower prices, quicker transactions, and more secure transactions are all part of development, as people who want to save money or who have limited access to regular banking services would particularly benefit from this.

5.4 *Challenges of Implementing Decentralized Finance for Unbanked Populations*

DeFi is being highly heralded as a potential game-changer for unbanked people, as it would allow them to access financial services that are not available to them through traditional banking systems, especially in the developing world. DeFi will nevertheless face several obstacles before it can be made available to the underserved, unbanked communities in developing nations (Wan et al., 2023). The initial hurdle is developing a user-friendly platform that is simple to use and comprehend. For unbanked communities, which might lack the technical know-how or practical expertise to operate sophisticated financial systems, this is especially crucial. In addition, maintaining the platform's dependability and security is difficult because any security lapses could have negative effects on users. DeFi is still a relatively new idea, and unbanked people are not well informed about it. This implies that individuals might not be aware of the risks or potential advantages of using DeFi. As a result, it is critical to develop educational programs that can promote knowledge of DeFi and its potential advantages.

The other obstacle that lies in making DeFi available to unbanked populations entails making sure the platform is accessible to them in their native tongue and that using it will not break the bank (Aquilina et al., 2023). For unbanked communities to conveniently access their money, it is also crucial to ensure that the platform can interface with current banking systems. Technology access is another issue, as users need to have access to their smartphones or computers as well as the internet to be able to use DeFi services. Because technological access is scarce in developing nations, this can be a significant obstacle in this endeavor. Users must also be knowledgeable about how to use the technology, which can be challenging for individuals who lack technical aptitude or access to training. The issue of liquidity is another daunting challenge since decentralized networks are frequently used to build DeFi services, and liquidity issues may arise. As a result, the unbanked masses in developing nations may find it particularly challenging because they do not have access to the enormous sums of capital required for transactions (Trivedi et al., 2021). That is why we believe that accessing DeFi services may also be challenging due to this issue of a lack of liquidity because there could not be enough users to fund the transactions.

The issue of trust is a challenge of monumental proportions, as the decentralized networks are the building blocks for DeFi services; thus, users must have faith in the network to protect their money. Since they may not possess the same level of technological trust as people in more developed nations, this can be difficult for unbanked populations in developing nations. There is a need for vigorous promotional activities as well as clearing all elements of doubt that potential users may have for it to be a success (Dube et al., 2023). Due to the lack of the same restrictions that safeguard users in conventional banking systems, there is also a danger of fraud or theft. Therefore, it is crucial to address these difficulties so that unbanked citizens in developing nations can use DeFi services efficiently. This can involve expanding access to technology, offering instruction on how to use it, and establishing rules to safeguard users against fraud and theft.

6 Empirical Data from Key Informants

The researchers interviewed 10 key informants to gather empirical data from the various stakeholders to enrich the state of Zimbabwe context data and argue for the suitability of the contextual settings for DeFi (Table 1). These key informants included two fintech experts, and one of these experts is heavily involved in forex trading and bitcoin cryptocurrency. One of the key informants was a banker, one was a highly skilled IT manager for a bank; one was a cross-border trader; two smallholder farmers; one vendor; one artisanal miner; and one micro, small, and medium enterprise (MSME) owner. These were purposively sampled for suitability, as they were found to meet the criteria required by the authors. The authors were interested in interviewing people who were a good fit in terms of representation of the marginalized groups in Zimbabwe. In addition to the key informants, the authors also conducted a focus group discussion (FGD) to verify the nuances generated from the in-depth interviews (Table 2). However, the structure of our focus group discussion was unfocused since the nuances we needed to gather from the group had to do with the current challenges of financial inclusion faced by the marginalized communities in Zimbabwe as well as the potential for financial inclusion offered by DeFi as well as the challenges posed by the successful implementation of DeFi in the Zimbabwean context. That is why the composition of the FGD included two cryptocurrency experts and online forex traders, two bankers, one cross-border trader, one vendor, two university students, two smallholder farmers, and two registered MSME members.

The current level of financial inclusion among the unbanked in Zimbabwe and to pinpoint the difficulties encountered.

Table 1 Details of the participants in the in-depth interviews

Pseudonym	Age	Gender	Position profile	Highest Qualification	Date of interview	Fintech Knowledge	Financial Literacy	Entrepreneurial Knowledge	Entrepreneurial Working experience	Participant number
Chamunorwa	36	Male	Fintech expert	MSc Information Systems	24 November 2022	Very high	Very high	High	5 years	INTERV-P1
Namatai	33	Female	Fintech expert	BSc Data Science	28 November 2022	Very high	Very high	Very high	9 years	INTERV-P2
Maria	39	Female	Cross-border trader	BSc Human Resource Management	5 December 2022	High	Very high	Very high	14 years	INTERV-P3
Zvakanaka	43	Male	Artisanal miner	BSc Geography and Environmental Science	7 December 2022	High	High	High	16 years	INTERV-P4
Tsikamusava	47	Male	Successful smallholder farmer	Diploma in Agriculture	9 December 2022	Medium	High	Moderate	23 years	INTERV-P5
Chavurura	29	Male	Foreign currency and cryptocurrency trader.	BSc Hons Information Systems	13 December 2022	High	Medium	High	6 years	INTERV-P6
Kudakwashe	39	Male	ICT manager for a Bank	BSc Computer Science	15 December 2022	High	High	High	14 years	INTERV-P7
Chihera	45	Female	Bank ICT investment analyst	BSc Computer Science	5 January 2023	Very high	Very high	Moderate	18 years	INTERV-P8

Pseudonym	Age	Gender	Position profile	Highest Qualification	Date of interview	Fintech Knowledge	Financial Literacy	Entrepreneurial Knowledge	Entrepreneurial Working experience	Participant number
Marujata	33	Female	Vendor	Vocational Training Certificate	8 January 2023	High	High	High	9 years	INTERV-P9
Moyombembe	41	Male	Medium enterprise owner	BCom Business Management	10 January 2023	High	Very high	Moderate	18 years	INTERV-P10

Table 2 Details of the FGD participants

FGD Participants Pseudonyms	Age	Gender	Position profile	Highest Qualification	Financial inclusion Knowledge	DeFi Knowledge	Financially excluded	Working experience	FGD Participant number
Masharo	39	Male	Cryptocurrency expert and foreign currency trader	BCom Accounting	Very high	High	No	15 years	FGD-P1
Mandivavarira	36	Female	Cryptocurrency expert and foreign currency trader	BSc Economics	Very high	High	No	13 years	FGD-P2
Muchazondida	48	Female	Banker	BCom Business Management	Very high	High	No	23 years	FGD-P3
Chigohi	41	Male	Banker	BCom Financial Management	Very high	High	No	16 years	FGD-P4
Nyakasikana	22	Female	University student	Studying BCom Banking and Finance	High	High	Partially	5 years	FGD-P5
Flavia	23	Male	University student	Studying BCom Accounting	High	High	Partially	3 years	FGD-P6
Ntando	40	Male	Cross-border trader	BCom Marketing	Very high	High	No	14 years	FGD-P7
Shingai	37	Female	Vendor	BCom Entrepreneurship	Very high	Low	Yes	14 years	FGD-P8
Rupanga	56	Male	Smallholder farmer	Master farmer certificate	High	Low	Yes	27 yes	FGD-P9
Chenaimoyo	48	Female	Smallholder farmer	Ordinary level of education	High	Very low	Yes	23 yes	FGD-P10
Olivia	49	Female	MSME	BCom Business Management	High	High	No	25 years	FGD-P11
Chitovanedzinavene	53	Male	MSME	BED Education	Very high	Low	No	28 years	FGD-P12

The key informants reported that the current level of financial inclusion among the unbanked in Zimbabwe is low, as they are limited to informal borrowing "Chimbadzo", which is a very costly and high-risk model for both the borrower and the lender. Both key informants and the participants in the focus group discussion pointed out that the bulk of the population in Zimbabwe is rural because of the harsh economic climate, where even for the working class, it is very difficult to make ends meet. As participants, especially from the financial services sector, pointed out, in their banking institutions, some account holders are earning even negative salaries in some instances. Participants allege that the bulk of the rural adult population in Zimbabwe does not have an account at a formal financial institution. They cited the major reason for that as a lack of financial literacy, which also leads to a lack of faith in established banking institutions, especially among Zimbabwe's unbanked rural populace. Financial inclusion is also significantly hampered by the high cost of financial services, which, according to participants, seem to take more from clients than they do from banks.

There is also a lack of suitable financial products and limited access to technology among the rural populace. The bulk of the financially excluded is said to be dogged by a lack of official proof of identity documents, especially proof of residence, a shaky economy, rural poverty, gender inequality, and high transaction costs for financial services, which are highlighted as the main obstacles to achieving financial inclusion in Zimbabwe. However, the participants pointed out that telecommunications giant Econet's mobile money platform, Ecocash, has provided a major conduit for the bulk of the population to get financially included. Although the Women's Bank of Zimbabwe was established to advance women's financial needs, there seem to be obstacles to most women obtaining access to this money. Here are some excerpts from focus groups and in-depth interviews that were conducted regarding the research objective provided above.

> Most people in Zimbabwe do not have bank accounts [...] they normally manage their financial affairs informally through cash transactions and informal borrowing. **FGD-P8.**

> In Zimbabwe, most marginalized people reside in the rural areas, and they are unbanked and in most cases they lack the required paperwork to open a bank account, and even if they do, many of them lack the funds required to keep a minimum balance. **INTERV-P5.**

> I believe that the majority of Zimbabwe's unbanked population is marginalized, and they do not understand the concept of decentralized finance. [...] if they are to embrace it, they have to be taught... **FGD-P9.**

> Decentralized finance is good and has the potential to open up financial services to the unbanked in Zimbabwe and lower transaction costs and fees. [...] I think that if the unbanked in Zimbabwe are given the proper training and resources, they are likely to embrace decentralized finance. **INTERV-P6.**

To determine whether decentralized finance could bring financial inclusion to Zimbabwe's unbanked people.

The research participants suggested that the actual decentralized financial system is still operating in its early stages and that its effects on financial inclusion are not yet fully understood. Zimbabwe allows the purchase, sale, and usage of cryptocurrencies without breaching the law. They pointed out that the Zimbabwean government and private companies are not yet compelled to make use of cryptocurrency as a means of payment for goods and services since it is not yet recognized as legal tender by the monetary authorities in Zimbabwe. However, they acknowledged that DeFi has the potential to provide the unbanked with access to financial services that would otherwise be unavailable. The decentralized financial system has been beneficial in increasing the financial inclusion of the unbanked in Zimbabwe, as it provides them with access to financial services that are otherwise not available to them. The decentralized financial system has had a positive effect on the financial inclusion of some of the unbanked people in Zimbabwe, as it has provided them with access to financial services that were previously unavailable. Below are some extracts taken from focus groups and in-depth interviews that were conducted regarding the above research objective.

> [...] for the unbanked to effectively embrace decentralized finance, they need to be equipped with the right knowledge and resources [...] This could include things like training on how to use the technology, providing access to education, and access to the necessary technology. **FGD-P4.**

> Most of the people who are unbanked in Zimbabwe are not familiar with the concept of cryptocurrency, and so they are unlikely to embrace it without further education and support. **INTERV-P2.**

> I think the primary benefit that decentralized finance could bring to the unbanked in Zimbabwe is greater access to financial services and products, which would enable them to open their business activities and make more money. **FGD-P3.**

To examine how decentralized finance affects Zimbabwe's unbanked population's ability to access financial services.

The participants pointed out that the decentralized financial system has significantly improved the financial inclusion of some of Zimbabwe's unbanked population by giving them access to financial services that they were unable to obtain in the past. This includes MSMEs, cross-border traders, university students, some segments of smallholder farmers, and some vendors. However, participants pointed out that the bulk of the population from these marginalized groups is left out. Hence, they suggested that there is a need to expand access to digital technologies for marginalized masses, as DeFi is **ONLY** accessed via the internet using ICT tools. The participants also suggested that there is a need to establish rules to safeguard the unbanked from potential online hazards, as this can allay the fears of most of the population. Therefore, giving financially excluded people access to digital technology and providing a safe operating environment in which to use it is a key issue that should be resolved. That is why we believe that to ensure decentralized finance is handled responsibly and operates successfully in Zimbabwe, laws must be crafted and put in place to provide a cushioning effect for users. Some excerpts from focus groups and in-depth interviews were conducted regarding the research objective.

> I think to reach more unbanked people in Zimbabwe decentralized finance could be promoted through educational campaigns and community outreach activities. **FGD-P6.**

> Providing the appropriate education and technology to the unbanked in Zimbabwe is the most efficient approach to using decentralized finance to help people become financially included. **INTERV-P10.**

> There is a lack of user protection, and the risk of fraud are two perceived risks linked to decentralized finance for the unbanked in Zimbabwe. **FGD-P11.**

To assess how well the decentralized financial system can work to increase the financial inclusion of the unbanked in Zimbabwe.

The participants suggested that the decentralized financial system has been beneficial in increasing the financial inclusion of some of the unbanked population in Zimbabwe, as it provides them with access to financial services that are otherwise not available to them from the centralized financial system. However, a good number of marginalized individuals are still left out, and therefore, to further increase financial inclusion among the marginalized population, it is necessary to create a more secure and reliable digital infrastructure to provide the backbone for operations as a starting point. In addition, there is a need to establish regulations that provide some element of protection to the unbanked from potential financial risks, as some participants pointed out that there are many cases that have been happening in this sector, as many people have equally lost their hard-earned money to some bogus operators of crypto-currency traders, including some legitimate ones such as Golix.

Participants contend that by allowing financial services and goods that are not offered through conventional banking systems, Zimbabwe's decentralized financial system can have the potential to promote financial inclusion for those who are now financially excluded. This system might offer a more effective and safe way to safeguard the value of money in a volatile economy, send money, and make payments. Additionally, DeFi can also give access to financial services such as credit and some other services that may not be offered by conventional banking institutions. This would make it possible for Zimbabwe's unbanked population to gain access to financial services and goods that they would not otherwise have. Additionally, the decentralized financial system can act as a substitute for existing banking systems, which are frequently inefficient, expensive, and unstable. As a result, this could help reduce the cost of financial services and make them more accessible to the unbanked. The following are snippets from the focus groups and in-depth interviews that were held concerning the objective.

> I think for users of the system to feel confident that their money is protected, it must be trustworthy and secure. [...] My friend lost money invested in one of the cryptocurrency business organizations. **INTERV-P1.**

> Trust, security, scalability, and interoperability, in my opinion, are the essential elements of a successful decentralized finance system for financial inclusion. **FGD-P2.**

> It must also be scalable to support a high volume of transactions. **INTER-P3.**

> [...] that system must be able to integrate with the other financial systems like Ecocash [interoperable] to communicate with other networks and financial systems. **FGD-P7.**

To create a framework for the deployment of decentralized finance to help Zimbabwe's unbanked communities become financially included.

The information gleaned from the research participants on this objective suggests that there is a need to establish a guiding framework for the operationalization and implementation of decentralized finance in a developing context for the concept to work effectively and rip dividends for citizens and the country at large. Participants suggested that the framework will ensure that the safety and security of decentralized finance platforms and the users that interact with them are more important than leaving everything as it is. Thus, participants pointed out that there is a need to craft rules and regulations for operating DeFi platforms. This should include regulations that cover money laundering activities, the prevention of fraud and scamming activities, and other compliance measures. Participants suggested that the framework should encompass the establishment of a robust infrastructure that allows for the seamless deployment and operationalization of DeFi platforms to support scalability. This should include a network of payment processors and other financial institutions that can provide the necessary liquidity and financial services to facilitate transactions.

In addition, the framework should make provision for the need to create awareness and educate users on how to use DeFi platforms, which is essential for the financial inclusion of unbanked marginalized communities in Zimbabwe. This should include providing training and resources that explain the basics of DeFi in a way that is easy to understand for those with limited financial literacy. Participants pointed out that it is imperative to ensure that DeFi platforms are accessible to all users, regardless of their socioeconomic background. This should include providing incentives for users to join and use DeFi platforms, such as lower transaction fees and access to legitimate financial services. However, participants further suggested that there is also a need to engage with local communities, especially marginalized groups, to understand their needs and preferences. This should include conducting market research to understand the needs of users, as well as engaging with local stakeholders to ensure that DeFi projects are tailored to their specific needs. Some of the needs of the unbanked marginalized people in Zimbabwe include access to affordable and reliable digital devices, internet and data services, digital skills education about decentralized finance, and the provision of a safe and secure environment in which to use DeFi facilities.

The next section will provide a discussion of the research findings.

7 Discussion

The research established that both the body of literature and empirical data from participants largely defined financial inclusion as access to affordable financial services, such as savings and credit, that allow individuals to participate in the formal economy. The findings show that the financially excluded population in Zimbabwe is largely marginalized by rural people who are unbanked due to a lack of access to banking services and/or a lack of understanding of the banking system. Closer scrutiny reveals that there are segments among the financially excluded marginalized population that encompass MSME vendors, smallholder farmers, cross-border traders, artisanal miners, university students, and women. These people face challenges in accessing finance due to high costs, a lack of collateral security, and proper identification documents, especially proof of residency. Some of them have a negative perception of the banking system; hence, they mistrust the banking system.

Decentralized finance can promote openness, efficacy, and safety when conducting financial transactions. It can also relieve underdevelopment in Zimbabwe by giving the unbanked population access to financial services. This has the potential to unleash entrepreneurial activities among the populace, which can lead the country toward the attainment of its Vision 2030 and the SDG framework. This is because the research highlighted the conceivable advantages of using DeFi to boost financial inclusion, including access to more affordable financial services, improved transparency, and simpler access to credit. However, in the same vein, participants cited a few obstacles to using DeFi, including the unbanked population's lack of technological literacy, access to dependable internet, and lack of faith in the system. Hence, they proposed measures that should be taken to guarantee the effective implementation of DeFi to assist the unbanked in the African nation of Zimbabwe, such as providing education and training on DeFi, broadening access to reliable internet and mobile money services, and increasing trust in the system through regulation and oversight.

Participants were generally upbeat about the possibility of DeFi improving financial inclusion among the financially excluded in Zimbabwe, and they emphasized the need for crafting a framework that can be used as a guide for the successful implementation and operationalization of DeFi in a developing context such as Zimbabwe. Hence, they suggested the significance of incorporating important components for a successful framework for the deployment of DeFi, including education, trust, access to technology, and regulation. It is necessary to create a framework that considers the requirements of Zimbabwe's unbanked population. The numerous financial services that can be provided to the unbanked, such as access to digital wallets, micro-loans, and other financial products, should be considered. The framework should also ensure that unbanked people have access to education and training so they can successfully use decentralized finance. Hence, building a more trustworthy and secure digital infrastructure is required to further expand financial inclusion and establish regulations that protect the unbanked from potential risks. This may result in more financial products being made available to the financially excluded in Zimbabwe. A framework must be established that considers the unique needs of the unbanked communities in Zimbabwe. Hence, we believe that this can unleash the entrepreneurial potential of the country, which can then result in the harnessing of its human resources.

8 Establishing a Framework for Decentralized Finance in Developing Countries

The thrust of our book chapter was particularly to propose a guiding framework that can be used to facilitate the operationalization and implementation of decentralized finance facilities and services for the financial inclusion of financially excluded marginalized communities in developing countries. We conducted a literature review on decentralized finance and other fintech variances in the context of developing countries and carried out a background exploration of Zimbabwe to situate our work in a developing context. We then conducted empirical research by conducting 10 in-depth interviews and buttressing that with a 12-member focus group discussion to provide contextual empirical support for our work. Based on this analysis, we believe the proposed framework should encompass certain key tenets that should be taken into consideration for the envisaged financial inclusion of the bulk of the marginalized communities (Fig. 4). These key canons that we established include the following:

A. First, there is a need to identify and engage with local financial institutions and other stakeholders, such as ICT and telecommunications operators, as they provide the vehicles on which DeFi can ride. This step involves engagement with the Central Bank [Reserve Bank of Zimbabwe] first so that it champions the outreach to local financial institutions and other key stakeholders to understand the challenges and opportunities of implementing and operating DeFi for financial inclusion and have buy-in from everyone as well as secure their support.
B. Second, there is a need to establish a legal framework for the deployment of decentralized finance to ensure the security and stability of operations and services. This should encompass setting up a regulatory framework and creating a legal infrastructure that protects users and their funds. The regulatory framework would ensure that decentralized finance activities are conducted in a safe, secure, and transparent manner. However, we think there may be a need to bring an aspect of control and regulation to the operational rules to be adhered to by all players and users. Thus, all operators existing and aspiring may need to be registered with the central bank for approval and endorsement to conduct their operations. We believe this will weed out all dodge operators and bring confidence to DeFi operations, which will attract many participants to the platforms.
C. Third, there is a need to ensure that a robust infrastructure that can support and sustain decentralized financial services activities has been put in place. This step involves building the technical infrastructure [Electricity, Telecommunication, and ICT] for facilitating the deployment of decentralized finance, such as cryptocurrency, blockchain technology, forex trading, currency swaps, and smart contracts. This also includes fashioning the necessary tools and applications for the users. This infrastructure should be scalable and interoperable, giving both operators and users access to safe and dependable networks, trustworthy data sources, and trustworthy financial services.

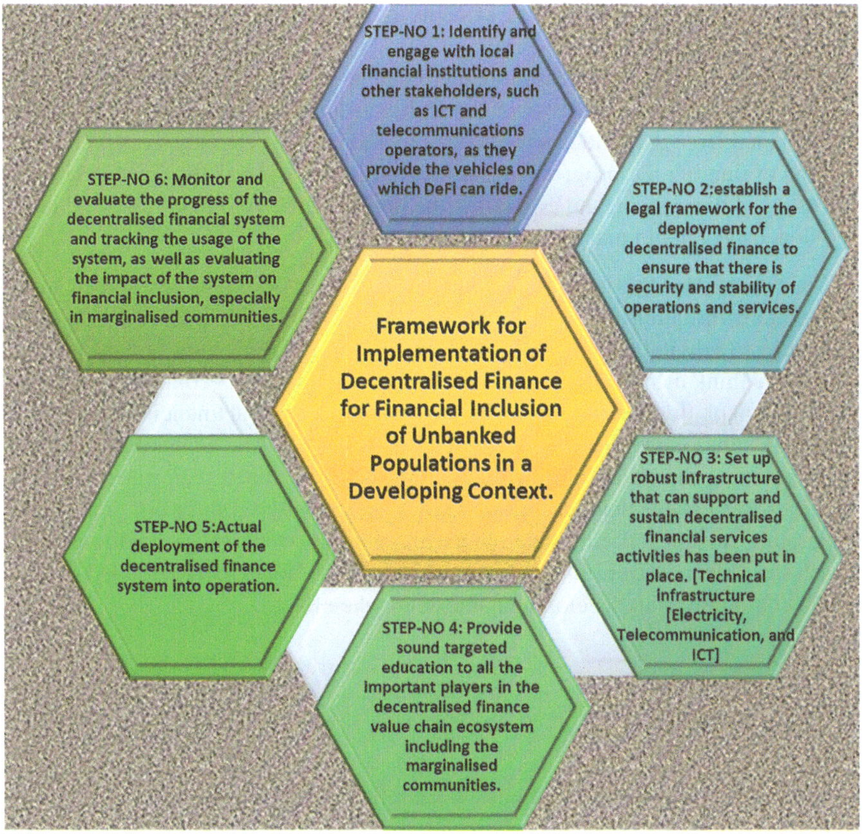

Fig. 4 Framework for implementation of decentralized finance for financial inclusion of unbanked populations in a developing context. (Author's construction)

D. The fourth key tenet of the proposed framework is the need to ensure that there is the provision of a proper, sound education to all the important players in the decentralized finance value chain ecosystem, but primacy should be given to the financially excluded marginalized communities to ensure that there is a successful application of DeFi in developing contexts. This education and training can involve providing system analysts and developers, financial consultants, and other stakeholders with training. This may result in the creation of a very good user experience for both the users and operators of the platforms. We believe that the success of DeFi depends on a good user experience. This includes creating user-friendly user interfaces, offering customer assistance, and ensuring that the environment is as secure and dependable as possible.
E. The fifth key tenet is the implementation of decentralized finance, and this step involves the actual deployment of the decentralized finance system into operation. This includes setting up the necessary infrastructure and applications, as

well as integrating the existing systems to include the banks and other financial service operators.

F. After successful implementation, there will be a need to monitor the operational mode, evaluate the progress of the DeFi system, and take note of any lessons obtained from the field's operational experience. This step involves monitoring and evaluating the progress of the decentralized financial system, tracking the usage of the system, and evaluating the impact of the system on financial inclusion, especially in marginalized communities.

We believe that the implementation of our framework could also result in the digital transformation of the operational landscape, as more people are likely to have access to digital gadgets such as smartphones, affordable data, and the internet. Hence, we think that this will eventually lead to more people becoming content with using digital platforms to conduct vital tasks such as personal financial transactions. This may subsequently result in more people, especially the TechnoServe generation, exploring digital asset portfolios in the quest to launch their entrepreneurial activities. We believe that our book chapter has proposed a framework premised on a literature review and empirical evidence, and this set the stage for the possible successful launch of DeFi for the financial inclusion of financially excluded marginalized communities in developing contexts to take off.

9 Conclusion

According to the research's findings, decentralized finance is regarded as a possible way to enhance financial inclusion among Zimbabwe's unbanked population. Decentralized finance has an array of benefits, according to the participants, including quicker and more affordable access to financial services, more access to international markets, and improved security. The risks of adopting decentralized finance, such as those of consumer protection, cybersecurity, and trust, were raised by the participants. Therefore, decentralized finance is nevertheless regarded as a workable approach to broadening financial inclusion among the unbanked in Zimbabwe. Participants noted several critical factors that must be considered for the effective implementation of decentralized finance in Zimbabwe, including consumer protection, trust, cyber-security, and access to international markets. The research participants also came up with an assortment of possible ways that Zimbabwe's unbanked population could participate in the decentralized financial network and obtain credit and other financial services. However, this can only happen when potential users have access to training and education on the importance of and how to use decentralized finance. Overall, the results suggested that decentralized finance could be an effective technique for increasing financial inclusion among Zimbabwe's unbanked population.

Therefore, the framework that we created, which includes the essential elements for ensuring that decentralized finance facilitates the financial inclusiveness of financially excluded communities, constitutes the main contribution of our book chapter. Our chapter recommends that by considering the decentralized finance complexities and the inherent nuances contained therein within the context of marginalized communities in developing countries such as Zimbabwe, the deployment and operationalization of DeFi may be successfully implemented using the proposed framework. This may ultimately assist in identifying and tackling the problems of entrepreneurial development and growth, which may result in the entrepreneurial revolution and culminate in achieving the Sustainable Development Goals. In this book chapter, we propose a guiding framework that can be used to facilitate the operationalization and implementation of decentralized finance facilities and services for the financial inclusion of financially excluded marginalized communities in developing countries. This framework should encompass key tenets that should be taken into consideration for the envisaged financial inclusion of the bulk of the marginalized communities.

We believe that by taking the identified steps, all-encompassing financial inclusivity for marginalized communities [MSMEs, smallholder farmers, artisanal miners, vendors, cross-border traders, and university students] may happen in Zimbabwe, and perhaps other countries in similar circumstances may also successfully implement our framework to achieve financial inclusivity using decentralized finance for their nations by adapting our ideas to their situations. Therefore, we suggest that our framework may be used as a template for the implementation and operationalization of DeFi to ensure that financially excluded communities in SSA are included to unleash entrepreneurial potential into reality. However, based on the vast array of critical tasks necessary, this research has drawn attention by demonstrating how challenging it is to truly understand decentralized finance; because doing so resembles the analysis and comprehension of a revolution that is already unfolding. Many things change in an ongoing revolution, and most of those changes can occur quickly, which makes it difficult to anticipate what the subsequent episodes will encompass. Although forecasting the outcome of a scenario such as this is intricate, we believe that researchers should continue to hypothesize about things that may be looming on the horizon, problematize already-existing situations, and investigate possible avenues because failing to do so might signal the end of the discipline of academia. Thus, we believe that developing countries, particularly in SSA, which is where Zimbabwe belongs, have the chance to implement comprehensive decentralized financial systems for the financial inclusivity of financially excluded aspiring marginalized people as a result of the ongoing evolution and revolution occurring around financial technology. Successful implementation of decentralized finance may enable these countries to unleash the full potential of their entrepreneurial capabilities, which can enable them to diversify their economies. Thus, we believe that this will improve the country's economy and educational systems and subsequently create new employment avenues. This study is supported by extensive engagement with representatives of financially excluded members of society, MSMEs and fintech experts, bankers' representatives, and academia in Zimbabwe. It draws on 5 months of literature review research and analysis involving ten structured interviews and a focus group discussion with 12 participants. The chapter's major topics are in line with those of the book; hence, we believe that it makes a significant contribution to the overall book project.

References

Abdulhakeem, S. A., & Hu, Q. (2021). Powered by Blockchain technology, DeFi (decentralized finance) strives to increase financial inclusion of the unbanked by reshaping the world financial system. *Modern Economy, 12*(01), 1–16. https://doi.org/10.4236/me.2021.121001

Aquilina, M., Frost, J., & Schrimpf, A. (2023). Decentralised finance (DeFi): A functional approach. *SSRN Electronic Journal, 1–26*. https://doi.org/10.2139/ssrn.4325095

Astalin, P. K. (2013). Qualitative research designs: A conceptual framework. *International Journal of Social Science & Interdisciplinary Research, 2*(1), 118–124. indianresearchjournals.com

Boar, C., Holden, H., & Wadsworth, A. (2020). Impending arrival–a sequel to the survey on central bank digital currency. *BIS Papers, 107*, 19.

Denzin, N., & Lincoln, Y. (2005). *The sage handbook of qualitative research*. Sage Publications.

di Prisco, D., & Strangio, D. (2021). Technology and financial inclusion: A case study to evaluate potential and limitations of Blockchain in emerging countries. *Technology Analysis and Strategic Management, 0*(0), 1–14. https://doi.org/10.1080/09537325.2021.1944617

Dube, M., Musungwini, S., Mudzimba, E., & Watyoka, N. (2023). Mixed reality in confronting consumer security and privacy issues in digital marketing: Integrating the best of both worlds for better interaction with users chapter 12. In *Confronting security and privacy challenges in digital marketing (pp. 252–266)*. https://doi.org/10.4018/978-1-6684-8958-1.ch012

FinScope. (2022, September). *Finscope micro, small and medium enterprises survey*.

Furusa, S. S., & Coleman, A. (2018). A strategic framework for effective utilisation of eHealth tools by medical doctors in Zimbabwe's public hospitals. *Indian Journal of Public Health Research and Development, 9*(8), 284–288. https://doi.org/10.5958/0976-5506.2018.00734.9

HSBC. (2018). *Blockchain–transforming the future of trade finance*.

Iglesias-Pradas, S., Hernández-García, Á., Chaparro-Peláez, J., & Prieto, J. L. (2021). Emergency remote teaching and students' academic performance in higher education during the COVID-19 pandemic: A case study. *Computers in Human Behavior, 119*, 106713. https://doi.org/10.1016/j.chb.2021.106713

Kabanda, G. (2021, September). *Model structure for block chain technology and cryptocurrency for the financial services sector in Zimbabwe*. 1–32.

Kachingwe, S. (1986). And humanities journals. This item is from the digital archive maintained by Michigan Zimbabwe women : A neglected factor in social development*. *Journal of Social Development in Africa, 1*, 27–33.

Kawasmi, Z., Gyasi, E. A., & Dadd, D. (2019). Blockchain adoption model for the global banking industry. *Journal of International Technology and Information Management, 28*(4), 112–154. https://www.proquest.com/scholarly journals/blockchain-adoption-model-global-banking-industry/docview/2419751773/se-2?accountid=11144%0A; http://sfx-49gbv.hosted.exlibrisgroup.com/sfx_sub?url_ver=Z39.88-2004&rft_val_fmt=info:ofi/fmt:kev:mtx:journal&genre=ar

Mashapure, R., Nyagadza, B., & Chikazhe, L. (2022, October). *Challenges hindering women entrepreneurship sustainability in rural livelihoods: Case of Manicaland province challenges hindering women entrepreneurship sustainability in rural livelihoods: Case of Manicaland province*. https://doi.org/10.1080/23311886.2022.2132675.

Mavilia, R., & Pisani, R. (2020). Blockchain and catching-up in developing countries: The case of financial inclusion in Africa. *African Journal of Science, Technology, Innovation, and Development, 12*(2), 151–163. https://doi.org/10.1080/20421338.2019.1624009

Mazuruse, G. (2023). Women entrepreneurship development and sustainable rural livelihoods in Zimbabwe. *Arab Gulf Journal of Scientific Research, 41*, 557. https://doi.org/10.1108/AGJSR-07-2022-0112

Mhlanga, D. (2021). ArtificialIntelligencece ie industry 4.0, and its impact on poverty, innovation, infrastructure development, and the sustainable development goals: Lessons from emerging economies? *Sustainability (Switzerland), 13*(11). https://doi.org/10.3390/su13115788

Mujeyi, K., & Sadomba, W. Z. (2019). Unemployment and informal entrepreneurship in Zimbabwe: Implications for regional integration. *Advances in African Economic, Social and Political Development, 251–266*. https://doi.org/10.1007/978-3-319-92180-8_17

Musungwini, S., Furusa, S. S., Gavai, P. V., & Gumbo, R. (2022). Inclusive digital transformation for the marginalised communities in a developing context. *IGI Global, 95–122*. https://doi.org/10.4018/978-1-6684-3901-2.ch005

Musungwini, S., & Van Zyl, I. (2017). Mobile Technology for Development 'experiences from Zimbabwe vending markets a naturalistic enquiry. *International Journal of Business and Management Studies, 06*(Number 01), 101–111.

Musungwini, S., Zyl, I. van, & Kroeze, J. H. (2022). *The perceptions of smallholder farmers on the use of Mobile technology: A naturalistic inquiry in Zimbabwe*. 530–544. https://doi.org/10.1007/978-3-030-98015-3_37.

Musungwini, S., Zhou, T. G., Ruvinga, C., & Z. M. (2014). Harnessing Mobile technology (MT) to enhance the sustainable livelihood of rural women in Zimbabwe : Case of Mobile money transfer (MMT). *International Journal of Computer Science and Business Informatics, 14*(2), 46–57.

Njerekai, C. (2020). An application of the virtual reality 360° concept to the great Zimbabwe monument. *Journal of Heritage Tourism, 15*(5), 567–579. https://doi.org/10.1080/1743873X.2019.1696808

Ozili, P. K. (2022). Decentralised finance research and developments around the world. *Journal of Banking and Financial Technology, 6*(2), 117–133. https://doi.org/10.1007/s42786-022-00044-x

Qin, T., Wang, L., Zhou, Y., Guo, L., Jiang, G., & Zhang, L. (2022). Digital technology-and-services-driven sustainable transformation of agriculture: Cases of China and the EU. *Agriculture (Switzerland), 12*(2), 1–16. https://doi.org/10.3390/agriculture12020297

Qin, K., Zhou, L., Afonin, Y., Lazzaretti, L., & Gervais, A. (2021). CeFi vs. DeFi–comparing centralised to decentralised finance. In *Proceedings of ACM Conference (Conference'17)* (Vol. 1, Issue 1). Association for Computing Machinery. http://arxiv.org/abs/2106.08157

Qureshi, S., & Xiong, J. (2018). Global development global financial inclusion and human development: The bitcoin effect. *Proceedings Annual Workshop of the AIS Special Interest Group for ICT in Global Development*. https://aisel.aisnet.org/globdev2018/8

RBZ. (2016). *Zimbabwe national financial inclusion strategy*. Policy Document.

Salami, I. (2020). Decentralised finance: The case for a holistic approach to regulating the crypto industry. *SSRN Electronic Journal, 1–7*. https://doi.org/10.2139/ssrn.3733647

Shinde, M. (2023). Decentralised finance coming to the Rescue of the Unbanked. *SSRN Electronic Journal, 1–8*. https://doi.org/10.2139/ssrn.4391851

Snyder, H. (2019). Literature review as a research methodology: An overview and guidelines. *Journal of Business Research, 104*(July), 333–339. https://doi.org/10.1016/j.jbusres.2019.07.039

Tipedze, M. T., Ngirazi, A., Tagarira Mutenga, J. T., & Satande. (2020). The effect of monetary and exchange control policies on the quality of financial reporting in Zimbabwe. *Journal of African Interdisciplinary Studies (JAIS), 2*(12), 16–27.

Trivedi, S., Mehta, K., & Sharma, R. (2021). Systematic literature review on application of Blockchain technology in E-finance and financial services. *Journal of Technology Management and Innovation, 16*(3), 89–102. https://doi.org/10.4067/S0718-27242021000300089

Wan, S., Lin, H., Gan, W., Chen, J., & Yu, P. S. (2023). *Web3: The next internet revolution*. 1–11. http://arxiv.org/abs/2304.06111

Dr. Samuel Musungwini is a lecturer in the Department of Information and Marketing Siences under the Faculty of Business Sciences at Midlands State University (MSU) in Zimbabwe. He has over 17 years of university teaching experience which entails Curriculum design, Module design, and content creation. Musungwini is an accomplished researcher having published more than 40 research articles. This includes attending and presenting at top international conferences. He is currently a research reviewer for 8 top Scopus-indexed journals. More on this is found here https://www.researchgate.net/profile/Samuel-Musungwini. He is a holder of a Bachelor of Science in Information Systems, Master's in Information Systems Management, and a Post Graduate Diploma in Tertiary Education all from MSU. He is a holder of a Ph.D. in Information Systems from University of South Africa (Unisa). His research interests are ICT4D, Information Systems, mAgriculture Cloud Computing, and Digital Emerging technologies like FinTechs.

Dr. Furusa Samuel Simbarashe is a lecturer in the Department of Information and Marketing Sciences at Midlands State University (MSU) in Zimbabwe. Furusa has over 14 years of university teaching experience. He is a holder of a Bachelor of Science in Information Systems, Master's in Information Systems and Post Graduate Diploma in Tertiary Education all from MSU. He is a holder of a Ph.D. in Information Systems from University of South Africa (Unisa). His research interests are e-health, Artificial intelligence and security.

Islamic Digital Currency and Entrepreneurship

Abubakar Jamilu Baita and Shellvy Lukito

1 Introduction

The decentralization of finance has disrupted the traditional financial model and brought to fore the emergence of new payment outlets. Blockchain technology proves beneficial to business models, financial transactions, and other economic activities. It simplifies and fast-tracks payment systems, reduces transaction costs, promotes digital start-ups, strengthens transparency through smart contracts, and increases efficiency. Currently, the business environment favors innovative entrepreneurs who are digitally oriented. In line with this, Gupta (2018) noted that online commercial activities have contributed to the growing number of transactions, as has the growing mobility among individuals across the globe. Therefore, if businesses grasp the sensitivity connected with the reality of the unbanked, blockchain technology presents an incredible opportunity to address this dilemma in a novel way (Larios-Hernandez, 2017).

Larios-Hernandez (2017) observed that entrepreneurs could create new revenue streams by financially including low-income consumers as they adopt decentralized, blockchain-based services. Given that distributed organization is the mechanism that preserves informality and family funding, distributed ledgers might not be able to replace formal financial services, but they might complement them. Furthermore, the author explained that blockchain companies have the potential to enable funding by making it lawful, safe, private, transparent, and in accordance

A. J. Baita (✉)
Faculty of Economics and Business, Universitas Islam Internasional Indonesia, Depok, Indonesia

Department of Economics, Yusuf Maitama Sule University Kano, Kano, Nigeria

S. Lukito
Faculty of Economics and Business, Universitas Islam Internasional Indonesia, Depok, Indonesia

S. Basly (ed.), *Decentralized Finance*, Financial Innovation and Technology,
https://doi.org/10.1007/978-3-031-49515-1_5

with the contextual norms of informality when formal institutions fail to give viable solutions to unbanked persons. In a paradoxical turn of events, many entrepreneurial blockchain-based initiatives depend on eluding regulatory supervision in the same way that informal practices do. This would foster a new definition of formality since it makes use of the peer-to-peer architecture of blockchains.

Moreover, statistics by Triple A (2023) indicated that crypto owners reached 431 million in 2023, accounting for 4.2% of the world's population. As presented in Fig. 1, Asia represents 60% of global crypto owners, followed by North America, which accounts for 13% of crypto users. Africa, representing 9% of global ownership, has 38 million owners. Oceania has the fewest owners (3%), with 15 million users. Demographically, 72% of crypto owners are below 34 years of age. It revealed that US 46, India 27, Pakistan 26, Nigeria 22, and Vietnam 20 are the top five countries adopting crypto. These countries account for approximately one-third (32.71%) of crypto owners, representing 141 million. It is estimated that the crypto market will increase by 56.4% between 2019 and 2025. Additionally, foreign remittances of digital coins are 388 times swifter and 127 times more economical compared to the conventional system of remitting funds. Digital transboundary settlements stood at $298 billion in 2021 and are estimated to reach $428 billion in 2025; similarly, 15.8% of persons sending remittances adopt digital currency platforms. Additionally, the market share of bitcoin represents 47% of the total industry.

A report revealed that the number of digital coins reached 9000 in 2023. However, 20 coins alone constitute 90% of the total crypto market. Within 3 years, ranging from 2018 to 2020, the number of users of digital coins nearly doubled globally (Statista, 2023). The report further showed that buyers in Africa, Asia, and South Africa have the highest tendency to use digital currencies in 2022. IMF showed that the capitalized market value of digital currency reached $2.5 trillion in 2021 (Thomson Reuters, 2023). In addition, Polaris Market Research (2023) reported that the market size of cryptocurrency wallet is $8.49 billion in 2022; it is projected

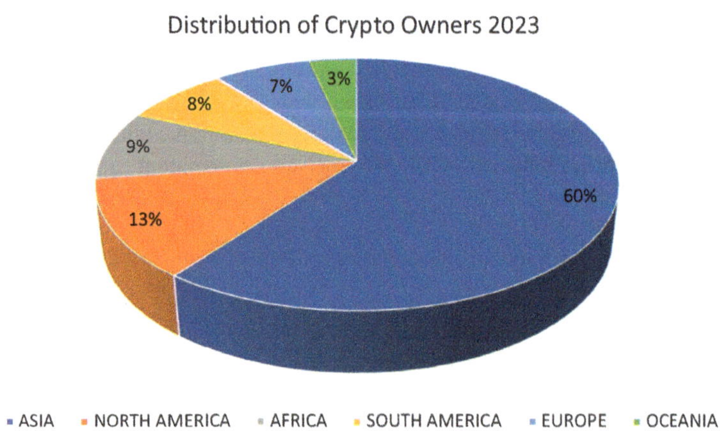

Fig. 1 Global distribution of cryptocurrency ownership

to have a cumulative growth of 24.31% between 2022 and 2030. At present, it represents one-quarter of bitcoin total revenues, and the sales value is estimated to reach $48.42 billion in 2030. In fact, the crypto adoption rate is largely attributed to the increased use of crypto wallets. The number of global users of digital currency wallets rose from 76.32 million in 2021 to 84.02 million in 2022, representing a 10% increase. According to Polaris Market Research, there are numerous factors influencing the expansion of crypto adoption. First, corporations open more digital channels to facilitate payments. Second, competition among traditional banks is intensifying, and clients are losing trust in financial entities. Third, there is an increase in illicit money movements, which is now easier through crypto.

Recently, ethically interested investors have decided to offer variant Sharia-compliant cryptocurrencies in the blockchain ecosystem. These coins include Islamic Coin (a native of Haqq Network Blockchain), Sidra Bank, Caiz Coin, and IslamiCoin. Therefore, this study aims to explore the development of Islamic Coins in the decentralized finance ecosystem. In particular, the chapter focused on the emergence of Sharia-compliant digital coins and the connection between digital currency and entrepreneurship. To achieve these objectives, the author used a case study of Islamic Coin by examining its whitepaper, websites, blogs, and social media accounts.

The structure of the chapter is composed of five sections. Section two explains the link between blockchain and digital currency. Section three discusses the role of digital currency in promoting entrepreneurship. Section four delves into the case study of Islamic Coin. In this section, the authors traced the background of Islamic Coin, explored the collaborative and community-building activities, explained the grant to empower both potential and existing entrepreneurs in the ecosystem, and identified some potential challenges to Islamic Coin.

2 Blockchain and Digital Currency

2.1 What Is Blockchain?

Blockchain is a technology that serves as the foundation for developments in the realm of cryptocurrency. Typically, exemplified by the most prominent crypto forms, such as bitcoin, Ethereum, and other comparable crypto forms. Note that the function or use of blockchain is not limited to functioning as a cryptocurrency but can also be utilized in other fields, such as digitalization and technology. Second, blockchain is a technology that focuses on maximizing the use of computing technology to create a collection of groups, or, as the term blockchain suggests, a collection of interconnected blocks. In summary, a group of interconnected blocks containing various records of a set of transactions can monitor the location of an asset within a business network.

Blockchain in another context is resistant to modification and tampering, even by its administrators, while the sequentially connected blocks are referred to as a blockchain. It is technically low-cost effective, and its application in the financial sector is anticipated to increase service efficiency (Yoo, 2017). As a decentralized digital ledger, it records transactions securely and transparently. It is a distributed database that allows multiple parties to access the same information, making it an ideal platform for secure and efficient transactions (Oh & Shong, 2017).

2.2 *Concept of Digital Currency*

It is not an overemphasis that digital finance is significantly accelerating, and digitalization has become a life-blood of almost every aspect of life. From an economic perspective, the digital economy can benefit the economy. The digital economy has the potential to transform manual business practices into automated ones. People in business can rely on the system to operate their businesses. Productive activities that hitherto require human labor can now be automated and performed by blockchain or artificial intelligence. Gupta (2018) recorded that digital currencies, also known as virtual currencies, originated from bitcoin, which is digital currency based on blockchain technology. Chen (2018) claimed that digital currency has become a buzzword in recent years with the rise of cryptocurrencies. However, digital currency includes more than just cryptocurrencies. It includes a range of electronic payment methods, from e-wallets to digital tokens.

Literally, digital currency is a currency that is completely digital and has no physical form. It can be used to buy goods and services, transfer money, and store value. There are different types of digital currencies, including cryptocurrencies, e-wallets, and digital tokens. Cryptocurrencies are decentralized digital currencies that use cryptography to create currency units and verify the transfer of funds. E-wallets are digital wallets that store various payment methods, such as credit cards and cryptocurrencies. Digital tokens are digital assets that represent a unit of value or ownership of a particular asset or company. In this context, digital currency can be described as a decentralized virtual coin that is not issued by the central authority or banks. This makes it more secure and less prone to fraud and hacking. Additionally, digital currency transactions are often faster and cheaper than traditional bank transactions (BitDegree.org, n.d.).

Although digital currencies are characterized as decentralized and scalable, Emanuella (2021) showed that central bank digital currencies (CBDC), the digital versions of traditional currencies, are evolving government digital currencies. Currently, CBDCs are being explored by central banks around the world. Following Emanuella (2021), this study conceived digital currency as a decentralized or non-centralized virtual currency in which transactions are conducted in a peer-to-peer (P2P) manner without the need for a third party. This decentralized system is powered by blockchain technology. Additionally, encryption is secured by cryptography, making it difficult to tamper with or counterfeit.

2.3 *Blockchain and Digital Currency*

Blockchain technology and digital currency are two of the most discussed topics in recent years. As technological advancements continue to shape the world we live in, blockchain and digital currencies are becoming increasingly important in our daily lives. The potential of blockchain technology to disrupt traditional industries is enormous. It has the potential to radically transform business and financial transactions by supplying a secured and transparent platform for the exchange of value. Digital currencies also have the potential to change the way we think about money by providing a faster, safer, and more accessible alternative to the traditional banking system. However, there are also challenges with the adoption of digital currencies. Regulatory concerns, security risks, and volatility are factors that could slow digital currency adoption. Despite these challenges, the benefits of digital currencies cannot be ignored. As blockchain technology and digital currencies continue to evolve, we can expect more innovation and disruption across industries (Chen, 2018).

In addition to strengthening digital currencies, Chen (2018) remarked that blockchain provides technology that enables innovators to create digital tokens to replace valuable assets that could reshape entrepreneurial innovation. These tokens are important because they (1) open new avenues for entrepreneurs to raise funds and engage stakeholders and (2) innovate new ways for innovators to build, install, and distribute decentralized apps. Essentially, both blockchain and tokens are creating new disruptive innovations that may empower entrepreneurs and accelerate innovation.

Chen (2018) pointed out that blockchain technology and digital currency are two of the most exciting and transformative technologies of our time. They have the potential to change the way we transact, exchange value, and think about money. While digital currency adoption faces challenges, its benefits cannot be overlooked. As we continue to explore the possibilities of blockchain technology and digital currencies, we can expect further innovation and disruption across industries.

3 Digital Currency and Entrepreneurship

3.1 *An Overview*

Digital currencies have had a significant impact on entrepreneurship. It promotes global entrepreneurship, provides access to finance, and lowers barriers to entry for small businesses (Chen, 2018; Lee, 2019). Digital currencies continue to proliferate as financial technologies become more sophisticated and widely used. The major benefit of digital currency to entrepreneurial development is "trust" (Gupta, 2018).

In the same vein, Lee (2019) observed that digital currencies have had a major impact on entrepreneurship. It facilitates global entrepreneurship by providing a way to conduct business across borders without the need for traditional banking infrastructure. Digital currencies also open up financing for entrepreneurs who may not have access to traditional finance. This lowers the barriers to entry for small businesses, allowing them to compete with larger companies. Additionally, digital currencies enable entrepreneurs to raise capital through Initial Coin Offerings (ICOs) (i.e., crowdfunding), which allows companies to raise capital by issuing digital tokens to investors. This has become a popular method of fundraising. The tech industry has seen many start-ups use ICOs to raise millions of dollars.

Emerging financial products, including digital payment platforms, wallets, and ethically compliant digital currency, are causing disruption in the business environment, which has implication for entrepreneurial activities (AIBC, 2023). Aldulaimi et al. (2022) observed that the application of blockchain technology has facilitated business transactions for both consumers and entrepreneurs in Bahrain. They believed that digital transactions need to be supervised and approved by Sharia experts to guarantee their execution; this will minimize Sharia risks. In addition, Islamic FinTechs in Bahrain increasingly engage in providing digital services, including digital payments, digital currencies, and smart contracts. Similarly, Larios-Hernandez (2017) observed that the unbanked nonetheless maintain patterns that tend toward peer-to-peer interactions, which digital technology may adapt to and use to engage the digitally poor in decentralized peer-to-peer services. The reputation-based peer-to-peer trust networks of the past may be modernized and expanded using digital technologies, most notably the blockchain architecture.

Bernstein and Catalini (2022) observed that digital currencies can promote innovative products and propel competitive financial services. They provide lower-cost payments for both local and international transactions. They can also enable real-time settlements, thus addressing a major flaw in the system of payments. Due to the drop in revenues brought about by the pandemic, small entrepreneurs in the United States have resorted to alternative means to reach customers outside of their local communities via digital platforms. They further remarked that consequent to small entrepreneurs' inadequate access to credit and delay in payment, they were exposed to strain their cash flow crunch, business shocks, and gloomy growth prospects.

Digital currency may allow entry to new population groups such as younger clients who appreciate openness in their interactions. Recently, Deloitte (2021) reported that approximately 40% of consumers who use digital currency are new business clients, and their buy is double that of buyers who use credit cards. In 2020, estimates have shown that over 2300 US-based businesses adopted bitcoin, excluding bitcoin ATMs. Likewise, a growing number of businesses across the globe are utilizing digital currencies for a variety of reasons in the areas of finance, business operations, and transactions. However, there are also some challenges and risks associated with its use, such as bitcoin regulatory uncertainty, volatility, and security risks (Chen, 2018; Lee, 2019).

3.2 Pros and Cons of Digital Currencies

Traditional payment systems were deemed inefficient and rather costly (Gupta, 2018). He identified key factors constraining the centralized financial system, including (1) limited supply of cash predominantly for domestic transactions. (2) Time lag between payment and clearance. (3) Inefficiencies due to third-party verification and intermediary agents. (4) Vulnerability to fraud and cyberattacks. (5) Large unbanked population.

Digital currency offers both risks and prospects (Deloitte, 2021). The benefits of digital currency are numerous. They are shaping the digital and financial architecture of the modern-day business world. One of the main advantages of digital currencies is their speed and security. Transactions can be completed quickly and efficiently without intermediaries such as banks. This also means transaction fees are generally lower than traditional currencies. Anyone with an internet connection can use digital currencies, making it a global phenomenon. However, digital currencies also have disadvantages. Its volatility makes it a risky investment, while a lack of regulation means it is vulnerable to fraud and hacking. Additionally, it is not yet widely accepted, which means it may not be as convenient as traditional currencies in some cases (Jung et al., 2019).

Likewise, Gupta (2018) identified three important benefits of scaling up digital currency. First, it saves on the cost of business operations as it removes middlemen from the supply chain. Second, transactions are made more effective by just recording information once and making it accessible to all parties involved using a distributed network. Third, the original record (i.e., ledger) is unchangeable for safety and security. That is why it is not possible to modify a transaction; rather, it can be undone by performing another transaction to avoid double-spending.

Ozili (2022) noted that scaling up digital currency will foster financial inclusion. First, it helps low-income and financially excluded individuals save money, thus improving their financial situation. Due to the lower fees, a sizable number of this group of individuals may adopt digital currency. Second, the adoption of cryptocurrency in accessing financial services will circumvent the KYC hurdles, which constrain unbanked persons from having accounts with banks. Third, it facilitates the transfer of foreign remittances, which is yet another way in which it promotes financial inclusion.

However, digital innovation is not free from downsides. Regulatory hurdles and security concerns stifle the widespread adoption of digital currencies. Digital currency is still a relatively new technology, and its use lacks clear regulations. This creates uncertainty and confusion among entrepreneurs and investors. Another challenge is volatility and market volatility. Digital currencies are known for their volatility, with rapid and unpredictable price movements. This can make it difficult for business owners to plan and budget effectively. Again, there are security risks associated with digital currencies, such as hacking and fraud. This can cause significant financial loss to the entrepreneur (Silva & Silva, 2022; Cheng, 2022).

Ozili (2022) pointed out three key challenges that constrain digital currency from promoting financial inclusion. First, individual preference will largely influence the acceptance and utilization of digital currency despite its inclusiveness. Second, digital financial services are contactless; as a result, market participants cannot access a physical human agent if they want to make enquiries. Third, weak regulation of digital currencies has an adverse impact on access to financial services. Fourth, it may not be beneficial to many people who are not tech-savvy.

4 Islamic Finance and Digital Currency

There are divergent views on the extent to which cryptocurrencies comply with Sharia principles. Khan (2022) argues that cryptocurrency is not Sharia-compliant. He holds similar opinions with Islamic scholars who claimed that fraud, evasion of taxes, and illicit financing are possible with cryptocurrencies, as they are not issued by a recognized government. Due to its extreme price fluctuations, it is unfit to serve as a currency. Hence, these scholars judged bitcoin impermissible due to these concerns. The author points to three principles of money that are violated by digital currencies. First, it can be deduced from Sharia principles that valuable metals such as gold and silver, or any item with an enormous supply, can serve as money. Gold and silver are the best choices for currency; however, in the event of an inadequate supply of those metals, commodities can serve as a substitute. Nevertheless, digital currency is not backed by gold or silver; hence, it cannot function as money. Second, the intrinsic true worth of money ought to be set by the Almighty. However, digital currencies have no underlying value. Third, tenet states that speculating is forbidden in Islam. However, the worth of virtual currency depends largely on speculative behavior about the rest of the market.

In contrast, Dar (2023a) outlined four conditions that qualify any financial transaction as Sharia-compliant. The transaction should not bear interest, be free from gambling and injustice, make mutual contractual obligations transparent, and avoid impermissible assets. While commenting on the potential of fintech in accelerating the growth of Islamic finance, Dar (2023b) posited that "missing this opportunity may prove to be fatal for Islamic finance". He viewed that Sharia authenticity should be promoted by connecting digital financial innovation with real economic activities rather than limiting it to monetary activities. Thus, seizing this opportunity goes beyond having Sharia-compliant digitally innovative products.

Moreover, Mohamed and Ali (2022) concluded that *fiqh* views on virtual currency perceived cryptocurrency as legitimate currency like physical currencies. Nonetheless, there were concerns about crypto's lack of central regulation, its tendency to trigger speculative behavior due to its volatile nature, the possibility of financing terrorist activities, and circumventing rules against money laundering. The authors further explained that Sharia views currency as any tangible or intangible thing that (i) is commercially valuable, (ii) can be stored, and (iii) can be subjected to ownership. As a result, they concluded that any digital assets such as digital coins, virtual tokens, and digital securities can be regarded as currency.

AlHashmi, who co-founded Islamic Coin, claimed that a digital currency can be in accordance with Sharia principles if it is created with the appropriate purposes, such as true value, as opposed to mere trade or speculations. Similarly, Sharia-compliant finance provides special chance for the global Muslim community and the rest of the world to create financial instruments, which avoid the kinds of problems encountered in 2008. Hence, any financial product that complies with the standards of Islamic Finance can be leveraged for both transactions and charity (Wallstreet Online, 2022). Blockchain could accelerate the competitiveness of the Islamic finance industry.

In the same vein, specialists in Islamic technology and finance, such as Islamic scholars, financial specialists, and developers, collaborate to establish cryptocurrency architecture and set standards for compliance (Clarke, 2023). This group will make certain that the coin is not based on interest-based loans but rather on a framework of gain or loss pooling. This means that rather than earning a fixed reward for their investment, investors will be entitled to a portion of the enterprise's gains and losses.

5 Case Study of Islamic Coin

5.1 Background

In April 2022, Hussein Al Meeza, Mohammed Alkaff Alhashmi, Andrey Kuznetsov, and Alex Malkov introduced Islamic Coin, an ethically oriented digital currency called "Islamic Coin" created under the Haqq Blockchain network. The idea behind this digital currency was to facilitate business transactions and scale up payment among the Muslim population and non-Muslims alike. However, the core goals of Islamic Coin were to financially empower the global Muslim society, facilitate business transactions, and foster entrepreneurial and charitable activities.

Islamic Coin is characterized by four distinguishing features. First, it is free from devaluation and cannot be minted indiscriminately. Thus, its fair market value protects it from the influence of the interest rate. Second, it is produced and supplied at a fixed rate and made available to the validators and delegators. Third, it cannot generate an interest stream, which is in stark contrast with other conventional currencies that can bear interest. Fourth, 10% of this digital currency will be used to finance Muslim charitable activities.

Due to its proof of staking, commitment to charity, and decentralization, Islamic Coin, the native currency of the Haqq Blockchain, has obtained the Fatwa from prominent authorities. Bloomberg (2022) observed that Islamic Coin is the first cryptocurrency, which not only conforms to Islamic teachings but also uses blockchain technology and innovation to directly benefit the Muslim community.

Within 100 years (i.e., 50 eras), Islamic Coin will supply a total of 100 billion coins. Initially, 20 billion coins will be minted and supplied to the market during the launch (expected to be in the second quarter of this year). The initial private sales reached $200 million as of 30th April 2023. The 20 billion initial coins will be allocated as shown in Fig. 2.

In Fig. 2, 11 billion $ISLM will be equally apportioned to business partners and funding the business ecosystem. Then, 4 billion will be sold to private investors, including high net worth individuals (HNWIs) and small-scale buyers. Initially, 2 billion will be allocated to the Evergreen organization to support charitable activities, while business originators will receive 2 billion.

5.2 *Governance Model for Evergreen DAO*

A novel innovation of Islamic Coin is that 10% of all newly created coins on the Haqq network are donated to the Evergreen autonomous decentralized organization (DAO). This is in response to addressing environmental sustainability. In this system, the stakeholders put the money to fund Islamic internet projects and charitable projects, which promote Islam. As Clark (2023) succinctly stated, charitable-oriented activity mimics the zakat model.

Again, the charity fund (Evergreen DAO) has its unique governance process. In this model, three stakeholders, namely, the community, Sharia board, and council, are involved in governing the charity organization. Smart contracts are applied in the governance process to ensure trust in managing the funds. The governance model provides that three stages must be passed through before committing expenditure to finance projects or charity. First, a stakeholder of Islamic Coin will forward a proposal. Second, the council members will scrutinize the proposal and vote on it;

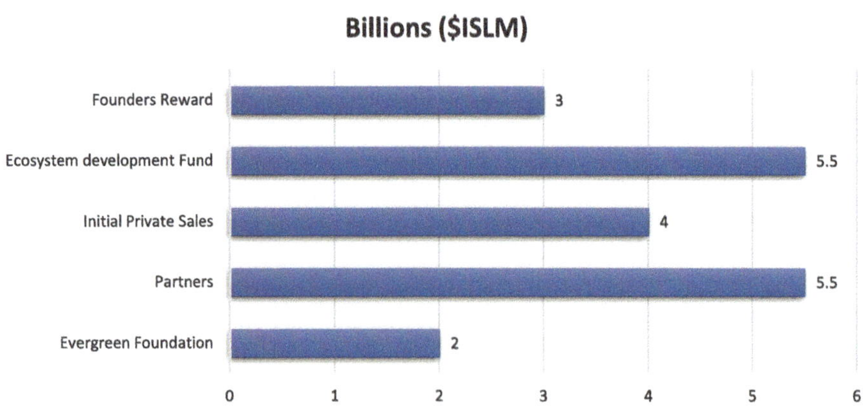

Fig. 2 Composition of initial coin offer

this process is essentially participatory and democratic. In the third stage, the proposal is implemented if it is found viable and voted for.

Stage 1: Proposing a Spending Plan

Every owner of Islamic Coin has the right to submit a spending plan. First, the request must be presented to a forum outside of the Haqq blockchain. The proposal, together with details of the budget and outcome, should be forwarded to the governance smart contract. Deposit is required for presenting a proposal. The actual deposit is the product of proposal's cost and 5% rate of deposit. However, the coefficient is subject to future changes based on the prevailing dollar value of Islamic Coin ($ISLM) and budget. Finally, if the proposal is accepted, the entire deposit will be frozen and inaccessible for different projects.

Stage 2: Council Voting Process

The plan requires council approval via the Evergreen DAO Smart Contract. The process ensures equal votes for every member. At least 60% of the council members must endorse the proposal. In contrast, a minimum of 50% vote is sufficient to turn down a proposal. However, the plan is abandoned if it is neither voted for nor rejected in a week.

Stage 3: Implementation Process

At this stage, project implementation is based on smart contracts, which are open to council members. When three-fifths of members approve the spending plan within a week, the full amount of such proposal is allocated for the stated goal. Thus, the project's initiator can request the deposit. This process encourages stakeholder engagement in the governance process while deterring scammish projects.

5.3 Collaboration and Community Building

To deepen Islamic market penetration, the Haqq network strategically collaborates with DDCAP, an established ethical finance company. The Haqq Association (2023) reported that Islamic Coin and DDCAP have agreed to partner to provide market infrastructure for ethical digital currency and deepen the Islamic market for financial products. The partnership will develop a Sharia-compliant digital platform that will substitute SWIFT and venture into creating tokens and central bank digital currency. While the DDCAP has a stronghold in providing ethical solutions, the Haqq blockchain is set to provide environmentally sustainable digital innovation, including Islamic Coin. In 2022, the Haqq blockchain was awarded the "Most Promising ESG Crypto at The Middle East Blockchain Awards" and the "Golden Excellence Award" by the United Arab Emirates. On April 25, 2023, Haqq Blockchain collaborated with Halborn Security. The partnership aims to integrate security infrastructure into the Haqq blockchain to provide security protection for users. On April 27, it announced another collaboration with SAMPRA and Holiday Swap. SAMPRA issues halal certification based on blockchain and deploys blockchain to track compliance. Holiday Swap agreed to bring together more than 650,000 active wallets on the Haqq Blockchain. Another initiative is an agreement for the establishment of the Blockchain Academy at the International Islamic University Malaysia. The goal is to promote blockchain and digital currency literacy among Muslims.

In addition, Islamic Coin initiated a "Haqq Ecosystem Fund" to promote the entrepreneurial ecosystem and fund digital start-ups and other projects aligned with Islamic digital currency. Prospective grants are thoroughly examined based on ethical and Sharia criteria. The grant, amounting to $40 million (i.e., $20 million USDC+USDT and $20 million Islamic Coin), is expected to foster the expansion of the Haqq ecosystem. Accordingly, Haqq Wallet, Haqq Node, and Haqq Shell are some of the fundamental Haqq infrastructure products that receive extra attention. Additionally, the initiative is also paying special attention to both new ideas and established ventures that will build on the Haqq Network. The funding will collaborate with blockchain-minded fintech entities or any nonprofit-oriented initiative that is consistent with Islamic principles.

Haqq Network has an active online community hub to solidify its community. Islamic Coin reaches out to several social media outlets to increase awareness and intimate members about developments in the Coin's features and its innovation. Presently, there are seven prominent media outlets for community engagement and information dissemination. These include Islamic Coin Channel, Telegram, Discord, Twitter, LinkedIn, YouTube, and a blog (medium.com/Islamic-coin). Table 1 shows the number of followers/members in six social media accounts. The data were gathered on 30th April 2023 and may be subject to change over time.

Table 1 shows that more than four-fifths (85.74%) of the Islamic Coin community members follow the Twitter handle, representing nearly one million followers. Islamic Coin Channel is the second most patronized media platform, with 114,641 subscribers, which represent approximately one-tenth (9.56%). Both Twitter and Islamic Coin channels constitute 95.3% of the online community members. However, LinkedIn and YouTube have the fewest community members, accounting for less than 1% altogether.

Although Islamic Coin has not yet been launched in the market, it hosted a creative strategy for engaging community members called #GIVEAWAY. Unlike

Table 1 Distribution of subscribers/followers of Islamic Coin

S/N.	Media Handle	Members/Followers	Percent
1	Islamic Coin Channel	114,641	9.56
2	Telegram	27,186	2.26
3	Twitter	1,028,047	85.74
4	Discord	20,098	1.68
5	LinkedIn	3227	0.27
6	YouTube	5830	0.49
TOTAL		1,199,029	100

Source: Authors' computation

airdrops and mining, the first member to answer a quiz or puzzle in Telegram is rewarded some number of Islamic Coins ($ISLM) falling within 40–100. Additionally, followers with the best twitter posts about Islamic Coin are rewarded between 400 $ISLM and 1000 $ISLM. This creative strategy has significantly driven traffic as its twitter followers reached one million members. In addition, it introduced the "Ambassador" program, which selects active individuals to write short articles or post a short video that promotes Islamic Coin. This is indirectly a kind of digital marketing for advertising Islamic Coin. In return, Islamic Coin rewards the "Ambassadors" some number of ISLM.

5.4 Potential Challenges

Despite optimism in launching Islamic Coin into the cryptocurrency market, there are many challenges ahead. These may be from the perspectives of the regulatory, market, and real sectors.

(i) Fear of Speculations. Despite *fatwa* supporting Islamic Coin, one major concern is that the coin can still be manipulated for speculative activities; however, this is forbidden due to the presence of gharar. There is concern that some potential Islamic Coin users may buy-and-hold this coin for speculative purposes by expecting price appreciation to gain from the rising price margin. This will adversely affect its prospects in the real economy. Unless actions are strategized, Islamic Coin will be engrossed in users' speculative behavior, which may undermine its original purpose of Sharia compliance and empowering entrepreneurs.

(ii) Participation of Entrepreneurs: Islamic Coin is predicted to reach nearly 2 billion Muslim population. Islamic Coin white paper showed that Muslim crypto users stood at 25 million in 2021. This implies low adoption of digital currency among the Muslim population. Again, specific data about the size of Muslim entrepreneurs are not available. Unless Islamic Coin is used by many entrepreneurs as well as large organizations, it will not significantly promote entrepreneurial activities. Our personal observation showed that many crypto users, particularly in developing countries, perceive digital currency as a get-quick-rich passive investment. Real entrepreneurs require digital coins to reach customers within and across borders.

(iii) Corruption: It is documented that crypto usage may potentially raise corruption (Alnasaa, et al. 2022). This may pose a challenge to the adoption of Islamic Coin because there is fear that countries with weaker regulation of corruption may be vulnerable to financial fraud and money laundering. This concern is prevalent in the cryptocurrency industry in both developed and developing economies. Nevertheless, industrialized economies have better technologies to illicit financing.

(iv) Price Volatility: One of the key obstacles of the existing digital currency market is a high level of price instability. Crypto prices are highly volatile, and as a result, digital holders suffer a significant loss of value. The challenge to Islamic Coin is to develop a mechanism that will ensure price stability, at least in the short, to have buyers' confidence. Otherwise, buyers may be willing to adopt Islamic digital currency, despite claims of being ethical and Sharia-compliant.

(v) Market Penetration: A report shows that bitcoin alone accounts for 47% of the crypto market share, and only 4.2% of the world population owns digital coins (Triple A, 2023). In addition, the available number of digital coins exceeds 9000. This is a market hurdle for Islamic Coins to cross, as it faces stiff competition with long-established and highly capitalized digital coins. Although some royal family members in the UAE joined the journey, this is not sufficient to penetrate the market.

6 Conclusion and Recommendations

The chapter explored the emergence of Islamic digital coins in the decentralized finance ecosystem and the development of Islamic Coins under the Haqq Blockchain. The study specifically focused on the role of digital currency in promoting entrepreneurship. The goal of Islamic Coin is to promote the digital financial inclusion of Muslims along with non-Muslims by supporting the real economic sector. It is based on fair and ethically acceptable processes, which can be stored and spent. From the case study, we showed that strategic collaboration and community building are building blocks for increasing awareness and expanding the adoption of Islamic Coin. Within a year of incorporation (Islamic Coin will be launched in the second quarter of 2023), Islamic Coin has attracted more than one million followers, particularly on its Twitter account, which accounts for 85% of the online community hub. Our investigation showed that Islamic Coin has enormous potential to promote entrepreneurial activities, particularly among Muslim internet users. Additionally, ethically minded individuals who were hitherto averse to crypto may likely use Islamic Coin because of its being Sharia-compliant. However, this does not mean that other crypto coins are completely unethical. In our understanding, the striking difference between conventional crypto and Islamic Coin is "ethical screening". Conventionally, virtual currencies support both ethical transactions such as trade and unethical activities such as interest and gambling. In contrast, Islamic digital currencies are designed to support Sharia-compliant economic activities only. In addition, Islamic Coin has integrated charity funding (10% of total supply) to support projects that aligned with community development and digital innovation.

Some practical challenges have been highlighted; consequently, we offer the following recommendations:

1. Companies operating Islamic digital currencies should seriously inform people about the harmful effects of speculations in Islam and to the economy. In particular, many people perceive digital currency as a get-rich-quick gateway, and the story is not different with respect to Islamic digital coins. However, such perception kills entrepreneurship and craftsmanship and promotes laziness and lack of industry. Therefore, there should be campaigns with wider outreach, particularly to youth, about the importance of digital currency in simplifying payments and empowering start-ups. This can help in educating users on the entrepreneurial opportunities available in crypto usage.
2. Many developing countries, including Muslim-majority nations, have weak regulation on the control of corruption, and digital currencies are decentralized. However, stakeholders can set up special tracking mechanisms that will detect illicit transactions. United States has gone far in this aspect, and Haqq Blockchain should collaborate with experts to curtail fraud, money laundering, and any other illicit activities. Possibly, the company can use an integrated system that can track, identify, and bar users who are found doing illicit transactions.
3. We hold a similar view to Mohamed and Ali (2022) that Islamic digital currency should be pegged to gold. This is very crucial, as it will tremendously reduce price fluctuation. This is an ideal situation, although it can increase the cost of business. However, it will be beneficial in the long term because entrepreneurs who need stable prices are likely to be attracted.
4. There is a criticism that 10% of Islamic Coin, under Evergreen DAO, which is set aside for funding charity, will only benefit the founders and major investors. The council members who manage the funds should not only be concerned with trust but also ensure that the funds finance projects with large social impact.

References

AIBC. (2023, March 23). *Islamic banking launches shariah-compliant digital coins*. https://aibc.world/news/islamic-banking-launches-shariah-compliant-digital-coin/

Aldulaimi, S. H., Aldulaimi, F. H., Abdeldayem, M. M., Muttar, A. K. & Shakir, M. (2022). *Entrepreneurship in Islamic financial products: Evidence from the Kingdom of Bahrain*. ASU International Conference in Emerging Technologies for Sustainability and Intelligent Systems.

Alnasaa, M., Gueorguiev, N., Honda, J., Imamoglu, E., Mauro, P., et al. (2022). *Crypto, corruption, and capital control: Cross-country correlations*. IMF Working Paper (WP/22/60), 110492.

Bernstein, S. & Catalini, C. (2022, May, 25). How digital currencies can help small businesses. Harvard Business Review

BItDegree.org. (n.d.). *Crypto 101 Beginner Handbook by BitDegree*. Retrieved April 12, 2023.

Bloomberg (2022, June 24). *In major breakthrough, Islamic coin gains fatwa from leading global muslim scholars*. https://www.bloomberg.com/press-releases/2022-06-24/in-major-breakthrough-islamic-coin-gains-fatwa-from-leading-global-muslim-scholars

Chen, Y. (2018). Blockchain tokens and the potential democratization of entrepreneurship and. *Business Horizons, 61*. Retrieved April 16, 2023, from, 567. https://doi.org/10.1016/j.bushor.2018.03.006

Cheng, P. (2022). Decoding the rise of central Bank digital currency in China: Designs, problems, and prospects. *Journal of Banking Regulation., 24*, 156. https://doi.org/10.1057/s41261-022-00193-5

Clarke, A. (2023). *Islam and crypto: How digital assets can comply with Islamic financial law*. https://cointelegraph.com/news/islam-and-crypto-how-digital-assets-can-comply-with-islamic-financial-law?utm_source=Telegram&utm_medium=social

Dar, H. (2023a, April 16). *Islamic finance thought of the day. No. 106*. Cambridge Institute of Islamic Finance. https://www.linkedin.com/posts/humayon-dar-b52a323_islamic-finance-tod-106-activity-7053409146938740736-Sud_?utm_source=share&utm_medium=member_android

Dar, H. (2023b, April 19). *Islamic finance thought of the day*. No. 109. Cambridge Institute of Islamic Finance. https://www.linkedin.com/feed/update/urn:li:activity:7054565332513878016?updateEntityUrn=urn%3Ali%3Afs_feedUpdate%3A%28V2%2Curn%3Ali%3Aactivity%3A7054565332513878016%29

Deloitte. (2021). *Corporates using crypto: Conducting business with digital assets*. Deloitte Development.

Emanuella, C. S. (2021). Central Bank Digital Currency (CBDC) Sebagai Alat Pembayaran di Indonesia. *Jurist-Diction, 6*. Retrieved April 2023, 2243.

Gupta, M. (2018). *Blockchain for dummies* (2nd ed. IBM Limited Edition). John Wiley.

Haqq Association (2023, April 26). *Islamic Coin and DDCAP Group announce significant partnership for the global Islamic market*. https://finance.yahoo.com/news/Islamic-coin-ddcap-group-announce-143000171.html?

Jung, K.-J., Park, J.-B., Phan, N., Bo, C., & Gim, G.-Y. (2019). *An international comparative study on the intension to using crypto-currency* (pp. 104–123). https://doi.org/10.1007/978-3-319-98370-7_9

Khan, S. N. (2022). The legality of cryptocurrency from an Islamic perspective. A research note. *Journal of Islamic Accounting and Business Research*.

Larios-Hernandez, G. J. (2017). Blockchain entrepreneurship opportunities in the practice of the unbanked. *Business Horizons., 60*, 865.

Lee, J. Y. (2019). A decentralized token economy: How blockchain and cryptocurrency can revolutionize business. *Business Horizons., 62*, 773. https://doi.org/10.1016/j.bushor.2019.08.003

Mohamed, H., & Ali, H. (2022). *Blockchain, fintech, and Islamic finance: Building the future in the new Islamic digital economy* (2nd ed.). Walter de Gruyeter.

Islamic Coin. (2023). *Haqq whitepaper*. https://islamiccoin.net/wp.

Oh, J., & Shong, I. (2017). A case study on business model innovations using Blockchain: Focusing on financial institutions. *Asia Pacific Journal of Innovation and Entrepreneurship, 11*, 335–344. https://doi.org/10.1108/APJIE-12-2017-038

Ozili, P. K. (2022). CBDC, fintech and cryptocurrency for financial inclusion and financial stability. *Digital Policy, Regulation and Governance., 25*, 40. https://doi.org/10.1108/DPRG-04-2022-0033

Polaris Market Research. (2023). *Crypto wallet market size: Global analysis report 2022–2030*. Retrieved from https://www.polarismarketresearch.com/#:~:text=The%20number%20of%20crypto%20wallet,from%2076.32%20million%20in%202021

Silva, E. C., & Silva, M. M. (2022). Research contributions and challenges in DLT-based cryptocurrency regulation: A systematic mapping study. *Journal of Banking and Financial Technology, 6*, 63–82. https://doi.org/10.1007/s42786-021-00037-2

Statista. (2023). *Cryptocurrency–statistics & facts*. Retrieved from https://www.statista.com/topics/4495/cryptocurrencies/#topicOverview

Thomson Reuters. (2023). *Cryptos on the rise 2022*. Retrieved from https://www.thomsonreuters.com/en/reports/cryptos-on-the-rise-2022.html

Triple A (2023). *Global cryptocurrency ownership data 2023*. Retrieved from https://triple-a.io/crypto-ownership-data/#:~:text=As%20of%202023%2C%20we%20estimated,420%20million%20crypto%20users%20worldwide

Yoo, S. (2017). Blockchain based financial case analysis and its implications. *Asia Pacific Journal of Innovation and Entrepreneurship, 11*, 312–321. https://doi.org/10.1108/APJIE-12-2017-036

Wallstreet Online. (2022, July 11). *Newly launched Shariah-compliant Islamic Coin wins the ethics debate*. https://www.wallstreet-online.de/nachricht/15680059-newly-launched-shariah-compliant-islamic-coin-wins-the-ethics-debate

Abubakar Jamilu Baita obtained both degree and masters from the Department of Economics, Bayero University Kano. He currently undergoes a Ph.D. programme in the Faculty of Economics and Business, Universitas Islam Internasional Indonesia. He is also a permanent staff in the Department of Economics, and served as Part-Time Lecturer in the Institute of Continuing Education (ICE), Yusuf Maitama Sule University Kano - Nigeria. He has presented papers in national and international conferences, and published research articles in refereed journals. His research interests include green and sustainable finance, Islamic finance, and financial development.

Shellvy Lukito is a junior researcher with a strong inclination for delving into the realm of study. Following the successful completion of her undergraduate studies in Sharia Economics at the SEBI School of Islamic Economics, Indonesia. Shellvy decided to pursue further academic endeavors within the realm of research. At present, Shellvy is a recipient of a scholarship as a master's student from the Ministry of Religion of the Republic of Indonesia, pursuing studies at the Faculty of Economics and Business, Indonesia International Islamic University.

Shellvy is actively engaged in various writing endeavors, including composing multiple opinion articles for various online mass media platforms in Indonesia. In recent years, Shellvy has dedicated herself to pursuing more education with the aim of becoming a researcher, aligning with her personal philosophy encapsulated by the phrase, "If you can't stand the fatigue of study, you will feel poignant of stupidity".

Blockchain Adoption in the Accounting and Auditing Industry: An Exploratory Study in France

Sami Basly and Paul-Laurent Saunier

1 Introduction

Blockchain technology, characterized as a distributed ledger shared synchronously across its entire user base, is rapidly gaining traction as a transformative force in various sectors. In contrast to traditional databases, this decentralized registry allows all participants to enter data based on a highly secure set of rules dictated by cryptographic protocols (Mission d'information commune sur les usages des blocchaînes et autres technologies de certification de registres, 2018). Lauded as a disruptive innovation with the potential to redefine competitive landscapes (Deloitte, 2016), Blockchain technology has been posited as a cornerstone for new economic and social architectures (Iansiti & Lakhani, 2017). It has even been classified as the "fifth pillar" in the computing revolution, following mainframes, personal computers, the Internet, and social media (Kokina et al., 2017).

Originally conceptualized as the underlying framework for the cryptocurrency Bitcoin, Blockchain's unique capacity to engender trust in a decentralized network sets it apart from other emergent technologies (Kokina et al., 2017). This attribute could serve as a democratizing catalyst, lowering barriers to entry and disrupting a plethora of industries by significantly reducing transaction costs, much like the Internet's impact on communication costs (Lundy, 2016). Market forecasts suggest that enterprise applications for Blockchain technology will escalate from \$2.5 billion in 2016 to nearly \$20 billion by 2025, contributing to 10% of the global GDP (Kokina et al., 2017; World Economic Forum, 2017). Although the financial services sector has been an early adopter, diverse applications in areas such as supply chain management and public administration—including land ownership and healthcare—are emerging (AlSaqa et al., 2019; Demirkan et al., 2010).

S. Basly (✉) · P.-L. Saunier
University of Paris Nanterre, Paris, France
e-mail: sbasly@parisnanterre.fr; pl.saunier@parisnanterre.fr

S. Basly (ed.), *Decentralized Finance*, Financial Innovation and Technology,
https://doi.org/10.1007/978-3-031-49515-1_6

Blockchain's transformative potential also has critical implications for the accounting profession and, more broadly, for financial services (Degos, 2017; Kokina et al., 2017; Desplebin et al., 2019; Schmitz & Leoni, 2019). The technology can enhance the credibility and timeliness of information disseminated to investors and other stakeholders. By recording transactions on a Blockchain, the risk of accounting manipulation and fraudulent activities could be substantially mitigated (Byström, 2019). Furthermore, the instantaneous nature of Blockchain-based transactions would enable real-time updating of financial records, rendering them immediately accessible to both internal and external entities, including auditors and regulatory agencies (Degos, 2017; Desplebin et al., 2019; Byström, 2019; Kokina et al., 2017; Dai & Vasarhelyi, 2017).

Academic scholarship on this subject has seen a surge, with over 1000 articles published in peer-reviewed journals between 2013 and 2018 (Firdaus et al., 2019). While extant literature primarily focuses on the technology's ramifications for auditors, there is growing acknowledgment that business accountants and management controllers will also see significant alterations in their roles, including substantial time-saving efficiencies (Kokina et al., 2017; Dai & Vasarhelyi, 2017). For instance, enhanced transparency and real-time transaction tracking could prompt shifts in management accounting practices.

In this article, we aim to present preliminary findings from an exploratory study investigating the uptake of Blockchain technology by accounting and auditing professionals in France. We will also delve into the attributes of Blockchain technology and smart contracts, elucidating their ramifications for the accounting and auditing sectors.

2 How Does Blockchain Technology Function, and Why Is It of Significance to the Fields of Accounting and Auditing?

The architecture and functional attributes of Blockchain technology facilitate the generation of trustworthy transactional records, predicated on consensus-based validation, verifiability, and an inherent feature of immutability. This paper aims to elucidate three cardinal features of the Blockchain, as delineated by Desplebin et al. (2019): namely, transparency, which entails the public availability of information shared among network participants; data protection, characterized by the prevention of data falsification, peer-to-peer verification, the impossibility of data erasure, and data anonymization; and decentralization, which implies the system's operation independent of any centralized administrative or governance mechanism. Moreover, the incorporation of smart contracts into Blockchain networks introduces the capability for the automated execution of decision-making processes and related transactional actions.

Blockchain serves as a decentralized digital ledger—a registry that maintains transaction entries characterized by verifiable integrity. It employs a globally distributed network of computational nodes to register transactions in a manner that renders them immutable post-approval. Utilizing the concept of "mechanical trust" (Degos, 2017), the system mitigates the need for a centralized intermediary to authenticate transactions. This decentralized validation is accomplished through an algorithmic method commonly referred to as "mining" leveraging the computational power of network nodes—identified as "miners"—who are economically incentivized to participate in block creation and validation. Each block, constituting a timestamped collection of validated transactions, undergoes scrutiny and validation by the network nodes prior to its addition to the chain. Upon reaching a network-wide consensus, a block is authenticated and sequenced chronologically into the existing Blockchain, each block embedding the identifier of its antecedent block. The decentralization intrinsic to the system precludes any modification of authenticated blocks and ensures the system's immutable conduct. To enforce this immutability, a cryptographic hash function is employed, producing a unique cryptographic "fingerprint" for each block, known as a "hash". Before its addition to the Blockchain, each block is subjected to a computational challenge, which necessitates numerous attempts and considerable computational power for its resolution. Following successful resolution, the block is authenticated through the consensus of a majority of participating miners and is subsequently appended to the Blockchain network.

In theoretical terms, the Blockchain's architecture is designed to be immutable. Altering the contents of an existing block would necessitate commanding substantial computational resources from at least 51% of the network's nodes—a feat that is practically infeasible given the anonymous and decentralized nature of the participant nodes. Initially conceived to underpin Bitcoin cryptocurrency, Blockchain technology has evolved to encompass a range of structural variations. These can manifest as either permissionless systems, open to any participant, or permissioned systems that restrict participation to designated entities. In a private Blockchain model, data within the chain is exclusively accessible to predetermined stakeholders. This offers enhanced anonymity and data confidentiality, a feature increasingly being explored and implemented by financial and accounting sectors (Kokina et al., 2017; Dai et al., 2017).

Correspondingly, the transformative capacity of Blockchain is augmented when integrated with a complementary technology known as smart contracts. Defined by Buterin (2014) as self-executing contractual agreements governed by preset conditions, smart contracts have realized their full potential only in the advent of Blockchain technology. While earlier implementations required centralized oversight for execution, the decentralized nature of Blockchain allows for the autonomous activation and execution of smart contracts (Dai & Vasarhelyi, 2017; Nofer et al., 2017). These contracts operate based on a priori logic agreed upon by the transacting parties, which is then encoded and stored in the Blockchain. Once activated by users submitting requisite data, smart contracts evaluate these inputs against the established conditions, generating either a fulfillment or an error message, visible to all network nodes (Rozario & Vasarhelyi, 2018).

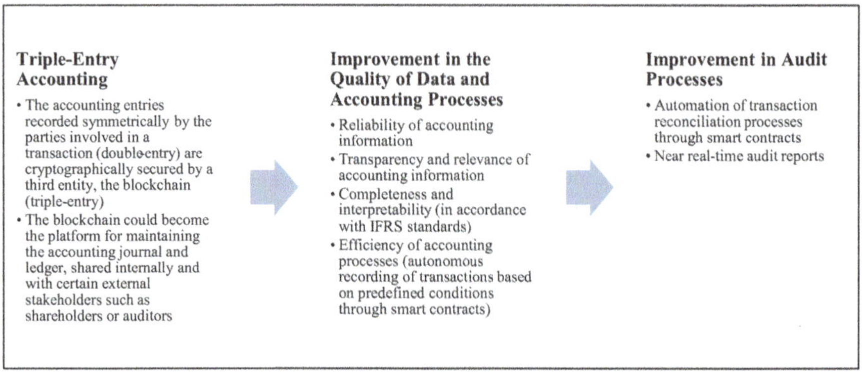

Fig. 1 How does Blockchain technology impacts accounting and auditing

Blockchain technology holds significant promise for revolutionizing the accounting and auditing domains by enhancing data reliability and transparency (Schmitz & Leoni, 2019) (Fig. 1). It presents an opportunity to evolve from the traditional double-entry to a triple-entry accounting system, in which transactional entries made by involved parties are cryptographically sealed by a decentralized third entity—the Blockchain itself (AlSaqa et al., 2019; Schmitz & Leoni, 2019). This potential transformation is underpinned by Blockchain's inherent characteristics, such as its immutable ledger shared both internally and with selected external stakeholders like shareholders or auditors (Desplebin et al., 2019; Rückeshäuser, 2017). Unlike traditional databases, Blockchain offers granular control over access rights, permitting stakeholders varying levels of access based on their roles and requirements, particularly in the context of private Blockchains. This enhanced security paradigm ensures that the integrity of accounting records is maintained, permitting only the addition of new blocks post-authorization, while precluding any alterations or deletions of existing blocks.

As elucidated by Bonsón and Bednárová (2019), Blockchain technology serves as a robust mechanism for ensuring data integrity while also enhancing its quality—specifically in terms of completeness and interpretability within the framework of International Financial Reporting Standards (IFRS). Furthermore, the technology allows for stratified access to information, thereby increasing its contextual relevance (Bonsón & Bednárová, 2019). Within a given Blockchain network, certain nodes, such as corporate executives or auditing firms, can be granted unrestricted access to comprehensive data, while other stakeholders may be limited to viewing only aggregated or summary data based on their pre-defined roles (Schmitz & Leoni, 2019). The incorporation of smart contracts into Blockchain platforms extends the technology's capabilities by automating the execution of multi-party contractual terms upon verification of specific conditions (Schmitz & Leoni, 2019). This enables autonomous accounting recording, aligned with predetermined criteria. For instance, a smart contract could be programmed to validate a sale only after confirming the shipment of the corresponding goods (Dai & Vasarhelyi, 2017).

Moreover, smart contracts can streamline the auditing process by automating transaction reconciliation, furnishing stakeholders with near real-time audit reports. This results in significant time-savings and minimizes the risk of human error, while also fostering collaborative audit work within organizations (Degos, 2017).

The extant literature exploring the factors that influence the adoption of Blockchain technology in the fields of accounting and auditing remains limited and predominantly centered on Anglo-Saxon contexts (Handoko & Lantu, 2021; Jumah & Li, 2020). There exists a pressing need for further research to elucidate the principal facilitators and obstacles to Blockchain integration within this sector. While some scholarly work has touched upon the prospective advantages of Blockchain for auditing procedures (Simões et al., 2021), scant attention has been paid to the pragmatic challenges and operational nuances of incorporating this technology into existing auditing processes. Additionally, much of the current research landscape in this domain is characterized by theoretical or qualitative methodologies (Perera & Abeygunasekera, 2022; Simões et al., 2021). The scholarly community would benefit from a greater emphasis on empirical studies to corroborate proposed frameworks and illuminate the practical implications of Blockchain technology adoption within accounting and auditing practices.

In light of the paucity of French-language academic research on this technology, our study seeks to explore its actual implementation among accounting and auditing professionals in France. The guiding questions for our exploratory research focus on the level of awareness among these professionals about the transformative potential of Blockchain and its ancillary technologies. We aim to ascertain whether they comprehend how these technologies could modify or even disrupt their current professional activities. Additionally, we endeavor to identify the perceived benefits and barriers to the wider adoption of this technology in the accounting and auditing sectors in France.

3 An Exploratory Study of Blockchain Adoption in France

To facilitate the empirical exploration of our research questions, a meticulously designed questionnaire was disseminated electronically to professionals engaged in sectors relevant to this study. These include, but are not limited to, chartered accountancy, auditing, statutory auditing, and management control. Participants were identified and contacted through the professional networking platform, LinkedIn. Our sampling strategy was twofold: initially, invitations were extended to 60 alumni who had graduated at least 3 years prior, given that the co-authors are academicians specializing in accounting and finance. Subsequently, a random selection procedure was employed to disseminate 150 additional questionnaire invitations through the same digital platform. The data collection process spanned from May to October 2021 and garnered 34 responses, of which 32 were both complete and suitable for further analysis.

3.1 Sample Description

The composition of the study's sample, as delineated in the appendices, encompasses a total of 32 respondents who are employed in various positions within the financial sector—including but not limited to chartered accountants, financial auditors, and management controllers. Among these roles, management controllers constitute the most prevalent category, accounting for 18.8% of the total respondents. They are closely followed by financial consultants/auditors and accountants, each constituting 15.6% of the sample.

With regard to professional tenure, the respondents exhibit a range of experience spanning from 1 to 20 years, with a mean value of 4.41 years. Notably, a significant plurality—31.3% of the sample—possesses 2 years of experience in their respective fields. The demographic constitution of the sample is gender-balanced, and includes individuals aged between 21 and 47 years, with an average age of 27.3 years. The majority of respondents fall within the age bracket of 24 to 27 years.

Educational qualifications among the participants reveal that a substantial majority—75%—hold Master's degrees or their equivalent. Moreover, the majority of the respondents, constituting 34.4%, are employed in accounting firms. In terms of organizational characteristics, the enterprises to which these respondents are affiliated are predominantly global in scope, with 65.6% operating internationally. The firms are also notably sizable: 53.1% employ more than 5000 individuals, and 65.6% report an annual turnover exceeding ten million euros.

3.2 Results

Adoption of Blockchain Technology

The findings indicate a moderated level of organizational adoption of Blockchain technology among the firms represented in the sample. Specifically, a predominant 43.8% of respondents reported that their respective companies neither currently utilize nor have plans to implement Blockchain technology in the foreseeable future. Conversely, a modest 28.1% of participants indicated that their organizations are presently utilizing Blockchain, while an additional 25% conveyed that their companies are actively exploring its potential application.

Within the subset of respondents whose companies are engaged in Blockchain experimentation or implementation, a further disaggregation reveals that 30.8% state their organizations are in the experimental stage of Blockchain technology adoption. A mere 9.4% anticipate transitioning to production-level Blockchain applications within a 12- to 24-month timeframe. Surprisingly, 46.2% within this subset assert that their companies have already operationalized Blockchain applications.

Corroborating this overall tepid adoption rate, 46.9% of the survey participants opined that their organizations have neither initiated Blockchain projects nor established dedicated teams for Blockchain-related ventures, nor do they intend to do so in the near term. Only a quarter of the respondents confirmed the existence of such specialized initiatives within their organizations. Furthermore, 46.9% declared that their organizations have not allocated financial resources for the development of prospective Blockchain initiatives or projects.

Use of Blockchain Technology

In addressing the question, "What specific benefits do you anticipate your organization or industry would derive from Blockchain technology?", the majority of respondents identify enhanced transactional integrity and visibility as the principal advantage, representing 18.02% of the responses. The capacity for improved data security—likely attributable to Blockchain's decentralized architecture—emerges as the second most commonly cited benefit, garnering 13.51% of the responses. Additionally, respondents perceive a notable advantage in time efficiency, which constituted 12.61% of the enumerated benefits. Other organizational and commercial advantages are articulated to a lesser extent by the survey participants, as delineated in Table 1.

When examining the distinct advantages pertinent to accounting and financial information, as outlined in Table 2, a majority of respondents attribute significant importance to the enhanced verifiability of accounting data, with an average intensity score of 3.594. This finding is congruent with the merits most frequently extolled by advocates of Blockchain technology. Such verifiability is intrinsically connected to the transparency and reliability of financial transactions. In accordance, the respondents identify these latter two attributes as criteria that stand to be ameliorated by the adoption of this technology, as further detailed in Table 2.

Table 1 Perceived benefits of Blockchain technology

Improved business efficiency	6	5.41%
Identification of new ways to automate business processes with partners	10	9.01%
Improved transaction integrity and visibility	**20**	**18.02%**
Increased transaction speed	11	9.91%
Better data protection thanks to Blockchain Capability	**15**	**13.51%**
Reduced transaction costs	8	7.21%
Collaborative relationships	6	5.41%
Enable the emergence of new business models	10	9.01%
Time saving	14	12.61%
Risk reduction	11	9.91%
Number of occurrences	111	100.00%

Table 2 Perceived benefits of Blockchain technology regarding accounting information (Likert scale/5 points)

Advantage	Average
Reliability	3.563
Transparency	3.469
Verifiability	**3.594**
Least manipulation or error	3.406
Immutability	3.25
Timeliness	3.406
Relevance	3.313

Table 3 Perceived benefits Blockchain technology in terms of processes/activities

Improved quality of accounting entry processes	19	16.52%
Automation of accounting entry processes using smart contracts	18	15.65%
Save time in the process of preparing financial statements	18	15.65%
Improved compliance of accounting information with accounting standards	10	8.70%
Automation of accounting review procedures thanks to smart contracts	7	6.09%
Improved audit efficiency	**20**	**17.39%**
Fraud detection made easy	16	13.91%
Improved efficiency of performance monitoring tools	7	6.09%
Occurrences	115	100.00%

The outcomes of the preceding analysis manifest tangibly in the specific applications of Blockchain technology across various processes and activities (Table 3). A majority of respondents indicate that the primary advantage of Blockchain adoption resides in improving the efficiency of auditing practices, accounting for 17.39% of responses. This observation is consistent with the results of multiple studies conducted in the Anglo-Saxon context, affirming that the most immediate implications of this technology appear to be concentrated within auditing functions. By bolstering the reliability, transparency, and verifiability of financial transactions, this technology appears to exert a substantial influence on the integrity of accounting audit processes. Subsequently, respondents also posit that the quality of accounting entry procedures stands to benefit, capturing the second-highest proportion of responses. These findings corroborate the notion that Blockchain technology can enhance accounting recording procedures, particularly through the integration of smart contracts, and more broadly expedite the process of financial statement preparation—each category accounting for 15.65% of responses.

Perceptions about the Future of Blockchain

On another dimension, although a substantial proportion of respondents (34.4%) acknowledge the utility of Blockchain technology, it does not appear to be regarded as a strategic imperative within their respective organizations. It is noteworthy, however, that an identical percentage (34.4%), comprised of 25% who deem the technology as important and an additional 9.4% who consider it critical, believe that this innovation holds significant or even pivotal importance for their institutions (Table 4).

With regard to the prospective trajectory of this technology (Table 5), a preponderance of respondents (50%) anticipates that it will fundamentally alter the scope and functions of professionals engaged in the accounting domain in the forthcoming years. Despite the current modest rate of adoption, respondents appear to acknowledge the technology's potential significance and its prospective applicability within the accounting sector.

Based on the feedback from the survey participants, the primary impediments to the adoption of Blockchain technology within their respective organizations primarily stem from a deficiency in comprehension regarding the technology's potential applications and functionalities. Subsequently, three additional obstacles are cited with equal frequency: first, the nascent status of Blockchain technologies, which have yet to establish a proven track record; second, the complexities associated with their integration, which often necessitates the modification or replacement of existing systems; and third, the imperative to identify viable use cases that are not only pertinent but also cost-effective and practically feasible for implementation within the given organizational or industrial context (see Table 6).

In addition to the aforementioned descriptive analyses, we conducted a correlational analysis to examine the relationship between the extent of Blockchain adoption and various organizational metrics. The results indicate that the level of Blockchain technology adoption does not exhibit a significant correlation with either the size of the organization, as measured by employee count, or its revenue. However, a noteworthy linkage was observed between the degree of adoption and the organization's allocated IT budget. Contrary to expectations, the adoption of

Table 4 Potential of Blockchain for the organization

	Frequency	%
It is not relevant to our organization	5	15.6
It can be useful but is not considered a strategic priority	11	**34.4**
It is important but not part of our strategic priorities	8	25.0
It is critical and is among the most urgent strategic priorities	3	9.4
Total	27	84.4
Do not know	5	15.6
32		100.0

Table 5 Future of Blockchain technology

	Frequency	%
Do not know	6	18.8
It will have no impact on the missions and tasks of professionals exercising these professions in the coming years.	3	9.4
It will have a weak impact on the missions and tasks of professionals exercising these professions in the coming years.	7	21.9
It will drastically change the missions and tasks of professionals exercising these professions in the coming years.	16	50.0
Total	32	100.0

Table 6 Barriers to the adoption of Blockchain technology

Blockchains are emerging technologies that have yet to prove themselves	13	11.61%
Lack of understanding of the possible uses/utilities of Blockchain	**19**	**16.96%**
We need to identify applicable use cases that are relevant, cost-effective, and practical to implement for our organization or industry	13	11.61%
Lack of qualified experts in Blockchain technology	12	10.71%
Its implementation and the need to modify/replace existing systems (ERP, etc.)	13	11.61%
The lack of standardized Blockchain practices within our industry	8	7.14%
Regulatory constraints	8	7.14%
Data privacy concerns	6	5.36%
Concerns about the security of data and exchanges	10	8.93%
Available Blockchain solutions	6	5.36%
Lack of funding	4	3.57%
Occurrences	112	100.00%

Blockchain technology does not appear to be contingent upon the organization's primary sector of operation, although a considerable association was discerned with respect to the organization's geographical scope. Furthermore, the bivariate analysis substantiates that the organizational metrics of size, turnover, and scope are significantly correlated with the importance ascribed to Blockchain technology by the company.

4 Suggestion for a Contingency-Based Approach to Blockchain Adoption in Accounting and Auditing Professions

This study constitutes the initial phase of an overarching research endeavor aimed at elucidating the significance and roles of Blockchain technology within the financial services professions. While corroborating initial assumptions about the nascent nature of this technology and its concomitant unfamiliarity among certain professionals, the study also unveils a noteworthy level of interest toward Blockchain within the professional community. Despite hindrances to its wide-scale implementation and its relatively limited adoption within the accounting sector in France, professionals appear to harbor optimism concerning the prospective utility of Blockchain in their respective fields.

Our findings imply the presence of some contingencies regarding the organizational uptake of Blockchain technology. Specific variables, such as the organization's operational scope and Information Technology (IT) budget, appear to correlate with both the extent of Blockchain adoption and the level of interest organizations manifest toward it. We advocate for a more granular investigation into these contingency factors, positing that it could unearth intriguing correlations between organizational attributes and Blockchain technology adoption behavior. Such an inquiry aligns with the established tradition of scrutinizing organizational technology adoption through the lens of structural contingency theory, which postulates that an organization's structural features are closely tied to its functional environments (Ngongang, 2013). Prior research enumerates six pivotal factors: organizational size, age, corporate culture, technological usage, and environmental context. Similarly, Mintzberg (1989) identifies influential aspects such as age, size, technology, environment, culture, and power dynamics, all of which collectively shape an organization's management system. This theoretical framework has been employed to explicate diverse accounting practices as well as the assimilation of digital tools within the accounting function. For instance, several studies (e.g., Chapellier, 1997; Lacombe-Saboly, 1994) have shed light on the heterogeneity of accounting information systems within Small and Medium-sized Enterprises (SMEs), pinpointing determinants such as organizational size, ownership structure, and indebtedness, with particular emphasis on the salience of the first factor. Similarly, the existing scholarly literature on Blockchain in accounting enumerates several factors shaping the inclination of accounting and auditing firms to embrace Blockchain technology. On the one hand, an auditor's proficiency in both accounting and auditing, coupled with their experience with accounting software and general understanding of Blockchain technology, positively correlates with the intent to adopt Blockchain (Jumah & Li, 2020). On the contrary, auditors' heightened degrees of professional skepticism, as well as reservations concerning transaction sample sizes in relation to the concept of materiality, appear to deter the adoption of Blockchain technology (Jumah & Li, 2020). Additional considerations, such as concerns over security and privacy, also serve as significant influencers in the decision-making process for adopting Blockchain in accounting. Moreover, the availability of specialized Blockchain-based accounting platforms stands as a critical facilitator in the proliferation of Blockchain technology within the accounting sector.

Drawing on this theoretical framework, we hypothesize a potential association between particular organizational traits and the extent of Blockchain adoption within accounting and auditing professions. Therefore, the scope of the organization, its size, its level of computerization, and its core business activities collectively exert an influence on the organization's degree of Blockchain adoption. Furthermore, the comprehensive literature review, in conjunction with the findings from our exploratory study, points toward the formulation of a research model (Fig. 2)

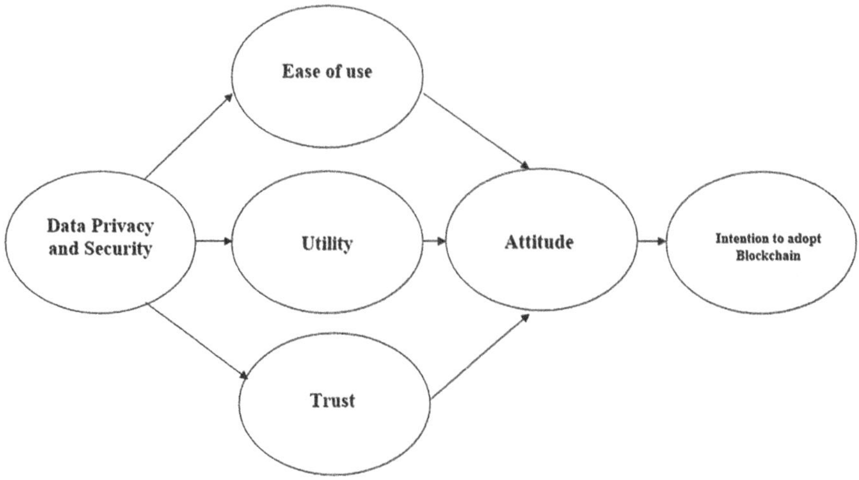

Fig. 2 Blockchain Technology adoption model in accounting and auditing

grounded in the principles of the Technology Adoption Model (TAM) (Davis et al., 1989).

This preliminary study is not without its limitations, most notably concerning the restricted sample size and the resultant inability to generalize the findings. While the initial phase of this research did not aim to secure a representative sample, this constraint is acknowledged and will be addressed in the project's subsequent stage. The second phase is explicitly designed to model Blockchain adoption within a contingency framework, thereby offering prospects for more comprehensive and generalizable insights.

Numerous unexplored research avenues regarding the adoption of Blockchain technology in the accounting and auditing industry warrant further investigation. First, there is a need for more empirical research to validate the frameworks proposed in the current literature and better understand the real-world implications of Blockchain adoption in accounting and auditing businesses (Bellucci et al., 2022). Research should also focus on how Blockchain technology can be integrated into existing auditing processes and the potential challenges that may arise (Lombardi et al., 2022). Furthermore, more in-depth research is needed on the specific regulations, accounting standards, and guidelines that need to be amended or developed to support Blockchain adoption in the accounting and auditing field (Jayasuriya & Sims, 2023; Bellucci et al., 2022). Sivaretinamohan and Sujatha (2022) also suggest exploring the potential of RPA (Robotic Process Automation) technology in automating business processes and improving task completion in auditing firms. Finally, there is a need for more research on the adoption of Blockchain technology in accounting and auditing businesses in developing countries, as their context and challenges may differ. These research avenues can help address the gaps in the literature and contribute to a better understanding of Blockchain adoption in the accounting and auditing industry.

Appendices

Appendix 1 Positions held by respondents

	Frequency	%
Financial auditor	1	3.1
Other	1	3.1
Audit employee	1	3.1
Employee in accounting verification	3	9.4
Auditor	2	6.3
Accountant	5	15.6
Financial consultant/auditor	5	15.6
Management controller	6	18.8
Internal controller	1	3.1
Chartered accountant	3	9.4
Accounting manager/director	2	6.3
Finance manager/director	1	3.1
Treasurer	1	3.1
Total	32	100.0

Appendix 2 Respondent companies

Business	Frequency	%
Accounting firm	11	34.4
Audit firm	4	12.5
Accounting office	1	3.1
Industrial company	4	12.5
Commercial company	6	18.8
Financial company	4	12.5
Other	2	6.3
	32	100

Appendix 3 Scope of companies

Scope	Frequency	%
Local	5	15.6
Regional	2	6.3
National	4	12.5
Global	21	65.6
Total	32	100

Appendix 4 Company size (number of employees)

	Frequency	%
1 to 9	3	9.4
10 to 249	6	18.8
250 to 5000	6	18.8
More than 5000	17	53.1
Total	32	100.0

Appendix 5 Company size (turnover)

	Frequency	%
Less than €50 K	0	0
€50 k - €100 k	1	3.1
€100 K - €1 M	4	12.5
€1 m - €5 m	1	3.1
€5 m - €10 m	2	6.3
Over €10 m	24	75
Total	32	100.0

References

AlSaqa, Z. H., Hussein, A. I., & Mahmood, S. M. (2019). The impact of *Blockchain* on accounting information systems. *Journal of Information Technology Management, 80, 11*(3), 62.

Bellucci, M., Cesa Bianchi, D., & Manetti, G. (2022). Blockchain in accounting practice and research: Systematic literature review. *Meditari Accountancy Research, 30*(7), 121–146.

Bonsón, E., & Bednárová, M. (2019). *Blockchain* and its implications for accounting and auditing. *Meditari Accountancy Research, 27*(5), 725–740.

Buterin V. (2014). *Ethereum white paper: A next-generation smart contract and decentralized application platform*. Available at: https://ethereum.org/en/whitepaper.

Byström, H. (2019). *Blockchains*, real-time accounting, and the future of credit risk modeling. *Ledger, 4*. https://doi.org/10.5195/ledger.2019.100

Chapellier, P. (1997). Profils de dirigeants et données comptables de gestion en PME. *Revue Internationale PME, 10*(1), 9–41.

Dai, J., & Vasarhelyi, M. A. (2017). Toward Blockchain-based accounting and assurance. *Journal of Information Systems, 31*(3), 5–21.

Dai, J., Wang, Y., & Vasarhelyi, M. A. (2017). *Blockchain*: An Emerging Solution for Fraud Prevention: Certified Public Accountant. *The CPA Journal, 87*(6), 12–14.

Davis, F. D., Bagozzi, R. P., & Warshaw, P. R. (1989). User acceptance of computer technology: A comparison of two theoretical models. *Management Science, 35*(8), 982–1003.

Degos, J. (2017). Les blocs chaînés et la future fiabilité des missions d'expertise comptable. *La Revue Du Financier, 39*(224–225), 13–24.

Deloitte (2016). *Blockchain technology: A game changer in accounting?* Rapport disponible à l'adresse. https://www2.deloitte.com/content/dam/Deloitte/de/Documents/Innovation/*Blockchain*_A%20game-changer%20in%20accounting.pdf

Demirkan, S., Demirkan, I., & McKee, A. (2010). Blockchain technology in the future of business cyber security and accounting. *Journal of Management Analytics, 7*(2), 189–208.

Desplebin, O., Lux, G., & Petit, N. (2019). Comprendre la Blockchain: quels impacts pour la comptabilité et ses métiers? *ACCRA, 5*(2), 5–23.

Firdaus, A., Ab Razak, M. F., Feizollah, A., Hashem, I. A. T., Hazim, M., & Anuar, N. B. (2019). The rise of "Blockchain": bibliometric analysis of Blockchain study. *Scientometrics, 120*(3), 1289–1331.

Handoko, B. L., & Lantu, J. E. (2021, July). UTAUT 2 model for predicting Auditor's Blockchain technology adoption. In *The 2021 12th International Conference on E-business, Management and Economics* (pp. 82-89).

Iansiti, M., & Lakhani, K. R. (2017). The truth about Blockchain. *Harvard Business Review, 95*(1), 118–127.

Jayasuriya, D. D., & Sims, A. (2023). From the abacus to enterprise resource planning: Is blockchain the next big accounting tool? *Accounting, Auditing & Accountability Journal, 36*(1), 24–62.

Jumah, A., & Li, Y. (2020). Auditors' adoption of Blockchain technology: A study on antecedents. *Americas Conference on Information Systems*.

Kokina, J., Mancha, R., & Pachamanova, D. (2017). Blockchain: Emergent industry adoption and implications for accounting. *Journal of Emerging Technologies in Accounting, 14*(2), 91–100.

Lacombe-Saboly, M. (1994). Les déterminants de la qualité des produits comptables des entreprises: le rôle du dirigeant (Doctoral dissertation, Poitiers).

Lombardi, R., de Villiers, C., Moscariello, N., & Pizzo, M. (2022). The disruption of blockchain in auditing–a systematic literature review and an agenda for future research. *Accounting, Auditing & Accountability Journal, 35*(7), 1534–1565.

Lundy L. (2016). *Blockchain and the sharing economy 2.0*. Rapport disponible à l'adresse:https://www.ibm.com/developerworks/library/iot-*Blockchain*-sharing-economy/index.html.

Mintzberg, H. (1989). *Mintzberg on management: Inside our strange world of organizations*. Simon and Schuster.

Ngongang, D. (2013). Facteurs de contingence, TIC et informations dans les entreprises tchadiennes. *La Revue des Sciences de Gestion, 259-260*, 153–162. https://doi.org/10.3917/rsg.259.0153

Nofer, M., Gomber, P., Hinz, O., & Schiereck, D. (2017). Blockchain. *Business & Information Systems Engineering, 59*(3), 183–187.

Perera, P. A., & Abeygunasekera, A. W. (2022). Blockchain adoption in accounting and auditing: A qualitative inquiry in Sri Lanka. *Colombo Business Journal, 13*(1), 57–87. https://doi.org/10.4038/cbj.v13i1.89

Rozario, A. M., & Vasarhelyi, M. A. (2018). Auditing with smart contracts. *International Journal of Digital Accounting Research, 18*(2018), 1–27.

Rückeshäuser N. (2017). *Do we really want Blockchain-based accounting?* Decentralized Consensus as Enabler of Management Override of Internal Controls. in Leimeister, J.M.; Brenner, W. (Hrsg.): Proceedings der 13. Internationalen Tagung Wirtschaftsinformatik (WI 2017), S. 16–30.

Schmitz, J., & Leoni, G. (2019). Accounting and auditing at the time of *Blockchain* technology: A research agenda. *Australian Accounting Review, 29*(2), 331–342.

Simões, M.P., Cavalcanti, J.A., Melo, J.F., & Reis, C.Q. (2021). Benefits of using Blockchain technology as an accounting auditing instrument. *Revista Ambiente Contabil*-Universidade Federal do Rio Grande do Norte-ISSN 2176-9036, 13(1).

Sivaretinamohan, R., & Sujatha, S. (2022). *Behavioural Intention towards adoption of Robotic Accounting for a profitable leading digital transformation.* 2022 First International Conference on Electrical, Electronics, Information and Communication Technologies (ICEEICT), 1–8.

World Economic Forum, World Economic Forum Annual Meeting, (2017). Report available at: https://www.weforum.org/events/world-economic-forum-annual-meeting-2017/

Sami Basly holds a Ph.D. in Management Sciences (University of Bordeaux) and is authorized to supervise Doctoral research (University Paris Nanterre). Before joining the University Paris Nanterre, he was a lecturer at the University of Bordeaux. He is interested in family businesses, digital entrepreneurship, and digital technologies. He has conducted research on family businesses, internationalization, and digital transformation, and has published his findings in many national and international journals (Management International, Review of Entrepreneurship, Journal of Entrepreneurship, etc.).

Paul-Laurent Saunier, Ph.D., is an Associate Professor of management at the University of Paris Nanterre. He received his Ph.D. with honors in 2012 from the University of Orleans. His research interests include management control, service quality management, and family firms. He is currently head of the Business and Administration department at the Institute of Technology of Ville d'Avray-Nanterre.

New MTFs Based on DLT Technology as Operational Spaces for Decentralized Finance: A European Perspective

Elisa Facciotti, Domenica Federico, and Antonella Notte

1 Introduction

Financial markets, in recent years, have been one of the areas most invested in and receptive to the changes brought about by digital innovation. This evolution has led to the identification of alternative trading venues to regulated markets, such as multilateral trading facilities (MTFs), increasing the places of exchange between economic operators for the fundraising of financial resources.

In particular, alternative trading venues, given their nature as places for trading financial instruments characterized by specific speed and operational efficiency, have historically constituted a favorable environment for experimentation with new technologies.

This evolution is part of the changes initiated by financial technology (FinTech), indicating the close relationship between finance and new technologies. One of the main and current manifestations of the FinTech phenomenon is decentralized finance (DeFi), which allows users to carry out financial transactions directly without the intervention of financial intermediaries. This is possible thanks to Distributed Ledger Technology (DLT), whose potential has aroused the interest of the European Commission, so much so that it has been included as an enabling factor in the European Fintech Action Plan.

The chapter is the fruit of the joint work of all the authors. However, Antonella Notte mainly contributed to paragraphs 1 and 2, Domenica Federico to paragraphs 3 and 8, and Elisa Facciotti to paragraphs 4, 5, 6, and 7.

E. Facciotti (✉) · D. Federico · A. Notte
eCampus University, Novedrate (Como), Italy
e-mail: elisa.facciotti@uniecampus.it; domenica.federico@uniecampus.it; antonella.notte@uniecampus.it

S. Basly (ed.), *Decentralized Finance*, Financial Innovation and Technology,
https://doi.org/10.1007/978-3-031-49515-1_7

The combination of new trading venues alternative to regulated markets and DLT technology is revolutionizing—also through a process of disintermediation—the financial services industry and the capital market and is prompting national and supranational institutions to introduce ad hoc regulation of the activities carried out therein. In particular, DLT technologies, through the digital representation of a right or a value in a cryptographic code, which can be stored and transferred in an unlimited temporal and geographical context without the supervision of a central body, produce a series of advantages: first, greater liquidity, as they allow for the fragmentation of ownership securities and the creation of a secondary market, more easily than traditional methods; furthermore, a decrease in transaction costs due to the automation of smart contracts; then, greater transparency through cryptography, which guarantees the protection of recorded information and its nonrepudiation; finally, an increase in investment opportunities, as the reduction of transaction costs will also allow for very small investments, with a consequent significant widening of the potential investor base.

The aim of the chapter is to illustrate the evolution of financial markets thanks to the development of technologies, with particular regard to MTFs and the overall regulatory path that has seen them as protagonists.

The chapter begins with an overview of the evolutionary trends of financial markets that, through technology, have developed alternative configurations, such as multilateral trading systems, becoming a great opportunity for economic operators to increase the methods of fundraising financial resources. Subsequently, the work addresses the importance of the digitization of finance highlighted by the European Commission, defining its main innovations and outlining a specific regulatory regime for market infrastructures based on DLT. Finally, the chapter illustrates the Pilot Regime introduced by Regulation (EU) 2022/858, highlighting the need for careful regulatory activity for market infrastructures that use DLT technology for the negotiation and settlement of crypto-assets qualifying as financial.

2 The Role of Markets in Financial Instruments for Entrepreneurial Fundraising

The market is the place where the transfer of financial resources between economic operators in surplus and deficit takes place. The task of financial markets is to facilitate the meeting between the supply and demand of financial instruments and services. The prerequisite for ensuring this direct financial intermediation process is the perfect alignment of interests between surplus and deficit operators in terms of the nature of financing, duration, remuneration, and repayment. When this alignment occurs, the surplus operator transfers financial resources to the deficit operator in exchange for a financial instrument that reports the agreed conditions (Nadotti et al., 2010).

It is natural that the direct connection between the surplus unit and the deficit unit requires the interposition of specialized operators in the issuance, placement, and negotiation phase. In fact, financial system markets are organized as companies and today constitute an institutional subject of great importance. Markets can be distinguished from a technical point of view and based on different financial instruments (Banfi et al., 2022).

From a technical point of view, the most significant distinctions are those between the primary market and the secondary market and between the regulated market and the organized market. The primary market performs the function of financing in the form of debt or equity, as it is the place where the issuance of financial instruments takes place, while the secondary market performs the function of facilitating liquidity through the investment and divestment of financial instruments, as it is the place intended for subsequent negotiation of already issued financial instruments.

From this distinction, it is evident how financial markets not only help companies raise the money they need (primary issuance) but also allow investors to trade stocks and other securities among themselves (secondary transactions). The result of these secondary transactions is simply a transfer of ownership between one party and another and does not produce any effects on the availability of financial resources for companies (Brealey et al., 2023).

The regulated market responds to a series of minimum requirements (regular operation, daily publication of opening and closing prices) and is therefore governed by specific general rules and supervision, while the organized market (over the counter) is reserved for qualified operators and develops based on the specific needs of the contracting parties (e.g., derivative markets relating to swaps and options are over-the-counter markets).

From a technical point of view, markets can be further distinguished based on the type of operators (retail and wholesale), the geographical scope of reference (domestic and international), and the articulation of operating rules (regulated and organized).

From the perspective of the financial instruments traded, it is possible to distinguish between monetary (where short-term financial instruments are issued and traded), foreign exchange (where currencies of different countries are traded), financial (where long-term financial instruments are traded), and derivatives (where derivative instruments are traded).

The benefits provided by financial markets to economic operators, and in particular to the fundraising of companies, which are the epitome of units in financial deficit, can be evaluated in terms of efficiency (Williams, 2005).

First, when the needs of the units involved in the transactions are satisfied, we speak of allocative-functional efficiency. A financial market that is efficient from this perspective is one that can guarantee operators the maximization of their financing and investment objectives, and no further redistribution of resources is necessary.

Second, we speak of technical-operational efficiency when the financial market is able to achieve the function of containing transaction costs (a heterogeneous set of costs that an economic unit must bear to carry out an exchange operation) and, more generally, to facilitate financial transactions.

Financial markets have undergone a long process of evolution along two directions: institutional structure and price determination methods.

The first direction, namely, the institutional structure, was initially conditioned by the rather limited level of technological infrastructure that required the concentration of operators in a physical location where trading took place. This is how Stock Exchanges were born which, however, depending on the experience gained in their respective countries of origin, assumed the form of private exchanges (i.e., born on the initiative of specialized operators who decided to dedicate themselves to this form of trading of financial instruments), as in the case of the United Kingdom and the United States, or the form of public institutions, as in the case of the stock exchanges of continental Europe, including those that were established in Italy.

The second direction, i.e., the methods of price determination, concerns the rules followed for collecting orders and executing trades. Based on this, from a technical point of view, it is possible to identify a classification of markets as "order-driven" or "quote-driven": the former so called because the price arises from the flow of orders from buyers and sellers, and the latter so named because the price is proposed by intermediaries and eventually accepted by potential buyers and sellers. The next step was the one that allowed, thanks to the development of technology, to connect specialized intermediaries operating outside official markets, making the concentration of orders increasingly necessary.

Technology has therefore brought markets toward trading modes (especially aimed at determining the price for the exchange of financial instruments) no longer (and not only) based on the physical encounter of the parties admitted to trading but on the activation of telematic circuits in competition with each other.

3 Multilateral Trading Facilities for Trading Financial Instruments

The evolution of markets through technology has led to the configuration of market models that, alongside various regulated markets, have seen the development of alternative trading systems, becoming a great opportunity for economic operators to develop an alternative activity of fundraising of financial resources (Barclay et al., 2003, pp. 2637–2665).

Additionally, the discipline regarding financial instruments markets, from Council Directive 93/22/EEC of 10 May 1993 on investment services in the securities field (European Union, 1993) to Directive 2004/39/EC of the European Parliament and of the Council of 21 April 2004 on markets in financial instruments (following MiFID) (European Parliament, 2004), up to Directive 2014/65/EU of the European Parliament and of the Council of 15 May 2014 on markets in financial instruments and amending Directive 2002/92/EC and Directive 2011/61/EU (European Parliament, 2014) (following MiFID II), has clearly documented the evolutionary nexus between financial markets, technology, and the need for regulation.

Since the advent of the MiFID Directive, it has been mainly MTFs that have experimented with the adoption of technologically sophisticated and advanced trading platforms, thus placing themselves in direct competition with regulated markets (Fioravanti & Gentile, 2011, pp. 1–48).

An MTF is defined as a multilateral system operated by an investment firm or market operator that facilitates the meeting of multiple third-party buying and selling interests in financial instruments, with the aim of concluding a contract (Banfi et al., 2016). It is a multilateral system in which all operators interested in trading financial instruments can act in compliance with the rules defined by the market organizers in a certain and nondiscretionary manner, leading to the conclusion of a contract. In fact, in MTFs, commitments made by participants in the trades must be binding both in terms of quantity traded and price. The entity that operates an MTF does not engage in any transactions on its own behalf, instead acting as a mere intermediary between the buyer and seller without assuming any risks.

In particular, the main characteristics that identify MTFs are as follows:

- The "multilateral" nature of third-party orders on financial instruments that such systems allow to be matched.
- The fact that exchanges take place in accordance with nondiscretionary rules predetermined by the system operator.
- The regular functioning of the system supported by a stable organization.

The MiFID Directive allows for a similarity to be drawn between traditional markets and MTFs. In fact, from careful reading, it emerges that the European legislator considers MTFs as "real markets", as they are organized systems of rules and structures that provide ad hoc services, thus facilitating the matching of proposals to buy and sell financial instruments (Amorosino, 2008).

The definitions of regulated market and MTF are closely aligned in terms of organizational structure and operational modalities, as both apply the same notion of organized trading; are "systems" made up of a trading platform operating exclusively based on rules; allow the matching of interests (orders, price quotations, or expressions of interest) based on the rules of the system or through internal protocols and operating procedures of the system itself; and refer to "nondiscretionary rules", which do not allow the operator any discretion on how trading interests may interact.

Unlike regulated markets, MTFs can also be managed by entities other than market management companies, such as banks or financial intermediaries, provided that they are authorized to provide the specific investment service of managing multilateral trading systems. This definition makes it clear that these systems must be considered different from those that establish direct relationships between external parties and exchange organizers, as is the case with over-the-counter markets. In addition, with regard to the object of negotiation, both financial instruments listed on regulated markets and unlisted securities can be traded on MTFs. This means that MTFs allow for an increase in trading, improving the liquidity (Jain et al., 2020, pp. 481–502) of securities that are not listed on regulated markets and the efficiency of fundraising activities (Saunders et al., 2010).

For the operation of an MTF, in addition to the platform operator, the following figures can be identified (Giannelli & Sfameni, 2020):

- Traders or negotiators, who are authorized to enter buy or sell orders into the system on their own behalf or on behalf of their clients.
- Market makers and specialists, who, based on specific obligations imposed by the regulations of each MTF or based on discretionary assignments from issuers, support the liquidity of traded financial instruments.
- Sponsors or advisors who provide consulting services to companies that intend to list their financial instruments on a particular MTF.

MTFs can be divided into two main types: primary MTFs and passive secondary MTFs (Vegas, 2011). Primary MTFs are platforms that offer issuers a listing service that is entirely analogous and alternative to that provided by regulated markets. The requirements for admission to trading on these markets are less stringent than those required for access to regulated markets. For example, the instruments traded on the MTF do not necessarily have to be already admitted to trading on a regulated market. Companies that intend to request admission of financial instruments to trading on a Primary MTF must rely on specialized intermediaries (sponsors or nominated advisors) who have the task of carrying out due diligence on the information contained in the documentation prepared by the issuer for admission to trading and issuing statements about the truthfulness and completeness of such information. Examples of Primary MTFs are Euronext Growth Milan and EuroTLX (for nonequity securities) managed by Borsa Italiana S.p.A. Passive Secondary MTFs, on the other hand, are MTFs on which only financial instruments that are already admitted to trading on a regulated market are organized and managed. Admission to trading can occur without authorization from the issuer of the financial instruments, as no prior communication is needed. An example of a Passive Secondary MTF is Turquoise managed by Turquoise Global Holdings Europe B.V.

4 The Development of Decentralized Technologies in Financial Services: The Digital Finance Strategy of the European Commission

The evolution of markets thanks to technology and the identification of alternative trading venues falls within the broader system of changes initiated by FinTech, which has allowed for financial innovation that can translate into new business models, processes, products, and new market operators, characteristic of digital finance.

The development of new technology has made it possible to redesign the exchange process in the economic and financial system. A new trading platform known as DeFi has emerged. What makes DeFi innovative compared to traditional finance is the absence of intermediation. The distrust that has permeated the minds of investors following major financial crises has led them to seek refuge in new forms of investment capable of providing them with higher returns.

The advent of decentralized technologies in the field of financial services rests on the central role of DLT, whose potential has aroused the interest of the European Commission to the point of including it as an enabling factor in the European Fintech Action Plan.

Specifically, the European Commission, in its Communication of September 24, 2020 (European Commission, 2020), expressly highlighted that "The future of finance is digital". In particular, the European Commission adopted a package of initiatives on digital finance, which includes a specific strategy and legislative proposals on cryptocurrencies and digital resilience, aimed at promoting the development of a competitive European Union financial sector that provides access to innovative financial products while ensuring that consumers and the financial stability of the Union are protected.

The so-called "Digital Finance Strategy" of the European Commission includes, among its various priorities, the adaptation of the European regulatory framework to facilitate digital innovation in the financial sector, addressing the challenges and risks of this transformation in terms of improving the digital resilience of the financial sector (Locatelli & Schena, 2022).

The European Commission has divided the aforementioned "Digital Finance Strategy" into four priority areas that will guide the actions of the European Union to boost digital transformation, ideally to be completed by 2024.

The first priority identified is to address the fragmentation of the digital single market in the field of financial services to provide European consumers with access to cross-border services and to help European financial companies expand their digital operations.

The second priority aims to ensure that the European Union regulatory framework facilitates digital innovation in the interest of consumers and market efficiency.

The third priority sets the goal of creating a European space for financial data to promote data-driven innovation, starting from the European data strategy, which includes enhancing access to and sharing of data within the financial sector.

The fourth and final priority is to address the new challenges and risks related to digital transformation.

To implement the outlined strategy, the European Commission has developed a substantial package of legislative measures, the so-called "Digital Finance Package", in support of digital innovation and the digitization of finance. The Commission is aware of the urgency to overcome the isolated legislative interventions carried out by the EU Member States and to adopt a discipline capable of ensuring that the EU regulatory framework regarding financial services is suitable to promote innovation and does not create barriers to the use of new technologies.

The risk that the European Commission intended to avoid was real, as in the absence of rules at the EU level, a highly fragmented regulatory framework was developing in the discipline of the EU Member States. In particular, three Member States (France, Germany, and Malta) had already established national regimes that regulated certain aspects of financial instruments and services that were not assimilated to financial instruments under the MiFID II legislation, with substantial differences both in terms of the application of the different regimes—since the French regime is optional, while the Maltese and German regimes are mandatory—and in terms of scope of application, activities covered, obligations imposed on issuers or service providers and measures to ensure market integrity.

The "Digital Finance Package" includes a proposal for a regulation on:

- Crypto-asset markets (MiCA).
- Distributed Ledger Technologies (DLT)-based market infrastructures (Pilot Regime).
- Digital Operational Resilience (DORA).

The regulatory initiatives mentioned also represent the attempt by the European Commission to reconcile two different approaches to FinTech.

The first approach of the regulator toward FinTech is generally identified with the principle of "same business, same risks, same rules" (Perrazzelli, 2021, p. 2). According to this principle, if an innovative activity has the same economic function and risks as a regulated activity, the same rules of the latter must be applied regardless of the technology used. This is probably the most widespread approach at the international and European level and has the advantage of ensuring the application of uniform conditions to new and old operators, avoiding regulatory arbitrage unfavorable to subjects already active on the market. However, the exclusive application of this approach sometimes risks underestimating the importance and innovativeness of the technological component in financial activities.

The second approach to FinTech regulation is summarized in the principle of "new functionality, new rules". This solution starts from the assumption that an innovative service or product can entail both risks (or a combination of risks) not adequately protected and opportunities not captured by existing regulations. In these cases, the regulator is called upon to develop new rules that enhance the innovative characteristics of the phenomenon and prevent uncontrolled development.

It should be clarified that of the three regulatory initiatives started by the European Commission, as of the drafting of this document, the only ones approved are Regulation (EU) 2022/858 of the European Parliament and of the Council of 30 May 2022, on the Pilot Regime for market infrastructures based on distributed ledger technology, and Regulation (EU) 2022/2554 of the European Parliament and of the Council of 14 December 2022 on digital operational resilience for the financial sector and amending Regulations (EC) No 1060/2009, (EU) No 648/2012, (EU) No 600/2014, (EU) No 909/2014, and (EU) 2016/1011.

5 The Characteristics of DLT Technology and Impact on MTFs

Within the scope of multilateral trading systems, a relevant technology is that of DLTs.

Literally, DLT refers to a technology based on distributed registries, consisting of distributed and decentralized systems for recording and storing data. More specifically, this expression refers to a set of protocols that allow a network made up of nodes of actors to manage a data register (called "ledger"), using cryptography for the protection and authentication of transactions, without the mediation of a central subject responsible for supervision and control. The validation of transactions within the system is based on the participation of the various actors in the network through nodes that contain an identical copy of the register within themselves, periodically updating it through procedures and mechanisms of "shared consensus" (Vasapollo & Comellini, 2019).

When referring to DLTs as decentralized systems, this is explained by the fact that they do not presuppose the existence of a central entity (or node) that verifies the validity of various operations. In fact, in such systems, the validating action is autonomously carried out by the various nodes in the network, within which data relating to all transactions executed on the platform are contained. Essentially, the concept of "middleman" is absent in DLT. This aspect then allows for a second characteristic of DLT to be defined, namely, transparency. Given the shared nature inherent in such systems, every operation or transaction that occurs is immediately visible and traceable by the various participants in the network through their nodes.

In distributed ledgers, the nodes in the network, organized in a peer-to-peer architecture, perform each task by jointly processing activities according to predetermined rules. Each node holds a copy of the register, either integral or partial depending on its full or light nature, typically protected with cryptography. In such registers, resistance to external manipulations is particularly efficient since each modification is subject to approval by the entire community of nodes. This translates into a tendency toward immutability of the data contained within them. In particular, following each operation carried out within the system in compliance with certain mechanisms, any subsequent modification will require the completion of a new operation, along with the confirmation process by the nodes in the same network.

DLT is characterized by a high level of security, as a potential attack on one node does not alter the overall integrity of the data contained in the other participating nodes in the network. This peculiarity is inevitably linked to the absence in DLT of a central node responsible for data management.

To summarize the main characteristics of distributed ledger technology, the following aspects can be highlighted (Garavaglia, 2019):

- Decentralization: the guarantee of security and resilience through the distribution of data and roles among a plurality of nodes.

- Disintermediation: the simplification (also intended as efficiency) of processes by eliminating some actors.
- Programmability: the ability to program certain actions that are executed when certain conditions occur.
- Immutability: once written on the Distributed Ledger, data become virtually impossible to modify.
- Verifiability: the ease of consultation and verification of what is written in the Distributed Ledger.
- Accountability: the ability to verify who (or what) wrote on the Distributed Ledger and when it was done (timestamping).
- Traceability: each element on the Distributed Ledger is traceable in every part of it and can be traced back to its exact origin.
- Transparency: the content of the Distributed Ledger is transparent and visible to all nodes.

Based on the methods of access, modification, and validation of the register itself (i.e., the so-called "algorithmic governance" of the technology), DLT can be classified into two different types: "permissionless ledger" and "permissioned ledger" (Bank of Italy, 2022).

The characteristic that unites the aforementioned types of DLT is the existence, for both, of a distributed ledger governed by a decentralized logic that keeps track of all transactions. The nodes are connected to each other in a peer-to-peer mode without the intervention of a central server for the validation of transactions, which thus become irreversible (or immutable).

The "permissionless" DLT includes all those open systems where access is not conditioned in any way and the presence of a third-party "trusted" is not foreseen; the actors operating in the permissionless DLT are pseudonymized, making transactions not directly attributable to natural persons. In fact, while it is possible to identify the address from which the transaction originated, it is not equally directly and certainly identifiable the natural person who owns the private key associated with that address (Maimeri & Mancini, 2019).

In the case of the "permissioned" DLT, there is a "trusted" third party responsible for governing access to the Distributed Ledger. The validation of transactions is carried out by preselected entities that are specifically appointed: the actors who operate on the "permissioned" DLT are necessarily known, as they are identified in advance by the "trusted" third party (Garavaglia, 2019, p. 173).

In the general framework of DLT types, it is also necessary to introduce the concept of blockchain (Adamo et al., 2019), often used as a synonym or in conjunction with DLT. Blockchain represents a particular type of DLT, that is, one that allows access to the registry in "permissionless" mode. Specifically, we refer to it as a blockchain because the stored transactions are grouped together in a sequence of "blocks" linked together cryptographically, creating a chronological and unalterable record of all transactions made up to that moment (Bank of Italy, 2022, p. 5).

The management of transactions on DLT is based on the use of asymmetric cryptography. In asymmetric cryptography, each user has a unique pair of keys (one private and one public). The private key is kept secret by its owner, while the public key, generated from the private key, is communicated to the counterparty. The private key is used to decrypt the encrypted text with the public key. The public key can be openly shared, for example, by sending it over the network to another party. However, it can encrypt a message but cannot decode it. Only the corresponding private key can decode or unlock messages encrypted with the public key, which is why secrecy is required (Orlando & Capaldo, 2021).

In DLT technology, the public key "represents" the address to which it is possible to transfer the availability of assets. The private key allows the owner of the aforementioned address (and only him) to actually dispose of the received quantity. The private key must be kept securely to prevent anyone who comes into possession of it from disposing of quantities that are not theirs.

The particular complexity and innovation inherent in distributed ledger technology, as well as its potential applications in the financial world, have clearly prompted the European legislature to outline a regulatory framework aimed at both promoting the development of such technology and addressing potential risks arising from its widespread application.

One of the first European authorities to consider the impacts of DLT on market infrastructures was the European Securities and Markets Authority (ESMA) in its report entitled "The Distributed Ledger Technology Applied to Securities Markets" (hereinafter also referred to as the "DLT Report") of February 7, 2017. According to ESMA, the introduction of DLT systems, as stated in paragraph 3 of the DLT Report ("Possible benefits of DLT applied to securities markets"), could bring significant advantages in relation to the following profiles: improvement in post-trade process management; greater market transparency also from the supervisory authority's perspective; greater transaction security; reduced counterparty risks and collateral management, as well as a possible reduction in costs in the provision of financial services (European Securities and Markets Authority, 2017).

Paragraph 6 of the DLT Report ("Interaction between the existing EU-level regulatory regime and the application of DLT to securities markets") is specifically dedicated to examining the interaction between the current capital market regulations and the application of DLT.

The first area of focus highlighted by ESMA concerns the post-trading sector, consisting of clearing and settlement activities: according to ESMA, the approach already taken by the European legislator in the reference regulations (such as the EMIR Regulation, the Settlement Finality Directive, and the Central Securities Depositories Regulation) based on the principle of technological neutrality would not constitute an obstacle to the introduction of DLT technology.

The second area of evaluation in the DLT Report concerns the systems and rules relating to the registration and custody of financial instruments. The conclusions of the DLT Report seem to support the assumption that the introduction of DLT technology could make it easier to register and custody dematerialized instruments. However, this observation is accompanied by ESMA's invitation to review national legislation and urge many market participants to use the new technology (Annunziata, 2018, pp. 1–29).

Alongside the ESMA, the European Commission in Fintech Action Plan ("FinTech Action Plan: For a more competitive and innovative European financial sector"), in March 2018, also analyzed the potential of distributed ledger technologies applied to financial services infrastructure. In this regard, in paragraph 2.3 ("Enabling FinTech applications with the EU blockchain initiative") of the aforementioned document, the Commission recognizes the following:

> Distributed ledger technologies and blockchain have great potential to drive simplicity and efficiency through the establishment of new infrastructure and processes. These technologies may become central to future financial services infrastructure. The most impactful applications will require deep collaboration between incumbents, innovators and regulators to have a successful and beneficial implementation path. The scope of potential applications is very broad and should be monitored closely (European Commission, 2018).

At the European level, it is worth mentioning the Resolution of the European Parliament of October 3, 2018, on distributed ledger technologies and blockchain (European Parliament, 2018).

In particular, the Parliament, recognizing the innovative nature of this technology:

> Highlights the significance of DLT in financial intermediation and its potential for improving transparency and reducing transaction costs and hidden costs by better managing data and streamlining processes; [...].

In outlining guidelines for stimulating DLT policies in Europe, the European Parliament:

> stresses that any regulatory approach toward DLT should be innovation-friendly, should enable passporting, and should be guided by the principles of technology neutrality and business-model neutrality"; and "calls on the Commission to assess and develop a European legal framework in order to solve any jurisdictional problems that may arise in the event of fraudulent or criminal cases of DLT exchange; [...].

6 The Pilot Regime as a Space to Test DLT Technology in MTFs

The interaction between MTFs and DLT has reached its point of arrival in the context of the "Digital Finance Strategy" of the European Commission with the issuance of Regulation (EU) 2022/858 (European Union, 2014, 2022).

Regulation (EU) 2022/858 introduced the Pilot Regime, which represents a significant step in the evolution of MTFs from a fintech perspective, as it outlines a specific regulatory regime for market infrastructures based on DLT. The application of the provisions of the Pilot Regime has been in effect since March 23, 2023. The intent of the European legislator, through this regulatory intervention, is to introduce a specific set of rules for market infrastructures that use DLT technology for the trading and settlement of crypto-assets that qualify as financial instruments under Annex I Section C of the MiFID II Directive (known as "crypto-securities") (Amato & Benvenuto, 2022).

Specifically, the regulation establishes and regulates three new market infrastructures based on the use of DLT technology, namely, DLT MTF (multilateral trading facility DLT), DLT SS (settlement system DLT), and DLT TSS (trading and settlement system DLT), while at the same time initiating a Pilot Regime following the scheme of a regulatory sandbox.

From the perspective of building a secondary market for DLT financial instruments, Regulation (EU) 2022/858, in recital 13, clarifies that:

> A DLT MTF should be a multilateral trading facility that is operated by an investment firm or a market operator authorized under Directive 2014/65/EU and that has received a specific permission under this Regulation. A credit institution authorized under Directive 2013/36/EU that provides investment services or performs investment activities should only be allowed to operate a DLT MTF when authorized as an investment firm or market operator under Directive 2014/65/EU. [...].

Article 2 ("Definitions") of Regulation (EU) 2022/858 defines a "DLT multilateral trading facility or DLT MTF" as "a multilateral trading facility that only admits to trading DLT financial instruments". Only "DLT financial instruments" can be traded on an MTF DLT, and a "DLT Financial instrument" is defined as "a financial instrument that is issued, recorded, transferred and stored using distributed ledger technology". With that said, Article 3 ("Limitations on the financial instruments admitted to trading or recorded on DLT market infrastructure") expressly lists the characteristics that DLT financial instruments, admitted for trading on a DLT market infrastructure or registered in a DLT market infrastructure, must have at the time of their admission for trading or their registration in a distributed ledger.

Article 4 ("Requirements and exemptions regarding DLT MTFs") of Regulation (EU) 2022/858 represents a significant piece in creating the discipline of DLT MTFs: it implements complete equivalence between DLT MTFs and MTFs subject to the requirements set out in Regulation (EU) No 600/2014 and MiFID II Directive.

Regarding the specific context of the Pilot Regime as a regulatory sandbox, the salient aspects relate to the system of exemptions and authorizations outlined for the operation of a secondary market for DLT MTFs.

The application of the Pilot Regime does not cover the issuance phase of financial instruments, as the European legislator assumes that this phase can be adequately regulated by existing regulations and considers it sufficient to expand the definition of "financial instrument" expressed in Article 4(1)(15) of Directive 2014/65/EU (MiFID II), including "DLT financial instrument" as well, which will be "issued, registered, transferred, and stored using distributed ledger technology".

The equivalence of DLT financial instruments to financial instruments under MiFID II is confirmed under Article 3(7) of Regulation (EU) 2022/858 and by the application of Regulation (EU) No 596/2014 (Market Abuse Regulation—MAR) on market abuse to all DLT financial instruments traded on a DLT MTF or a DLT TSS. This will mean that the rules regarding transparency and market information obligations, as defined by MAR, will be applied to both issuers of financial instruments traded on ordinary market infrastructures and operators of DLT infrastructures.

Focusing on the specific category of DLT MTFs, Article 4 of Regulation (EU) 2022/858 outlines the mechanism of exemptions that can be granted to MTF operators under the Pilot Regime.

According to paragraph 1 of Article 4, the first exemption concerns the possibility for a manager of a DLT MTF to request the supervisory authority to waive the requirements applicable to an MTF under MiFID II, subject to the conditions set out in the aforementioned paragraph. For an investment firm or a DLT MTF manager to benefit from the exemption, they must comply with, in addition to the requirements set out in Article 4 (referred to in paragraphs 2, 3, and 4), what is provided for in Article 7 ("Additional requirements for DLT market infrastructures"). These additional requirements are aimed at introducing precautions and measures, particularly to protect end users. Among others, the duty is to (i) establish clear and detailed business plans; (ii) make available to the public up-to-date, clear and detailed written documentation defining the rules under which DLT market infrastructures operate; (iii) ensure that the overall IT provisions relating to the use of DLT are proportionate to the nature, scope, and complexity of their activity; (iv) have specific operational risk management procedures for the risks posed by DLT and crypto assets; and (v) establish and disclose a "transition strategy" for reducing the activity of a particular DLT market infrastructure or for transitioning or terminating the activity of a particular DLT market infrastructure, including the transition or return of its DLT activities to traditional market infrastructures. Finally, the exemption may be granted if the investment firm or market operator complies with any compensatory measures that the competent authority considers appropriate to achieve the objectives of the provisions for which the exemption was requested or to ensure the protection of investments, market integrity, or financial stability (Annunziata & Minto, 2022). The ESMA, pursuant to paragraph 6 of Article 4 of Regulation (EU) 2022/858, will develop guidance to define the compensatory measures to be applied.

The second exemption provided by the Pilot Regime for DLT MTFs, indicated in paragraph 2 of Article 4, concerns the exemption from the obligation of intermediation and therefore the possibility of allowing not only entities authorized under MiFID II, such as banks, investment firms, and professional investors but also natural and legal persons who can be qualified as nonprofessional investors to access the trading platform. For these subjects to trade on their own as members or participants in a DLT MTF, the European regulator requires compliance with certain requirements, in particular, these subjects:

- Have a sufficiently good reputation.
- Must have a sufficient level of trading capacity, competence, and experience, including knowledge of the functioning of DLT.
- Are not market makers in the DLT MTF.
- Do not use high-frequency algorithmic trading techniques in the DLT MTF.
- Do not provide others with direct electronic access to the DLT MTF.
- Do not trade for their own account when executing customer orders on the DLT market infrastructure.

– Have given informed consent to trading on the DLT MTF as members or participants and have been informed by the DLT MTF of the potential risks associated with the use of its systems to trade DLT financial instruments.

The third paragraph of Article 4 introduces a last significant exemption: an operator of a DLT MTF may request from the competent authority an exemption from the obligation to report the transactions referred to in Article 26 (Obligation to report transactions) of Regulation (EU) 600/2014.

If the exemption provided in paragraph 3 is granted, the DLT MTF must directly manage a distributed ledger in which the recordings of the individual transactions carried out through its systems will be recorded. The recordings will contain all the information provided for in paragraph 3 of Article 26 of Regulation (EU) 600/2014, leaving it to the DLT MTF's discretion to evaluate the relevance of the requested information, in consideration of the system used by the same DLT MTF and in reference to the member or participant who carries out the transaction. The DLT MTF must also ensure that the competent authorities have direct and immediate access to the distributed ledger where such information is stored: the competent authority will be authorized to access it as an observer and will bear the burden of making all information to which it has access available to ESMA promptly (without undue delay).

The use of DLT technology for managing an MTF is subject to an authorization process before the competent authority in accordance with the provisions of Article 8 (Specific permission to operate DLT MTF) of Regulation (EU) 2022/858. The European legislature is aware that, alongside the potential benefits, DLT technology can also bring risks and has therefore introduced certain specific information requirements aimed at transparency toward investors (Mattassoglio, 2021).

To obtain authorization for the management of a DLT MTF, a company authorized to provide investment services or to manage a regulated market, in accordance with MiFID II, must accompany the application with rather detailed documents and information. Paragraph 4 of Article 8, in particular, requires the preparation of a business plan in which the rules of the MTF DLT, including information regarding its operation, services, and activities provided, must be presented. The description of the functioning of the DLT market infrastructure will include details of the DLT used. Finally, to complete the application, the infrastructure manager must develop a transition strategy to be promptly implemented for the transition to a particular infrastructure or in case of gradual cessation in the event that the authorization granted or exemptions granted under the Pilot Regime are suspended or revoked, or in the event of voluntary or involuntary cessation of the activity of the MTF DLT.

The authorization process starts with the submission of a specific application to the competent national authority aimed at managing a DLT MTF, which evaluates its completeness within thirty working days. If the competent authority identifies deficiencies in the information provided, it sets an additional deadline for the applicant to integrate the authorization application or provide additional information. Following the receipt of a complete application, within ninety working days, the authority will assess the request in detail, deciding whether or not to authorize an operator to manage a DLT MTF. Once granted, the authorization will be valid throughout the European Union for a maximum period of 6 years.

Denial by the competent authority to grant authorization to an operator is determined for various reasons. Paragraph 10 of Article 8 of Regulation (EU) 2022/858 attributes the refusal of authorization to the case of significant risks for the protection of investors, for the integrity of the market or for financial stability; to the purpose, through the exemptions requested for the management of an MTF DLT, of circumventing the requirements established by current legislation; or finally, to the inability of the MTF DLT operator to allow its users to comply with the provisions of Union law or the national provisions specifically enacted on the subject.

Following the issuance, the authorization initially granted may be revoked at a later time, in its entirety or in relation to individual exemptions, upon the occurrence of certain circumstances, such as the emergence, in the operation of the distributed ledger technology, of a flaw that could represent a risk to the protection of investors, market integrity or financial stability and such flaw is not compensated by the benefits offered by the services or activities during the experimentation phase; the violation, by the manager of the MTF DLT, of the conditions on the basis of which the exemptions were granted; the admission to trading through the MTF DLT of financial instruments that do not meet the conditions laid down in Article 3(1) of Regulation (EU) 2022/858; the exceeding of the thresholds established for the application of the Pilot Regime and the concurrent failure to activate the transition strategy; or obtaining authorization to manage an MTF DLT based on misleading information or a substantial omission.

Finally, if an operator of an MTF DLT intends to make a substantial change to the operation of the DLT used or to the services or activities provided, such modification or the request for specific exemptions must be subject to further authorization following the authorization process previously described.

Overall, the Pilot Regime is undoubtedly an important initiative aimed at allowing market operators and regulators (European and national) to experiment with the potential of DLT technology in a "neutral marketplace" and at simultaneously measuring the risks associated with its use. From this perspective, the periodic semiannual communications and reports that infrastructure managers will have to submit to the competent national authorities, which in turn will transmit them to ESMA, will certainly be an essential tool for monitoring proposals for regulatory and technological interventions on market infrastructures.

At the top of the bottom-up information chain, ESMA will play a crucial role: in addition to being the collector of collected data, it must become a promoter of a supervisory culture, transferring the information acquired regarding the use of DLT to the various national authorities, promoting consistent methods and supervisory guidance. Ultimately, it will be ESMA's responsibility to verify the need for modifications to Union legislation on financial services (Annunziata & Minto, 2022, p. 6).

Alongside the push for regulatory innovation, two considerations regarding potential limiting factors must be made with regard to the Pilot Regime. The first reflection concerns the approach taken by the European regulator: namely, the Pilot Regime proposes a replication of traditional market structures on DLT technology without taking into account its specificities. Furthermore, the imposition of the same conditions applied to existing market operators could limit access to the market of DLT infrastructures by new operators and favor the limited number of subjects already operating in the sector. New market barriers could have a restrictive rather than expansive effect on competition and induce some European operators to establish their platforms outside the European Union's economic area.

The second consideration concerns the lack of provision in the Pilot Regime for an extension of operability for third countries, i.e., platforms established outside the European Union. This could limit the access of investors and companies from the European Union to liquidity offered by DLT trading platforms operating in countries outside the Union, such as Switzerland, the United Kingdom, or the United States.

7 Efficiency and Transparency in the Management of DLT-Based Market Infrastructures: New Challenges for European Financial System Stakeholders

As highlighted, the idea behind the Pilot Regime is to develop the potential of a secondary market capable of allowing investors to trade financial instruments on infrastructures based on DLT technology.

The use of DLT technology, by recording all operations in a decentralized ledger, allows for the acceleration and synthesis of trading and settlement almost in real-time, effectively zeroing the counterparty risk and thus allowing the merger of trading and post-trading activities (Consob, 2023, pp. 13–14).

The use of distributed ledgers can enable the achievement of a series of advantages: lower costs for the management of the phases of issuance, trading, and settlement of financial instruments, which can be simultaneously managed on the ledger, overcoming the need to resort to traditional intermediation chains; expansion of operations compared to traditional infrastructures; and reduction of national segmentations through access to platforms for a wider range of operators interested in trading (Cipollone, 2023, p. 4).

To capture these benefits, the regulation introduces a highly innovative element of discontinuity compared to the current situation: that is, the possibility that services related to the lifecycle of a financial asset are jointly provided by a single market infrastructure, the so-called DLT TSS; this DLT infrastructure can be accompanied by those that offer only trading services (DLT MTF) or only settlement services (DLT SS). This provision represents a significant innovation, as it collects and expresses one of the most distinctive features of DLT technologies: the ability to concentrate different phases of the operation of financial instruments on a single platform without the need—in order to manage the different responsibilities involved—to separate them into different technological, administrative, and regulatory environments; this is thanks to the intrinsic potential of distributed ledgers, which are able to structurally guarantee the certainty, accessibility, and immutability of the information and data related to the operations carried out by network participants.

In addition, with the aim of expanding the pool of potential trading participants, the Pilot Regime allows the possibility that a DLT multilateral trading system, if authorized by the competent authority, may also admit natural persons, in addition to legal persons, to trade on their own behalf (provided that they meet a series of requirements provided for by the regulation). This exemption surpasses the requirement provided by the MiFID II Directive, according to which traditional multilateral trading systems can only admit investment firms, credit institutions, and other entities that meet specific requirements (the so-called "intermediation obligation").

To fully exploit the potential of using DLT, the Pilot Regime also provides for further exemptions (such as in the field of settlement in central bank money, access and connections between market infrastructures, use of certain communication procedures with participants) aimed at allowing the management of all stages of the production chain of a financial transaction (initial registration of instruments, trading, and settlement) on a single register, with participants that may also include final investors.

This is clearly a radical change in the underlying infrastructure architecture of financial markets. Therefore, to control the undeniable risks associated with the new regime, the regulation also sets limits on experimentation, particularly in terms of the financial instruments allowed and the values that can be traded on DLT infrastructures (limits that do not exist for infrastructures operating with traditional technology). The so-called "exit strategy", that is, the risk management introduced by the Pilot, requires the DLT infrastructure to prepare a credible exit strategy in advance in case the pilot regime is suspended, the specific authorization is revoked, or the thresholds are exceeded. This strategy must contemplate the transition or conversion of DLT operations into traditional market infrastructures. This is a central element aimed at supporting the security of the treatment of securities in the experimental regime.

The regime is also subject to monitoring by national authorities, exercising supervisory powers over the infrastructures, as well as by ESMA, which, 3 years after the entry into force of the Pilot Regime, must submit a report to the European Commission on the progress of the experiment.

The European Commission, in turn, will submit a report to the Parliament and the Council and proposals on the opportunity to extend (for no more than three additional years), modify, interrupt, or make the Pilot permanent, introducing appropriate amendments to the existing legislation.

8 Conclusions

In the last decade, technological innovation has become increasingly important, leading to the development of a new technology capable of redesigning the exchange process in the economic and financial system, supported by a revolution both in terms of application and regulation.

In this context, the evolution of financial markets regarded MTFs and the overall regulatory path that has seen them as protagonists. Specifically, the analysis unfolded starting from the defining attempts carried out by the European legislator, through the MiFID Directive, aimed at outlining a precise discipline for a form of market that originally presented atypical elements compared to other trading venues.

MTFs, given their peculiar characteristics of greater flexibility in terms of organizational structure and functioning, have become a field of technological experimentation and have also aroused interest from operators who faced difficulties in accessing regulated markets, difficulties mainly related to dimensional and structural factors.

In addition to the systematic and definitional framing issue, MTFs have also raised interest in the technologies underlying their operation: in particular, ESMA and subsequently the European Commission, in the Fintech Action Plan, have engaged in an analysis of the potential of the specific DLT applied to the market infrastructure dedicated to financial services.

Faced with disruptive manifestations of technological evolution, regulators and supervisory authorities had to question the suitability of existing rules to regulate such new phenomena, trying to balance the opposite needs of protecting operators without hindering their competitiveness and innovation.

The European regulator, through the Pilot Regime, introduced by Regulation (EU) 2022/858, has preferred a methodological approach aimed at reclassifying innovative legal situations into existing and regulated categories while simultaneously opening the possibility for operators to verify—more accurately, test—whether the existing regulatory apparatus was suitable and compatible with these new technological phenomena. The experimentation model envisaged by the regulation is that of the regulatory sandbox, that is, a "protected space" in which products, services, or activities are tested under the control of the competent authorities and for a limited period, benefiting from any exemptions or special authorization regimes.

The new regulatory framework will promote the development of technologies based on distributed ledgers and, in particular, the issuance, trading, and settlement of crypto-securities, without disregarding the need to ensure investor protection, market transparency, and financial stability.

The European interest in testing, promoting, and regulating new trading venues emerges from recital no. 1 of the regulation, which states that "It is important to ensure that Union financial services legislation is fit for the digital age and contributes to a future- proof economy that works for citizens, including by enabling the use of innovative technologies. The Union has a policy interest in exploring, developing and promoting the uptake of transformative technologies in the financial sector, including the uptake of distributed ledger technology (DLT) [...]".

Indeed, the exploitation of new digital technologies based on distributed ledgers throughout the entire "life cycle" of security tokens—from issuance to trading and post-trading—seems, ultimately, destined to offer promising opportunities and efficiency gains for economic operators who will be able to take advantage of new fundraising platforms through DLT MTFs.

This chapter allows us to reflect on the evolution of financial markets thanks to the development of MTFs and the overall regulatory path that has seen them as protagonists, and it provides evidence of their role as places of exchange between economic operators for the fundraising of financial resources.

Our study intends to contribute to the scientific debate on the relevance of implications for policymakers, regulators, and other market participants in developing a better ecosystem related to the development and usage of MTFs.

References

Adamo, R., Federico, D., Intonti, M., & Notte, A. (2019). Blockchain: A new way to build trust in financial relations. *Global Journal for Research Analysis, 8*(3), 32–34.

Amato, G., & Benvenuto, R. (2022). Regolamento DLT: il regime pilota UE sulle nuove infrastrutture di mercato. *Diritto Bancario, 7*, 1–5.

Amorosino, S. (2008). *Manuale di diritto del mercato finanziario*. Giuffrè.

Annunziata, F. (2018). La disciplina delle trading venues nell'era delle rivoluzioni tecnologiche: dalle criptovalute alla distributed ledger technology. *Rivista Orizzonti del Diritto Commerciale, Associazione Italiana dei Professori Universitari di Diritto Commerciale, 3*, 1–29.

Annunziata, F., & Minto, A. (2022). Il nuovo Regolamento UE in materia di Distributed Ledger Technology. Analisi del nuovo DLT Pilot Regime. *Diritto Bancario, 7*, 1–6.

Bank of Italy. (2022, June). *Comunicazione della Banca d'Italia in materia di tecnologie decentralizzate nella finanza e cripto-attività.*

Banfi, A., Nadotti, L., Tagliavini, G., & Valletta, M. (2016). *Economia del mercato mobiliare*. Isedi.

Banfi, A., Biasin, M., Borroni, M., & Oriani, M. (2022). *Economia degli intermediari finanziari*. Isedi.

Barclay, M. J., Hendershott, T., & Mccormick, D. T. (2003). Competition among trading venues: Information and trading on electronic communications networks. *Journal of Finance, 58*(6), 2637–2665. https://doi.org/10.1046/j.1540-6261.2003.00618.x

Brealey, R., Myers, S., Allen, F., & Edmans, A. (2023). *Principles of corporate finance*. Mc Graw Hill.

Cipollone, P. (2023, April 4). Audizione sul disegno di legge n. *605 di conversione in legge del decreto-legge 17 marzo 2023, n. 25, recante disposizioni urgenti in materia di emissioni e circolazione di determinati strumenti finanziari in forma digitale e di semplificazione della sperimentazione FinTech*. Rome, Italy, Senato della Repubblica 6ª Commissione permanente (Finanze e Tesoro).

Consob. (2023, January 25). Tokenizzazione di azioni e azioni tokens. *Quaderno Giuridico*.

European Securities and Markets Authority. (2017, February 7). Report. *The distributed ledger technology applied to securities market*.

Fioravanti, S. F., & Gentile, M. (2011). L'impatto della frammentazione degli scambi azionari sui mercati regolamentati europei. *Quaderni di Finanza, 69*, 1–48.

Garavaglia, R. (2019). Finalità, funzionamento e tipologia di utilizzi delle Blockchain–Le nuove frontiere dei servizi bancari e di pagamento fra PSD 2, criptovalute e rivoluzione digitale. *Quaderni di Ricerca Giuridica, 87*, 1–349.

Giannelli, A., & Sfameni, P. (2020). *Diritto degli intermediari e dei mercati finanziari*. Egea.

Jain, P. K., Mekhaimer, M., & Mortal, S. (2020). Commonality in liquidity and multilateral trading facilities. *Financial Review, 55*(3), 481–502. https://doi.org/10.1111/fire.12225

Locatelli, R., & Schena, C. (2022). Il nuovo ecosistema finanziario per le PMI. In *Le opportunità della digitalizzazione e dello sviluppo sostenibile*. Franco Angeli.

Maimeri, F., & Mancini, M. (2019). Le nuove frontiere dei servizi bancari e di pagamento fra PSD 2, criptovalute e rivoluzione digitale. *Quaderni di Ricerca Giuridica della Consulenza Legale, 9*, 1–349.

Mattassoglio, F. (2021). Le proposte europee in tema di crypto-assets e DLT. Prime prove di regolazione del mondo crypto o tentativo di tokenizzazione del mercato finanziario (ignorando bitcoin)? *Rivista di Diritto Bancario, 2*, 413–455.

Nadotti, L., Porzio, C., & Previati, D. (2010). *Economia degli intermediari finanziari*. McGraw-Hill.

Orlando, S., & Capaldo, G. (Eds.) (2021). *Osservatorio Giuridico sulla Innovazione Digitale*. Sapienza Università Publisher.

Perrazzelli, A. (2021, May 4). *Le iniziative regolamentari per il Fintech: a che punto siamo?* Speech to the Digital Finance Lab, Varese, Università degli Studi dell'Insubria.

Saunders, A., Millon Cornett, M., Anolli, M., & Alemanni, B. (2010). *Economia degli intermediari finanziari*. McGraw-Hill Education.

Vasapollo, M., & Comellini, S. (2019). *Blockchain, criptovalute, I.C.O. e smart contract*. Maggioli Publisher.

Vegas, G. (2011, March 23). Indagine conoscitiva sul mercato degli strumenti finanziari. *Audizione alla Camera dei Deputati del Presidente della Consob*.

Williams, L. V. (Ed.) (2005). *Information efficiency in financial and betting markets*. Cambridge University Press.

Normative References

European Commission. (2018, March 8). *Communication from the commission–action plan: Financing sustainable*. COM(2018) 97 final, Brussels.

European Commission. (2020, September 24). *Communication from the commission to the European Parliament, the Council, the European Economic and Social Committee and the Committee of the Regions on a Digital Finance Strategy for the EU*. COM(2020) 591 final, Brussels.

European Parliament. (2004). *Directive 2004/39/EC of the European Parliament and of the Council of 21 April 2004 on markets in financial instruments amending Council Directives 85/611/EEC and 93/6/EEC and Directive 2000/12/EC of the European Parliament and of the Council and repealing Council Directive 93/22/EEC*. Official Journal of the European Union, L 145/1.

European Parliament. (2014). *Directive 2014/65/EU of the European Parliament and of the Council of 15 May 2014 on markets in financial instruments and amending Directive 2002/92/EC and Directive 2011/61/EU*. Official Journal of the European Union, L 173/349.

European Parliament. (2018). *European Parliament resolution of 3 October 2018 on distributed ledger technologies and blockchains: building trust with disintermediation (2017/2772(RSP))*. P8_TA(2018)0373.

European Union. (1993). *Council directive 93/22/EEC of 10 may 1993 on investment services in the securities field*, Official Journal of the European Communities, Vol. 36, L. 141.

European Union. (2014, June 12). Regulation (EU) no 600/2014 of the European Parliament and of the council of 15 may 2014 on markets in financial instruments and amending regulation (EU) no 648/2012. *Official Journal of the European Union.*

European Union. (2022, June 2). *Regulation (EU) 2022/858 of the European Parliament and of the Council of 30 May 2022 on a pilot regime for market infrastructures based on distributed ledger technology, and amending Regulations (EU) No 600/2014 and (EU) No 909/2014 and Directive 2014/65/EU.* Official Journal of the European Union.

Elisa Facciotti is Doctor in Law and subject expert in Economics of Financial Intermediaries at eCampus University (Italy). She has gained several years of experience in corporate governance of Italian listed companies, holding the position of Head of Legal and Corporate Affairs, Investor Relations Manager, and member of boards of directors.

Domenica Federico is Associate Professor of Economics of Financial Intermediaries at eCampus University (Italy) where she teaches Economics of Financial Intermediaries and Economics of Insurance and Social Security Companies. She carries out research in subjects and techniques of financial intermediation, ethical finance, and sustainable finance.

Antonella Notte is Associate Professor of Corporate Finance at the eCampus University (Italy) where she teaches Corporate Finance, Financial Risk Management, and Portfolio Management, Pension Funds, Supplementary Welfare. She carries out research in corporate finance, corporate social responsibility, and techno-finance.

DeFi Cybersecurity Technical and Nontechnical Risks

Khoula Al Harthy and Aparna Agarwal

1 Introduction

A decentralized financial application (DeFi) is a decentralized financial application built on blockchain technology's public ledger. This technology allows users to gain access to permission-less financial services without the need for a third party. DeFi is an open system for finance based on blockchain smart contracts. DeFi can be recombined into larger services, and each DeFi service locks assets as deposits and offers a different asset as liquidity by simplifying and swapping tokens to other tokens and deposited assets to benefactors. Benefactors use the tokens given for other concatenated DeFi services, such as lending, decentralized exchanges (DEXs), and derivatives. The DeFi environment utilizes Ethereum Request of Comment (ERC-20) tokens that denote the value of an asset. ERC-20 is used for fungible tokens that can be exchanged with other tokens, and it is created in the Ethereum blockchain.

The DeFi platform centralizes the user's account information, payment credentials, and other sensitive data such as passwords. This environment is prone to cyber threats. The security issues that are increasing are fraud prevention and data privacy. As a result, organizations use encryption to protect DeFi data. This technology is susceptible to the same risks and problems as other financial goods and services, including liquidity risks, volatility risks, and market hazards.

K. Al Harthy (✉)
Middle East College, Seeb, Oman

Computer Science and Creative Technologies Department, Global College of Engineering and Technologies, CPO Ruwi, Oman
e-mail: aparna@mec.edu.com

A. Agarwal
Middle East College, Seeb, Oman
e-mail: aparna@mec.edu.com

S. Basly (ed.), *Decentralized Finance*, Financial Innovation and Technology,
https://doi.org/10.1007/978-3-031-49515-1_8

The authors want to explore DeFi issues, namely, cybersecurity risks and problems, in this book chapter. This will include the DeFi adoption concerns and risk management plan.

The rising popularity of DeFi technology has attracted attention to a number of hazards as a result of global regulatory gaps. As a result, users must either accept the dangers and mitigate the repercussions or wait until rules in their respective nations are issued. One of the dangers in a DeFi system is managing and monitoring transactions with authorization. DeFi audits should also be implemented to ensure proper transaction management and authorization. Smart contract errors involve hazards and high vulnerabilities, which may be discovered through code errors, bugs, and backdoor attacks.

Hence, this chapter will contain different sections, such as DeFi adoption challenges, risks, and risk management recommendations.

2 DeFi Risks and Vulnerabilities

The article titled "Security Analysis of DeFi: Vulnerabilities, Attacks and Advances" by Li et al. (2022) provides a complete examination of the security risks and vulnerabilities that are inherent in decentralized finance (DeFi) system environments (Fig. 1). The authors address the distinctive difficulties that decentralized finance (DeFi) brings in comparison to conventional forms of finance, including the absence of centralized control and regulatory monitoring. The use of uncontrolled external calls in DeFi smart contracts, which might result in unexpected behavior and possibly catastrophic effects, was noted as one of the primary dangers in the study. Li et al. (2022) cite instances of attacks that exploit this weakness, such as the notorious DAO assault, which resulted in the theft of Ethereum worth a total of 50 million dollars in 2016. This article also examines other threats to data security posed by DeFi, including front-running attacks, flash loan assaults, and oracle manipulation. The authors present an overview of the advancements that have been achieved in DeFi security, including the development of tools for formal verification and the usage of models for decentralized governance.

The following part of the section discusses the technical risks of the DeFi environment.

Categories	Causes	Categories	Causes
Unchecked External Calls	Without checking return values	Reentry	Repeated calls before completed
Transaction State Dependency	Failure to check permissions	Nested Call	Unrestricted call depth
DoS Under External Influence	External exceptions inside loops	Missing Return	Denote return but no value
Unmatched ERC-20 Standard	Not follow the standard	Greedy Contracts	Receive but not withdraw Ethers
Strict Balance Equality	Balance check failed	Block Info Dependency	Status leakage
Misleading Data Location	Incorrect storage type	Missing Interrupter	No backdoor to handle crises
Transaction State Dependency	Error using tx .origin	Arithmetic Operations	Unmatched type to values

Fig. 1 Smart contract vulnerabilities in DeFi (Li et al., 2022)

2.1 Smart Contract Risks and Vulnerabilities

Mohanta et al. (2018) design the smart contract as a programming code that includes a set of roles and functions that represent an agreement between various nodes on the chain that specifies the terms and conditions of the relationship between them. This contract is code-based software that was developed as the foundation of chain transactions since it is at the center of many different DeFi protocols. It offers automated and decentralized financial services such as lending, borrowing, and trading. The smart contracts that are used in DeFi systems serve as third-party agreements. The most difficult aspect of maintaining smart contracts is ensuring compliance with all applicable legislation, agreements, and audits (Vasudevan, 2022). Exploitation of the blockchain's smart contacts is possible, and malicious actors might take advantage of these flaws to steal money or influence the market.

The following is a list of some of these dangers and hazards (Fig. 2):

3 Reentrancy Attacks

The attacker takes advantage of the fact that there is more than one way to access the contract and generates logs (Fig. 3). Attackers may utilize several access points to extract money that they do not own, which would result in large monetary losses for them. This is one of the weaknesses that smart contracts have, and it allows an attacker to take advantage of the multiaccess gap to exert excessive influence over transactions. Attackers are also able to benefit from the interplay of smart contracts with other external contracts developed by third-party programmers and integrated into the DeFi platform to enhance the services, functionality, or security of the DeFi ecosystem. These external contracts work to carry out a variety of various actions,

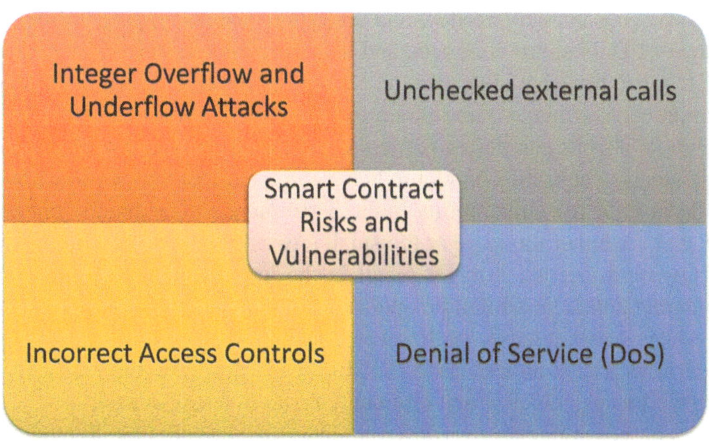

Fig. 2 Smart contract risks

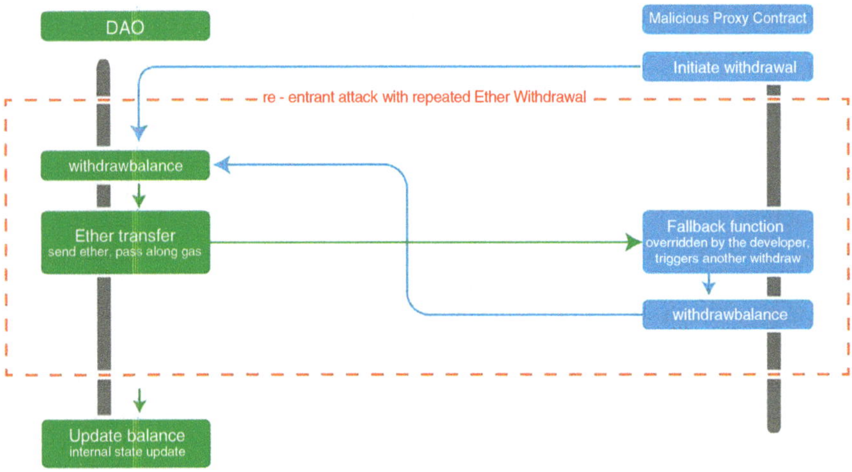

Fig. 3 Reentrancy Attacks (redfoxsec.com, 2022)

such as taking out loans and attacking wallets. According to the research conducted by Xu and Feng (2022), "In April 2021, the ForceDAO DeFi aggregator was exploited by a group of attackers who utilized reentrancy attacks to steal 367 thousand USD worth of tokens before the ForceDAO team took effective actions to prevent further attacks." In addition, "in September 2021, DAO Maker, a decentralized finance platform on Ethereum, had almost 4 million USD stolen from it due to insecure smart contracts".

4 Integer Overflow and Underflow Attacks

Attacks involving integer overflow and underflow are also capable of occurring in the context of DeFi smart contracts, and they may lead to the loss of cash or other sorts of security breaches. Because the entirety of the DeFi ecosystem depends on smart contracts to manage transactions and carry out complex financial operations, these kinds of attacks can pose a particularly difficult challenge in this space.

These attacks cause the contract to behave in a manner that was not anticipated. This is because of the vulnerability in the performance of arithmetic operations on integers that are either too large or too small (Ayoade et al., 2019). In the event that Integer Overflow occurs, it might result in the loss of tokens or money. When a smart contract conducts arithmetic operations on integers that are excessively large or excessively small, it leaves itself vulnerable to attacks known as integer overflow and underflow. These attacks have the ability to cause the contract to behave in unanticipated ways, which might ultimately result in a loss of cash.

Attacks based on integer overflow and underflow are possible in many different contexts inside DeFi, including the following:

A. Token Transfers: To carry out monetary transactions, decentralized finance systems depend on token transfers. Token transfers may sometimes include large integers, which can result in integer overflow or underflow vulnerabilities depending on the circumstances. For instance, if a smart contract is configured to handle token transfers that are of a value that is either more than or lower than its maximum or minimum value, this might result in unexpected behavior and could possibly enable an attacker to steal cash.
B. Automated market makers, often known as AMMs, are a popular feature in DeFi that gives users the ability to exchange tokens in an automated manner. However, these systems are susceptible to attacks that involve an integer overflow or an underflow of data. For instance, if the price algorithm of the AMM is not appropriately constructed to handle large numbers, this might lead to erroneous pricing, which in turn could possibly enable an adversary to influence the market.
C. Staking and yield farming are two popular activities in DeFi that entail locking up tokens in smart contracts to earn incentives. Staking and yield farming are two popular activities in DeFi that entail locking up tokens in smart contracts to earn incentives. However, these systems are vulnerable to attacks that involve either integer overflow or data underflow. Both of these types of attacks are possible. For instance, if the contract for staking or yield farming is not adequately built to handle enormous numbers, this might result in unexpected behavior, which could allow an attacker to take money from the system.

To defend DeFi from integer overflow and underflow attacks, developers are obligated to take the necessary measures to ensure that their smart contracts are appropriately constructed and thoroughly tested for vulnerabilities before being deployed. To prevent overflow and underflow problems, this requires the implementation of bounds checking and signed integer arithmetic. Additionally, this requires the implementation of input validation, the use of safe mathematical libraries, and the development of mathematical libraries.

5 Unchecked External Calls

When a smart contract interacts with other contracts or protocols without first checking their safety and reliability, this creates a sort of DeFi risk known as unchecked external calls. These may result in a loss of data. To accomplish a variety of goals, such as obtaining data or functionality from other contracts or connecting with other DeFi protocols, DeFi protocols make use of external calls. External calls may also be initiated by users. Unchecked calls to the outside world expose a company to a number of potential dangers, including

1. Malicious actors: External contracts or protocols may be controlled by malicious actors, and these actors can exploit any flaws they find to steal cash or jeopardize the security of the smart contract.

2. Vulnerabilities in smart contracts: External contracts or protocols may have defects or vulnerabilities, which may lead to a loss of cash or a breach in the security of the smart contract.
3. Reentrancy attacks: An attacker may be able to repeatedly contact a susceptible smart contract and drain its money if the contract is exposed to external calls. The DAO was hacked in 2016, resulting in the loss of ether worth a total of 50 million dollars, and the assault was caused by reentrancy attacks.

DeFi protocols should employ security features such as the following to limit the hazards posed by uncontrolled calls to external parties:

1. Code Audits: Audits of the source code smart contracts should be subjected to exhaustive source code audits to identify and remove vulnerabilities that might be exploited by hostile actors.
2. Whitelisting: Only trustworthy third-party contracts or protocols should be permitted to communicate with the smart contract; all other third-party contracts and protocols should be barred.
3. Gas restrictions: Smart contracts should impose gas limits on external calls to restrict the total amount of money that may be moved around.
4. Emergency stop: The DeFi protocols have to provide a mechanism for an emergency stop that may be utilized to freeze the smart contract in the event that there is a breach in the system's security.

6 Incorrect Access Controls

Incorrect access controls are a sort of DeFi risks that occur when a smart contract or platform does not correctly handle user access rights. This opens the door for users or third-party apps to do activities that are either not permitted or were not meant to be carried out by the smart contract or platform.

Access control is the process of developing and implementing rules that regulate how users may interact with a system or application. These rules might restrict what users can do or prevent them from doing. Access restrictions are necessary in DeFi to guarantee that users may only access the features and information for which they have been granted permission. The improper implementation of access restrictions may result in a number of dangers, including the following:

1. Unauthorized access: It is possible for hackers or attackers to obtain access to the system or data that they are not permitted to access, which may result in the theft of sensitive information or the loss of financial resources.
2. Abuse of privileges: Authorized users may abuse their rights by accessing or modifying data or by performing operations that were not intended for them.
3. Exploits of smart contracts: Attackers may attack weaknesses in the code of smart contracts to circumvent access constraints and obtain unauthorized access to money or data by using smart contract exploits.

DeFi protocols need to adopt security measures such as the following to reduce the dangers associated with erroneous access controls:

1. Role-based access control: Controls for access should be based on user roles. They specify the degree of access and permissions that are provided to each user. This is the first kind of access control that should be implemented.
2. Multisig wallets: These reduce the danger of illegal transactions by requiring several signatures or approvals before conducting transactions.
3. Time-locks: These provide the ability to postpone transactions, giving users more time to identify and revoke any unintentional or unlawful transactions.
4. Code Audits: Frequent code audit smart contracts should have their source code audited on a frequent basis to find and fix any flaws in the access controls.

7 Denial of Service (DoS)

A DoS is a danger that may be posed to a DeFi platform if an attacker sends an excessive number of transactions or requests to it. This can cause the platform's resources to be exhausted, which can result in the platform crashing or becoming unusable.

Malicious actors may perform denial-of-service attacks with the intention of interrupting or destroying a DeFi platform to cause monetary losses or reputational harm. DoS attacks may also be carried out unintentionally and occur as a consequence of flaws or vulnerabilities in the coding of the smart contract.

Denial of service attacks should be avoided as much as possible by implementing security measures on DeFi systems such as:

1. Load balancing: To prevent any one server or resource from being overloaded, DeFi systems should make use of load balancing methods to disperse the traffic that they receive.
2. Rate restriction: DeFi systems should have rate limiting to restrict the number of requests or transactions that may be handled within a specified time period. This helps to prevent the system from being overloaded with too many incoming requests or transactions.
3. Monitoring of the network: DeFi systems should monitor their network traffic and performance to identify and mitigate any abnormal spikes or patterns of activity that might suggest a denial-of-service attack.
4. Code audits: Defi systems must be subjected to frequent code audits to find and eliminate vulnerabilities that may be exploited in denial-of-service attacks.
5. Disaster recovery strategy: DeFi platforms need to have a disaster recovery plan in place so that they can swiftly restore services in the event that they are disrupted by a DoS attack or another kind of disruption.

Overall, distributed denial of service attacks pose a substantial danger to DeFi systems; thus, DeFi protocols need to adopt stringent security measures to thwart these attacks and reduce the damage they cause.

Implementing a number of security precautions is necessary for DeFi to protect itself against DoS (Denial of Service) attacks. This will prevent attackers from overloading the platform's resources and causing disruptions to its services. Common countermeasures against denial-of-service attacks in DeFi include the following:

1. Load balancing: DeFi systems should employ methods for load balancing to disperse traffic over numerous servers, thereby preventing any one server from being overloaded with traffic.
2. Rate limitation: DeFi systems need to include rate limiting so that they may restrict the number of requests or transactions that can be handled in a certain amount of time. This is done so that the platform can better manage its resources. Because of this, it will be far more difficult for attackers to overwhelm the platform with a large number of requests or transactions.
3. Network monitoring: Network DeFi systems should monitor their network traffic and performance to identify and mitigate any abnormal spikes or patterns of activity that might suggest a denial-of-service attack. Monitoring the network may also assist in locating the origin of an attack and preventing more damage from occurring.
4. Cloud-based DDoS protection: Protection against distributed denial of service attacks using cloud DeFi systems has the ability to leverage cloud-based DDoS (Distributed Denial of Service) protection services. These services are able to identify and stop DDoS assaults at the edge of the network, preventing attacks from accessing the platform's resources.
5. Implementing Captcha: Putting in place a captcha may assist in preventing automated assaults and limiting the pace at which requests are made to the platform.
6. Code audits: Defi systems must be subjected to frequent code audits so that vulnerabilities that might be exploited in denial-of-service attacks can be found and fixed.
7. Disaster Recovery Plan: Have a disaster recovery strategy in place: DeFi platforms need to have a disaster recovery plan in place so that they can swiftly restore services in the event that they are disrupted by a DoS attack or another kind of disruption.

Overall, avoiding and mitigating DoS attacks in DeFi calls for a multilayered strategy that combines frequent code audits and disaster recovery plans with technological safeguards such as load balancing, rate limiting, and network monitoring.

7.1 Oracles

Oracles are essential to the operation of DeFi systems because they provide off-chain data to smart contracts. In the event that the oracle is hacked, it may provide erroneous data to the smart contract, which may result in financial losses or other complications.

Oracles, on the other hand, present a potentially serious threat to the integrity of DeFi networks both individually and collectively.

Oracles are susceptible to manipulation in a number of different ways. For instance, an adversary could be able to compromise the data source on which the oracle relies, or they might be able to influence the oracle itself by hacking it or using social engineering to trick it into doing what they want. Both of these scenarios are possible.

The developers of DeFi are investigating a variety of potential methods to enhance the safety and dependability of oracles to reduce the impact of these hazards. Utilizing a number of oracles from a variety of sources is one method that may be used to achieve redundancy and verify that the data are correct. The use of decentralized oracles, which relies on a network of independent nodes to give data to the smart contract, is an additional strategy that may be implemented. Because a greater number of nodes need to be compromised to influence the data that are being delivered, decentralized oracles may be more resistant to attacks and manipulation than centralized oracles.

Oracles, although an essential part of DeFi systems as a whole, can pose substantial risks that need to be properly controlled and mitigated to guarantee the dependability and security of the system. Top of Form.

7.2 Decentralized Consensus

To confirm transactions and maintain the integrity of the blockchain, DeFi systems depend on decentralized consensus techniques such as Proof of Work and Proof of Stake. These processes are described in more detail below. In the event that these processes are broken, problems such as double spending or 51% attacks may result.

Because they offer a means to verify transactions and preserve the integrity of the blockchain, decentralized consensus mechanisms are a crucial component of blockchain-based decentralized finance (DeFi) systems. However, there are a number of dangers connected with decentralized consensus processes, and these dangers may have an effect on the safety and dependability of DeFi systems.

The possibility of forking is one of the dangers that comes along with using decentralized consensus techniques. A fork occurs when a piece of the network breaks off to establish a new blockchain, generally as a result of disputes about how the network should be managed or other technical concerns. If users are not cautious about following the right chain, forks may result in confusion, ambiguity, and even the possible loss of cash.

Transaction congestion and network latency are two examples of problems that may affect decentralized consensus systems. Both of these problems can slow down the processing of transactions, which in turn can have an effect on the dependability and performance of the system.

The developers of DeFi are investigating a variety of potential solutions, including sharing, sidechains, and layer-2 solutions, with the goal of enhancing the scalability and safety of decentralized consensus methods. This will help to alleviate the dangers that are now present. In addition, governance models are also being created to handle difficulties associated with network governance, such as the upgrading of protocols and the settlement of disputes.

7.3 Governance

Decentralized finance (DeFi) systems often depend on decentralized governance models, which may make these systems susceptible to risks and challenges that threaten the system's security and stability. The following is a list of some of the most significant dangers:

1. Collusion: Governance structures in DeFi systems often depend on voting by token holders to make decisions. This opens the door to the possibility of illegal collusion. It is possible for a small number of token holders to manipulate the system to their own advantage if they agree among themselves to control the result of the vote and conspire to do so. This work works by influencing the token holders to give their votes and control the outcome. The major issue in collusion is determining the integrity of the DeFi system, which leads to unfair decision-making.
2. Voter apathy: Even in circumstances in which voting is open and transparent, low voter participation might make it simpler for a small number of players to influence the result of the vote. It is possible for this to result in decisions that do not reflect the interests of the community as a whole.
3. Lack of accountability: It can be difficult to identify and punish bad actors who manipulate the system or participate in other types of misbehavior. This lack of accountability can be attributed to the fact that it can be difficult to identify bad actors who manipulate the system.
4. Complexity: Governance in DeFi systems may also be complicated, with several levels of decision-making and governance processes that can be difficult for users to comprehend and interact with. This can make it more difficult for users to participate in governance. The developers of DeFi are investigating a variety of potential solutions, including quadratic voting, reputation systems, and other types of governance that encourage participation while discouraging collusion, to reduce the potential impact of these dangers. In addition, the use of transpar-

ency and accountability measures, such as audits and disclosure requirements, may be an effective way to guarantee that choices on governance are made in an open and equitable manner.

5. Interoperability: Cross-chain interoperability protocols are the primary means through which DeFi systems communicate with one another. In the event that these protocols are not adequately protected, they may result in problems such as the theft of assets or other kinds of attacks.

7.4 Flash-Loan Attacks

Flash loans are an intriguing and potent feature of DeFi that enables users to borrow cash without providing security. This may be useful for users who want to execute intricate trading strategies or take advantage of arbitrage possibilities. However, flash loans are also becoming a favorite target for attackers who seek to manipulate the market or steal funds. These types of people are looking for a quick and easy way to get their hands on money. This danger is especially high because flash loans are almost immediately put into action, and the impact that they have on the market may be both large and rapid (Qin et al., 2020). This is the most prevalent kind of attack. This kind of assault has the potential to do enormous harm to the DeFi ecosystem, which might result in enormous financial losses for users, investors, and liquidity providers.

The creators of DeFi must apply the best practices for smart contract design to reduce the possibility of flash loan assaults. These best practices include input validation, multiple data sources for price feeds, and circuit breakers to avoid widespread harm. In addition, developers should perform routine security audits and put in place mechanisms that can identify flash loan attacks and mitigate their effects. They should only utilize platforms that have a good reputation and stay away from unfamiliar coins. They should also exercise caution when engaging with complicated DeFi protocols, guarantee the safety of their private keys, and use two-factor authentication to stop unauthorized users from accessing their wallets.

8 DeFi Nontechnical Risk

In addition to technical risks, decentralized finance (DeFi) systems must contend with a wide variety of nontechnical dangers that threaten both their safety and their long-term viability. These dangers include the following (Fig. 4):

1. Regulatory risk: Because DeFi systems are still mostly unregulated, they run the possibility of being subject to regulatory action or legal challenges, both of which have the potential to affect their capacity to function and their long-term survival.

Fig. 4 Nontechnical risk in DeFi

2. Market risk: DeFi systems are also susceptible to the risks of the market, which arises from the fact that changes in the price of cryptocurrencies may have an effect on the value of assets stored inside the system as well as the general health of the ecosystem.
3. Liquidity risk: To function properly, DeFi systems need a significant amount of liquid assets. If there is not enough liquidity in the system, it might become unstable or perhaps completely collapse.
4. Reputation risk: As DeFi systems are predicated on users' confidence in one another, any acts or situations that work to erode that trust have the potential to damage the system's reputation and credibility.
5. Operational risk: DeFi systems are also susceptible to operational risks, which includes problems such as software defects, human mistakes, and breakdowns in the system itself.

The creators of DeFi are investigating a variety of potential solutions, including insurance products, legal compliance procedures, and reputation management tactics, to reduce the impact of these risks that are not technological in nature. In addition, implementing rules for openness and disclosure may assist in guaranteeing that users have access to correct information on the system and the risks associated with it.

In general, whereas DeFi systems provide a wide variety of advantages, they are also exposed to a variety of nontechnical hazards, all of which need to be meticulously controlled and mitigated to guarantee their continued sustainability and success in the long run.

8.1 Regulatory Risk

It is a big issue that does not involve technology and affects decentralized finance (DeFi) systems. Because DeFi systems are currently, for the most part, unregulated, they might be vulnerable to regulatory action or legal challenges that could have an effect on their capacity to operate and their long-term survival.

The possibility of regulatory action being taken against cryptocurrencies and other blockchain-based systems is one of the most significant regulatory concerns to which decentralized finance platforms are exposed. There is a large amount of ambiguity around the manner in which these new technologies will be dealt with as regulators all over the globe struggle to determine how to govern them. There is a possibility that regulators would attempt to place limitations or requirements on DeFi networks. These restrictions or requirements might impede the usefulness of the systems.

The challenges may also be based on allegations of fraudulent behavior, unlawful activities, or other concerns, and they may result in considerable legal and financial expenses for the operators of the DeFi system.

The creators of DeFi are investigating a variety of potential remedies, including legal compliance procedures, lobbying activities, and requirements for openness and disclosure, to lessen the impact of these regulatory issues. DeFi systems' creators are also looking at methods to collaborate with authorities and bring themselves into compliance with the rules that are already in place. This is done with the goal of reducing the likelihood that regulators may take action on.

8.2 Market Risk

It is a big issue that does not involve technology and affects decentralized finance (DeFi) systems. Because they are dependent on cryptocurrencies, which are notorious for their unpredictability, DeFi systems are vulnerable to market risks.

The value of assets that are kept inside DeFi systems is subject to quick fluctuations, which may have an effect on the ecosystem's overall health and sustainability. For example, if the value of the assets that are being held inside a DeFi system declines dramatically, this may result in diminished liquidity, decreased participation, and perhaps even the breakdown of the system.

Black swan occurrences, also known as unanticipated market shocks, are another kind of market risk to which DeFi infrastructure systems are susceptible. These occurrences are notoriously difficult to forecast and have the potential to have a substantial influence on the value of cryptocurrencies as a whole, which, in turn, may have an effect on the value of assets stored in DeFi systems.

The creators of DeFi are investigating a variety of potential solutions, including the diversification of assets, the implementation of hedging measures, the use of stablecoins, and the usage of other assets that are less susceptible to price fluctuations. Many decentralized finance systems are investigating methods to reward participant engagement in the ecosystem, with the goals of improving liquidity and maintaining stability.

8.3 *Liquidity Risk*

Decentralized finance (DeFi) systems are exposed to a considerable amount of non-technical risk, which is known as liquidity risk. Because users need to be able to purchase, sell, and exchange assets inside the system for it to function properly, decentralized financial infrastructures (DeFi) need a high degree of liquidity.

If there is not enough liquidity in the system, it might become unstable or perhaps completely collapse. This may be the result of a number of different causes, such as swings in the market, abrupt shifts in the behavior of users, or problems caused by the system's internal technology.

Developers of decentralized exchanges utilize encouraging involvement in the ecosystem as one of the primary techniques to reduce the impact of liquidity risk. This may be accomplished by the implementation of a variety of incentives, such as yield farming or liquidity mining, which provide benefits to users in exchange for the liquidity that they contribute to the system.

Utilizing decentralized exchange protocols is another method that may be used to decrease liquidity risk. These protocols make it possible for users to trade assets directly with one another without having to depend on centralized middlemen. Because decentralized exchanges depend on a network of users rather than a single body to supply liquidity, they are potentially more resistant to shocks involving the availability of liquidity.

Finally, to foster higher interoperability and resilience in the face of liquidity shocks, several DeFi systems are investigating methods to bridge liquidity across various chains or protocols. This is done in an effort to combat liquidity shocks.

There are many different approaches that may be taken to reduce the risk of liquidity, although this is a substantial obstacle for decentralized finance systems as a whole. It is probable that as the DeFi ecosystem continues to develop and mature, we will see new methods to control liquidity risk that may support stability and sustainability within the ecosystem. These new techniques are expected to emerge in the next months and years.

8.4 *Operational Risk*

Decentralized finance (DeFi) systems are exposed to a substantial operational risk that is not technological in nature. The operational security of DeFi systems may be compromised by a variety of threats, including faulty code, operator mistakes, and hardware malfunctions.

One of the most important tactics that developers of DeFi utilize to reduce the operational risk of their products is to subject their systems to exhaustive testing and auditing. This might comprise a variety of testing approaches, including unit testing, integration testing, and penetration testing, with the goal of identifying and resolving possible flaws before they become operational problems.

Implementing stringent security measures, such as multifactor authentication, encryption, and access restrictions, is another tactic that may be used to reduce operational risk. These precautions may be of assistance in preventing unwanted access to the system and lowering the likelihood of data breaches or other security problems.

In addition, several DeFi systems are investigating the possibility of decentralizing their infrastructure to lessen their dependency on centralized bodies. Because it does not rely on a single point of failure but rather on a network of autonomous nodes, decentralized infrastructure may be more resistant to the operational hazards that may be encountered.

Finally, several DeFi systems are investigating different methods to put disaster recovery and business continuity plans into action. This is being done to guarantee that the systems can continue to function normally in the face of unforeseen occurrences or accidents.

In general, while operational risk is a substantial obstacle for DeFi systems as a whole, there are a variety of solutions that may be used to manage this risk. It is possible that we will see new methods to control operational risk in the DeFi ecosystem as it continues to develop and mature. These new techniques have the potential to support stability and sustainability within the ecosystem.

9 Impact on Entrepreneurship

With the increased adoption of financial technologies (FinTech) in markets and increased innovation opportunities for entrepreneurs, it also comes with technical and nontechnical risks that may impact business continuities and secure the resources of the proposed system, which are people, data, processes, and technologies.

The owners of small and medium organizations should take care of the following points while planning or adopting DeFi systems:

First, to avoid high money loss risk in systems developments through integrating the blockchain in current running platforms and systems. Or they can join ready platforms such as Biance, Ethereum, Solana, Corda, and other platforms. This will save time and effort and ensure the professional support of blockchain experts. Moreover, the entrepreneur seeking to avoid the complexities of developing and maintaining a blockchain-based system with decentralized consensus has several alternative approaches to consider.

Moreover, entrepreneurs may explore layer 2 solutions, which involve off-chain mechanisms such as payment channels and sidechains, to achieve scalability and faster transaction times while still relying on the underlying blockchain consensus. Alternatively, some entrepreneurs may choose to forgo full decentralization and consider permissioned blockchains, where a limited number of known participants control the consensus, making them easier to manage and scale. Another approach is to adopt a hybrid model, wherein centralized systems are combined with decentralized components, striking a balance between ease of use and the benefits of decentralization.

However, entrepreneurs can participate as validators or delegate voting power in blockchains that utilize a delegated consensus model. Despite these alternatives, entrepreneurs must carefully assess their specific use cases and goals to make informed decisions about the level of decentralization that best suits their projects (Popescu, 2020).

10 Conclusion

The authors have explored the DeFi issues, namely, cybersecurity risks and problems, in this book chapter. It provides a complete examination of the security risks and vulnerabilities that are inherent in the decentralized finance (DeFi) system environment. It also examines other threats to data security posed by DeFi, including front-running attacks, flash loan assaults, and oracle manipulation. The smart contracts that are used in DeFi systems serve as third-party agreements. Exploitation of the blockchain's smart contacts is possible, and malicious actors might take advantage of these flaws to steal money or influence the market. DeFi protocols need to adopt security measures to reduce the dangers associated with erroneous access controls. To enhance attack detection, especially against denial-of-service attacks, network traffic and performance should be monitored in DeFi systems to identify and mitigate any abnormal spikes or patterns of activity. Moreover, this chapter discussed the nontechnical risks faced by DeFi environments. The importance of having both technical and nontechnical risks is giving the reader an overview of DeFi cybersecurity governance and enhancing DeFi management, processes, and operations. Additionally, obtaining knowledge of these risks can enhance the DeFi audit process.

References

Ayoade, G., Bauman, E., Khan, L., & Hamlen, K. (2019, July). Smart contract defense through bytecode rewriting. In *2019 IEEE International Conference on Blockchain (Blockchain)* (pp. 384–389). IEEE.

Li, W., Bu, J., Li, X., & Chen, X. (2022, August). Security analysis of DeFi: Vulnerabilities, attacks and advances. In *2022 IEEE International Conference on Blockchain (Blockchain)* (pp. 488–493). IEEE.

Mohanta, B. K., Panda, S. S., & Jena, D. (2018, July). An overview of smart contract and use cases in blockchain technology. In *2018 9th international conference on computing, communication and networking technologies (ICCCNT)* (pp. 1–4). IEEE.

Popescu, A. D. (2020). Decentralized finance (defi)–the lego of finance. *Social Sciences and Education Research Review, 7*(1), 321–349.

Qin, K., Zhou, L., Livshits, B., & Gervais, A. (2020). Attacking the DeFi Ecosystem with Flash Loans for Fun and Profit", *arXiv e-prints*, 2020. https://doi.org/10.48550/arXiv.2003.03810.

Vasudevan, S. (2022). DeFi: A risky business or silver bullet for SMEs? In *2022 International Conference on Cyber Resilience (ICCR)* (pp. 1–5). IEEE.

Xu, J. and Feng, Y., (2022). *Reap the harvest on Blockchain: A survey of yield farming protocols.* IEEE Transactions on Network and Service Management.

Khoula Al Harthy has Ph.D. in Risk Management from Coventry University, UK. She is currently working in different sets of research related to blockchain applications and security. She is interested in BYOD environment and its challenges. She has worked for 14 years in the academic sector specially in teaching. She has more than 10 papers impacted research papers, and more than 20 with students.

Aparna Agarwal has received M.Tech. degree in Computer Science from Uttar Pradesh Technical University, Lucknow, Uttar Pradesh, India. She is currently pursuing a Ph.D. degree in Engineering and Technology from Parul University, Gujarat, India. She has been working in the Computing and Electronics Engineering Department, Middle East College, Sultanate of Oman, since 2016. She has more than 17 years of teaching experience. She has published more than 50 papers in International and National Journals/Conferences and 2 book chapters. Her research interests include Security and Trust in Online Social Networks, Information Security, Machine Learning, Artificial Intelligence, technology use in teaching and learning.

Integration of Blockchain with Last Mile Delivery Robots Toward Marketing Innovations

Behzad Esmaeilian and Sara Behdad

1 Introduction

Delivery robots (DRs) are becoming popular for the last-mile logistics of small and light items. They could play a significant role in supplementing or even replacing truck fleets. Prominent e-commerce and high-tech companies have been conducting experiments to pilot-test delivery robots in various applications. In July, 2015, the first commercial drone delivery was approved by the Federal Aviation Administration, which marked a significant milestone (Xu, 2017).

As technological progress continues in the field, several key points should be investigated to facilitate its practical implementation. These include conducting thorough market research, prioritizing user experience design, addressing regulations and standards, enhancing security, educating and creating awareness, and conducting proof-of-concept studies, to name a few. Integration of blockchain capabilities with robotic technology can overcome some of the aforementioned limitations. By considering these points, organizations can increase the likelihood of successful adoption of the technology. While previous studies have explored different factors that influence users' likelihood of adopting delivery robots, marketing strategies have received limited attention, if any.

This study aims to capture the opinion of future users of delivery robots about the type of marketing strategies that influence individuals' comfort levels and overall acceptance of such services. A questionnaire consisting of 16 questions was

B. Esmaeilian
Andrew F. Brimmer College of Business and Information Sciences, Tuskegee University, Tuskegee, AL, USA
e-mail: besmaeilian@tuskegee.edu

S. Behdad (✉)
Environmental Engineering Sciences, University of Florida, Gainesville, FL, USA
e-mail: sarabehdad@ufl.edu

S. Basly (ed.), *Decentralized Finance*, Financial Innovation and Technology,
https://doi.org/10.1007/978-3-031-49515-1_9

designed to test three different hypotheses. The study specifically targeted Generation Z participants, who are recognized as digital natives due to their familiarity and proficiency with technology. Finally, the chapter reviews the capabilities of blockchain technology in implementing marketing strategies and overcoming the current challenges of delivery robots in supply chains.

The remainder of the chapter is organized as follows. Section 2 provides a review of the literature. Section 3 discusses the questionnaire design and data collection process. Sections 4 and 5 describe the design features and marketing strategies preferred by users. Section 6 explains the blockchain capabilities to assist with implementing user preferences, and finally, Section 7 concludes the chapter.

2 Background

The growing implementation of service robots in a wide range of fields, such as package delivery, public safety, environmental data collection, and urban service planning, has encouraged the research community to pay attention to this topic. In this section, we provide a review of existing research on delivery robots. We have categorized the literature into six major topics: (1) design and development of delivery robots, (2) human-robot interactions, (3) ethical and social implications, (4) acceptance and adoption of delivery robots by end users, (5) applications of service robots, and (6) blockchain and robotic systems.

In this section, we present an overview of each group and discuss the key findings and contributions in the field. Figure 1 shows a summary of existing research and a future research roadmap to make the adoption of this technology viable in different application areas.

2.1 Design and Development

Research on the design and development of delivery robots focuses on creating autonomous robots that can navigate, transport items, and interact with their environment safely. A considerable number of studies have focused on the navigation and mapping of robots and developing algorithms and sensors to navigate in dynamic and unstructured environments (Imad et al., 2022; Milford & Wyeth, 2010a, 2010b; Sayed et al., 2020). This includes mapping technologies (Ramadhan et al., 2021; Hakli, 2022), obstacle detection (Neloy et al., 2020; Protasov et al., 2021; Seo & Jung, 2023), and path planning (Araki et al., 2017; Chen, et al., 2021b; Yang & Cheng, 2019) to provide safe and practical delivery. Another group of researchers focused on payload capacity and handling and identifying efficient methods for loading and unloading (Chen, et al., 2021a; Jeong et al., 2019). In addition, some studies explored approaches such as solar energy (Saif et al., 2021),

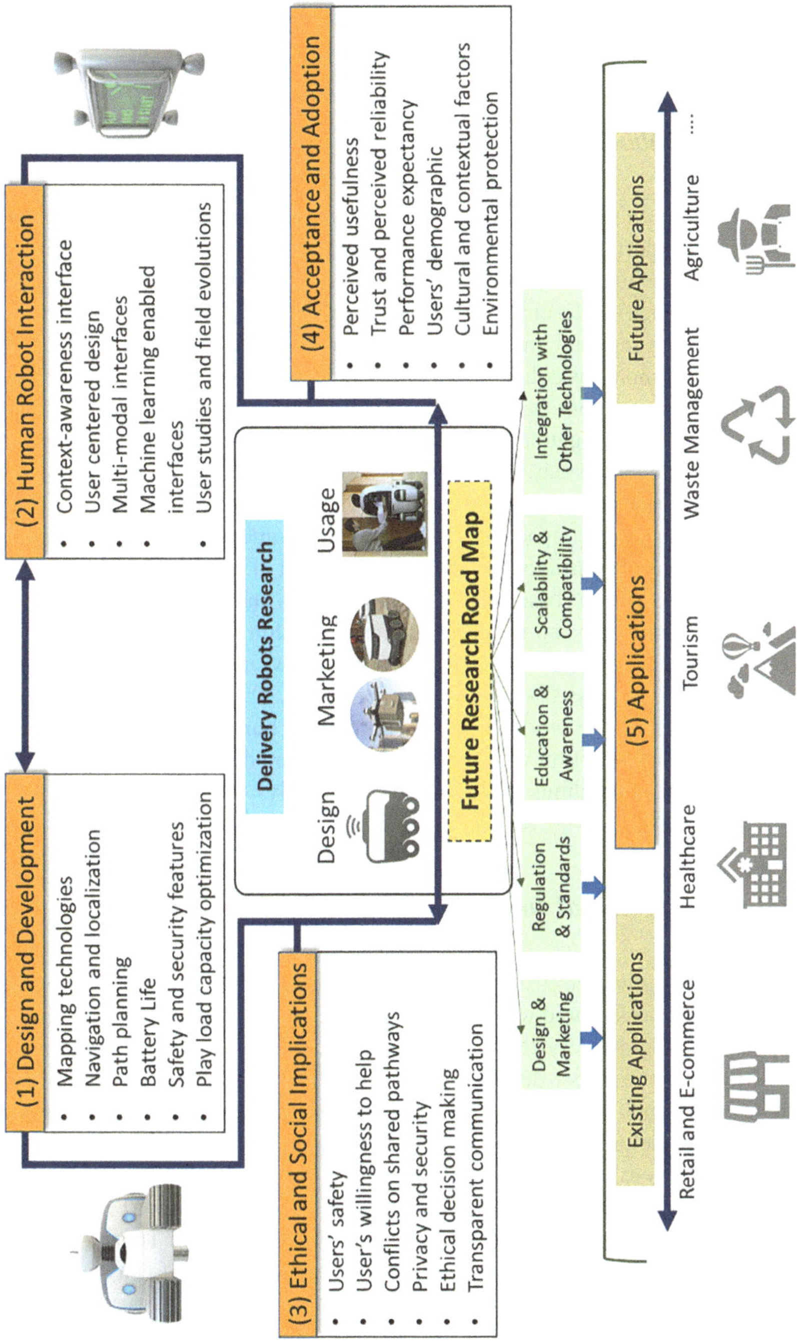

Fig. 1 The existing research and future roadmap for delivery robots

battery technologies and power systems (Cheah et al., 2019; Dowling, 1997; Zhu & Schmidt, 2021), and regenerative braking to improve energy efficiency (Hang et al., 2022).

2.2 *Human-Robot Interaction*

The studies in this area focused on exploring ways to enhance human-robot interaction (HRI) through designing functional HRI interfaces such as context-awareness and user-centered design (Green et al., 2000), the use of multimodal interfaces (e.g., speech, gestures, touch) (Jean et al., 2012; Ryumin et al., 2020), and the use of natural language processing and machine learning techniques (Kulyukin, 2006) to improve HRI in autonomous delivery robots. To name several studies, Kannan et al. explored the effective use of external human–machine interfaces (eHMIs) for demonstrating the robot's navigational intent to pedestrians, specifically focusing on how comprehensible the display and light-based eHMIs are under common navigation scenarios (Kannan et al., 2021). Yu et al. (2023) designed an augmented reality concept to understand the impact of visualizing robot intent and pedestrian path prediction on enhancing participants' trust. Gasteiger et al. (2022) involved stakeholders in designing a home-based robot for older adults and emphasized personalization, consistent imagery and speech, and customization as important factors to improve the future development of service robots. Law et al. (2022) focused on automating in-building cross-floor delivery using robots. They proposed a universal robot-oriented elevator-ride workflow that incorporates human-like touchpoints to facilitate automated interaction with elevators and explored potential scenarios for making robot travel in buildings more pedestrian-friendly.

2.3 *Ethical and Social Implications*

Research in this area has discussed the challenges that delivery robots face when navigating social spaces shared with humans and has explored the social and ethical implications of using delivery robots. For example, researchers investigated individuals' willingness to assist delivery robots in snowy conditions and examined contextual factors such as people's perceptions of robots as cute and helpful on humans' observed helping behaviors (Dobrosovestnova et al., 2022). In addition, existing research has explored the use of automated cue triggering to resolve situations where the robot's path is blocked by people. The results showed that verbal instructions have a positive effect on social attributions to the robot. There is a positive correlation between participants' willingness to allow the robot to pass and their perception of the robot's politeness, while a negative correlation exists between willingness and the ambiguity of the requests (Boos et al., 2022).

Previous studies have also examined concerns about conflicts and safety issues regarding pathways shared among pedestrians, cyclists, and robots. For example, Gehrke et al. (2023) conducted an analysis of one week of field-recorded video captured from ten locations on a university campus to examine the frequency and severity of interactions involving robots to inform facility management strategies for the safe integration of robots in shared-use environments. In addition to social, ethical, and security concerns, the literature has also investigated the capabilities of autonomous delivery robots and their potential for energy and emissions reduction. Research has discussed that delivery robots have the potential to reduce energy consumption and CO_2 emissions in urban areas (Figliozzi & Jennings, 2020).

2.4 Application of Delivery Robots

Currently, delivery robots are used in various industries ranging from e-commerce and retail to healthcare, hospitality, agriculture, and waste management. Studies have extensively elaborated on employing delivery robots in e-commerce and retail (Bogue, 2016; Mangiaracina et al., 2019). As noted by Rai et al., autonomous delivery vehicles gained traction in response to the COVID-19 pandemic, particularly in Asia and North America, but there were fewer initiatives in a European context (Rai et al., 2022). Delivery robots have also been used for transporting medical supplies, such as medication and lab samples, within hospitals and clinics (Javaid et al., 2022). To name a few studies that investigated this application, Law et al. conducted two case studies to investigate the usability, acceptability, and functionality of two delivery robots in different healthcare settings. The results showed that participants believed the robots could improve productivity and reduce staff workload in both settings, but improvements would be needed before long-term implementation (Law et al., 2021). Mann et al. investigated how people interacted with a robot and a tablet computer during healthcare instruction sessions. The findings indicated that participants had more positive interactions with the robot compared to the tablet computer. They exhibited increased speech and positive emotions while engaging with the robot. Moreover, participants reported higher levels of trust and enjoyment and expressed a greater desire for future interactions with the robot (Mann et al., 2015). Raje et al. examined the use of robots in the healthcare sector during the COVID-19 pandemic and concluded that the use of robots has a substantial effect in controlling the spread of the virus and provides advantages such as disinfection or cleaning (Raje et al., 2021). Regarding other applications, delivery robots are also being used in waste management to collect and transport waste and recycle materials in urban areas (Gupta et al., 2022). Alfeo et al. used simulation experiments with real-world GIS data and various garbage collection scenarios to show how utilizing a swarm of robots can enhance the effectiveness and independence of urban waste management systems (Alfeo et al., 2019).

2.5 Public Acceptance of Delivery Robots

A considerable number of studies have explored consumers' intention to adopt delivery robots and the factors driving this intention. To name a few, Koh and Yuen investigate the health and technology-related factors such as self-protection behaviors, task-technology fit, and outcome expectations that encourage consumers to adopt delivery robots (Koh & Yuen, 2023). Pani et al. used latent class analysis to identify six different consumer groups and determined what factors influence their willingness to pay for receiving online shopping deliveries using DRs. The factors considered include sociodemographic and locational factors, as well as attitudes toward familiarity, perceived trust, and technology (Pani et al., 2020). Edrisi and Ganjipour showed that consumers' intention to use delivery robots was positively affected by their attitude, level of innovativeness, and degree of optimism (Edrisi & Ganjipour, 2022). Romanjuk conducted an online questionnaire among Tallinn residents to understand their usage and perceptions of delivery robots. The majority of respondents actively use intracity delivery services but do not use the delivery robot service, mainly due to the service not working in their area. However, most respondents are willing to use the service if it meets their main factors of delivery service choice, which are delivery price and estimated time (Romanjuk, n.d.).

Martinez et al. investigated the influence of group dynamics on the acceptance and trust of food delivery robots. Their findings indicated that individual users exhibited higher levels of acceptance and trust compared to group users, as group members influence each other's perceptions, which leads to either more positive or negative attitudes toward the robots (Martinez et al., 2023). Kaiser et al. found that the factors of performance expectancy and effort expectancy influenced the acceptance of delivery robots. In addition, it was discovered that people were more willing to accept delivery robots for package delivery than for meal delivery (Kaiser et al., n.d.). Abrams et al. argued that current technology acceptance models are inadequate in explaining unplanned encounters between humans and delivery robots. These models rely on perceived ease of use, usefulness, and behavioral intention to use, which do not apply in situations where humans have no prior intention to use robots and meet robots spontaneously (Abrams et al., 2021). According to Waris et al. (2022), perceived usefulness, subjective norms, and attitude are key factors that significantly predict customers' adoption of drone food delivery services. (Chen et al., 2022) discussed that perceived ease-of-use positively impacts users' intention to adopt drone delivery services, whereas perceived usefulness does not have a significant effect. Leon et al. (2023) investigated how privacy, legislation, organizational trust, and usefulness impact consumers' intention to adopt last-mile drone delivery services. (Chen et al., 2023) examined the adoption of drone delivery services by Generation Z, who are digital natives and potential early adopters. They surveyed 83 Gen Zers in the United States, and the results suggest that the "seeing is believing" moment is crucial for their adoption. E-commerce vendors should emphasize on the advantages of speed and environmental protection to help Gen Zers develop their desire for drone delivery services.

2.6 Blockchain-Driven Robotic Systems

Recently, the research community highlighted the benefits of integrating blockchain and robotic systems. To name several studies, Alsamhi and Lee explored how blockchain can be applied to improve the operation of multirobot collaborations for combating COVID-19. The study proposed that blockchain technology can manage multirobot collaborations in a decentralized manner and facilitate information exchange (Alsamhi & Lee, 2020). In another study, Alsamhi et al. discussed the use of blockchain to facilitate decentralized coordination and communication among drones toward collaborative efforts in tasks such as monitoring, sanitization, and delivering supplies to combat COVID-19 (Alsamhi et al., 2021). Gray et al. (2021) proposed a blockchain-based system that employs a token economy to incentivize collaboration among robotic agents for self-governance and task execution even in adversarial settings. Alam et al. conducted simulation studies to explore the cybersecurity of autonomous robots by employing blockchain for coordinated path planning and implementing a consensus method to detect compromised robots in multirobot networks, particularly in spoofing attacks (Alam et al., 2020). Queralta et al. described the potential of next-generation mobile networks, particularly 5G and beyond, in revolutionizing the operation of robots by leveraging blockchain to increase their service management (Queralta et al., 2020). Stobel et al. introduced a proof-of-concept using blockchain to address the security of swarm robotics systems, particularly for Byzantine robots with potentially malicious behavior (Strobel et al., 2018).

While the literature acknowledges the potential of blockchain in robotic systems, there remains an unexplored area, with numerous untapped capabilities within blockchain that have yet to be fully integrated into these systems. Blockchain offers a promising solution to address security concerns such as data breaches, unauthorized access, and privacy issues for users. In addition, operational efficiency and data integrity are important for the smooth functioning of robotic systems, where blockchain features, including encryption, consensus mechanisms, and tamper-proof records, increase security by protecting sensitive data and creating secure communication within the robot network. It also provides identity management to ensure that only authorized robots operate within the system. Blockchain's immutable ledger improves supply chain traceability and provides end-to-end visibility for product verification. Smart contracts automate tasks and reduce the cost of verification.

Currently, most of the existing studies focus on improving the security and autonomy of robotic systems; however, the purpose of this study is to explore how blockchain facilitates the adoption of marketing strategies and services that users expect from such platforms. Despite the considerable amount of research on promoting the adoption of delivery robots in practice, there is still much to be explored. Previous research has primarily focused on developing technology without adequately testing the impact of marketing strategies. Previous studies have examined factors other than marketing that influence robot acceptance. Examples of those factors include demographic, performance, behavioral, and intention factors. In contrast, this study aims to specifically investigate the effects of marketing initiatives on robot acceptance. In addition to marketing strategies, the study also discusses the design features that shape users' perceptions and experiences with robots. Furthermore, the study discusses how integrating blockchain with a fleet of delivery robots paves the way for implementing marketing strategies compatible with users' needs.

3 Questionnaire and Data Collection

Before exploring the capabilities of blockchain, we aim to identify what marketing strategies would increase the acceptance of delivery robots by consumers. To achieve this, we developed a questionnaire consisting of 16 questions that aimed to test the three hypotheses listed in Table 1. In addition to marketing strategies, we also included questions to capture what design features of service robots would be of importance to users.

We conducted the survey using Google Forms from February to April 2023. Our target audience comprises students who represent the younger generation and are potentially more inclined to use the technology. Our focus was on participants from Generation Z. Generation Z is considered digital natives as they grow up with technology and have high proficiency in digital platforms. In addition, Generation Z is known for being early adopters of new technologies.

We invited over 600 students from three universities, one of which was an HBCU, to participate in the survey. Two email reminders were sent to encourage anonymous participation. We achieved a response rate of 27%. After removing outliers, we collected 126 valid responses for hypothesis analysis. The survey consisted of 16 questions to measure the respondent's familiarity with delivery robots and analyze their attitude toward design features and marketing strategies. Although the sample size of 126 is relatively small, it is consistent with previous studies, which allows for a focused analysis of students and mitigates the influence of

Table 1 The list of hypotheses on marketing strategies that promote users' acceptance of delivery robots

Hypothesis	Description
H1	Strategies such as offering discounts or providing additional services through service robots can enhance consumer acceptance of the technology for package delivery.
H2	Providing testimonials or case studies from other users who have successfully adopted the technology can help alleviate concerns and increase trust in the technology.
H3	Offering a gamified rewards system that allows customers to earn rewards for each delivery made with delivery robots increases customer engagement and adoption.

confounding factors such as income, age, and market segments in the general population. The lower number of responses can be attributed to the survey's length. Given the survey's length, a trade-off was made to prioritize collecting responses on a greater number of questions over a larger sample size.

4 Survey Findings: Key Design Features Valued by Users

In this section, we review several questions and the corresponding results on the design features that are important to customers. Six design-related questions were asked.

The first question explores the preferred type of delivery robot for receiving packages, specifically ground-based delivery robots or aerial delivery drones. Participants rate their interest in each option on a scale of 1 to 5 to provide their preferences for different robot types. The second question examines the trust factor associated with different service robot designs for package delivery. Participants are asked to choose between a traditional delivery truck design and a pet-like design (e.g., dog or cat). The options "neither" and "do not know/no opinion" are also provided to capture additional responses. Finally, the third question assesses the importance placed on various design features when considering the use of a delivery robot for package delivery. Participants rate the importance of each design feature, including size and shape, payload capacity, durability, battery life, security features, navigation technology, and aesthetics, on a scale of 1 to 10.

The findings indicate that users mention a higher level of comfort with ground-based delivery robots, with an average score of 4 compared to 3 for aerial robots. The preferred shape of delivery robots that users trust the most varied among respondents. The majority of respondents (over 57%) express a greater inclination to trust service robots that resemble traditional delivery trucks for package delivery. On the other hand, 15% expressed a preference for a robot that resembles a pet, such as a dog or cat, which may indicate a desire for a more relatable and friendly appearance. It is worth noting that 15% of respondents chose the option of "no opinion/do not know," which shows uncertainty or a lack of specific preference. In addition, 11% of participants indicated a preference for neither design option. Regarding design features, security features, navigation technology, and battery life are the most highly rated design features (Fig. 2).

In addition, we conducted a hierarchical clustering analysis to group the design features based on their perceived importance to potential users. The resulting dendrogram is illustrated in Fig. 3. The design features are divided into two separate groups based on their similarities. The first group includes size and shape, aesthetics, and payload capacity. The second group consists of security features, navigation technology, durability, and battery life.

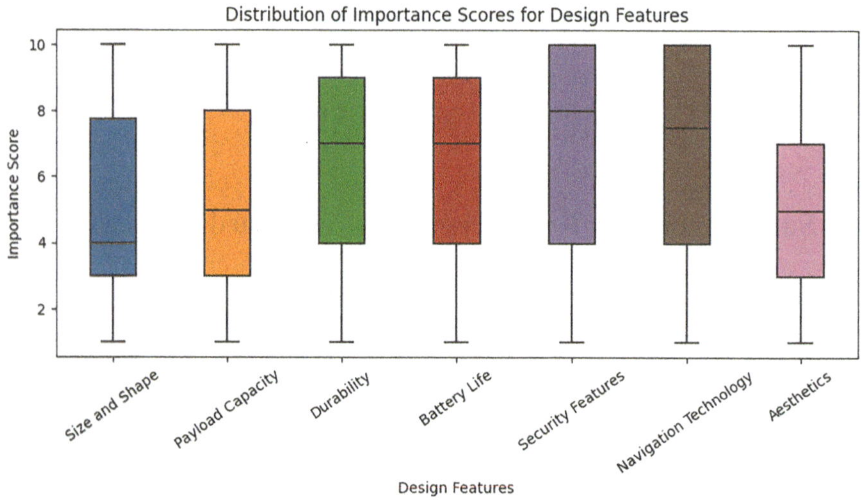

Fig. 2 The importance of various design features to users

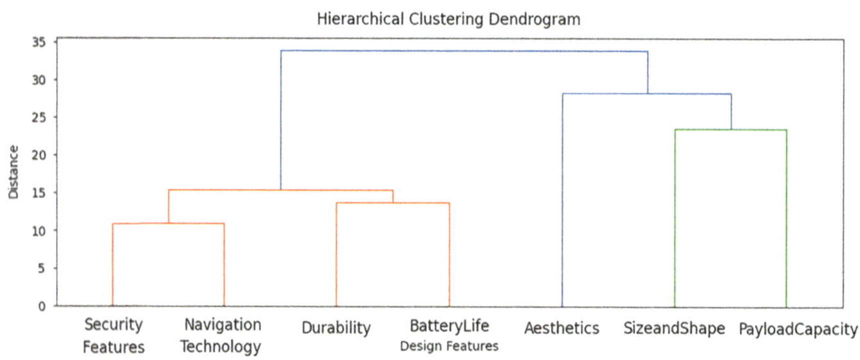

Fig. 3 The result of clustering of design features based on the perceived importance to potential users

In addition, we explored the impact of certain emotions and behaviors on consumers' positive interactions with service robots. Three key questions were included to capture this point. The first question assessed the respondents' comfort level in interacting with service robots to show their overall comfort. The second question aimed to understand the desired emotions and behaviors that users believe would improve their comfort when interacting with service robots. The respondents could choose from various options, such as friendliness and politeness, empathy and understanding, professionalism, and efficiency, or provide their suggestions. The final question examined the importance placed by users on service robots displaying emotions and behaviors similar to those of humans.

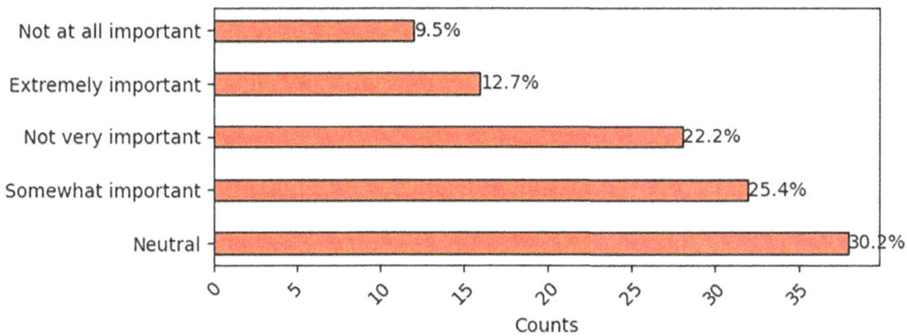

Fig. 4 The importance of displaying humanlike emotions and behaviors

Regarding the comfort level of interacting with delivery robots, a majority of respondents (over 80%) expressed being neutral, somewhat comfortable, or very comfortable. In terms of the desired behaviors or emotions from delivery robots, professionalism and efficiency were reported as the most important factors according to respondents (50%). Friendliness and politeness ranked second in terms of importance (29%). In regard to displaying human-like emotions and behaviors, a significant portion of respondents (over 60%) indicated that it was either not very important, not at all important, or neutral (Fig. 4).

5 Survey Findings: Key Marketing Strategies

This section describes the three main marketing strategies investigated with a set of hypotheses.

H1: *Strategies such as offering discounts or providing additional services through service robots can enhance consumer acceptance of the technology for package delivery.*

Three questions were included in the study to test hypothesis 1, which focuses on the role of strategies such as offering discounts or providing additional services in improving consumer acceptance of package delivery robots. The first question examines the respondents' inclination toward using a package delivery robot if it offers additional services beyond basic package delivery. The second question explores the specific additional services such as parcel wrapping, personalization options, same-day or express delivery, and loyalty program rewards that respondents expect from a package delivery robot. Finally, the third question assesses the importance of the environmental impact of package delivery when using a delivery robot.

The results indicate that 40% of respondents expressed a greater likelihood of using delivery robots if additional services were offered. On the other hand, 17% stated that they would not be more likely to use them, while 42% mentioned that their decision depends on the specific additional services provided. In terms of the additional services respondents would expect from a delivery robot, 70% mentioned same-day or express delivery as their preference. In addition, 12% expressed interest in personalization options, 8% mentioned parcel wrapping, 6% highlighted loyalty program rewards, and the remaining respondents specified other additional services (Fig. 5). Regarding the importance of environmental impact, 53% considered it to be very important or extremely important. Furthermore, 39% expressed that it was somewhat important, while the remaining respondents stated that environmental impact was not important at all.

H2: *Providing testimonials or case studies from other users who have successfully adopted the technology can help alleviate concerns and increase trust in the technology.*

Hypothesis 2 suggests that providing testimonials or case studies from other users who have successfully adopted the technology can help alleviate concerns and increase trust in service robots for package delivery. To test this hypothesis, two questions were included. The first question aimed to assess the participants' comfort level with the idea of receiving packages delivered by a service robot. Respondents were provided with five options ranging from "very comfortable" to "very uncomfortable" to express their level of comfort. The second question presented a scenario involving a busy professional named John who uses a delivery robot for his package delivery needs. The scenario highlighted features such as notifications, remote monitoring, and remote signatures for package delivery that John has used. Participants were then asked to evaluate their comfort level with the idea of receiving packages delivered by a service robot based on the knowledge of John's successful experience. Similar to the previous question, respondents were provided with five options to express their comfort level.

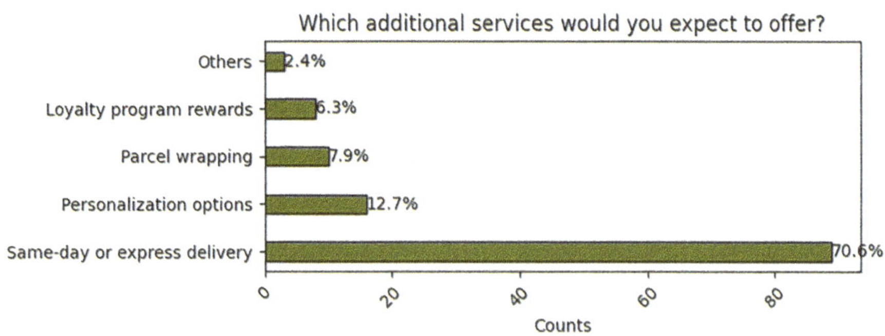

Fig. 5 The additional services respondents would expect from a delivery robot

The results of the survey indicate that initially, 37% of respondents reported feeling somewhat comfortable with the idea of receiving packages delivered by a service robot. In addition, 24% stated that they were very comfortable, 23% were neutral, 12% felt somewhat uncomfortable, and only 2.4% expressed being very uncomfortable (Table 2).

However, after learning about the successful experience of John, who used a delivery robot for his package delivery needs, the responses underwent a considerable shift. The percentage of respondents who reported feeling very comfortable increased to 35.7%, while 31% expressed being somewhat comfortable. Furthermore, 24.6% remained neutral and indicated no significant change in their comfort level. Only 6.3% reported feeling somewhat uncomfortable, and only 1.6% stated being very uncomfortable (Table 2).

The shift toward a higher percentage of respondents feeling very comfortable or somewhat comfortable indicates that success stories and positive user experiences can help alleviate concerns and increase trust in the technology.

We also conducted a paired t test to compare the comfort level before and after hearing about John's success. The p value of almost zero suggests that we cannot reject the significant difference in Comfort Level before and after hearing about John's success.

H3: *Offering a gamified rewards system that allows customers to earn rewards for each delivery made with delivery robots increases customer engagement and adoption.*

Hypothesis 3 suggests that offering a gamified rewards system where customers can earn rewards for each delivery made with delivery robots will lead to increased customer engagement and adoption of the technology. To explore this hypothesis, three questions are provided. First, respondents are asked to imagine making an online purchase and are given the choice between traditional postal service and delivery robots. The traditional postal service option has no rewards, while the delivery robot option offers the chance to win a reward with each delivery.

Then, in the next question, assuming respondents choose to receive their package using a delivery robot, they are asked about their interest in different reward options as part of the delivery robot service. They are presented with several reward options,

Table 2 Comparison of participants' stated comfort levels before and after knowledge of John's successful experience

How comfortable with service robots?	Participants' initial comfort level	Participants' comfort level based on John's successful experience
Very uncomfortable	2.4%	1.6%
Somewhat uncomfortable	12.7%	6.3%
Neutral	23%	24.6%
Somewhat comfortable	37.3%	31.7%
Very comfortable	24.6%	35.7%

such as a chance to win a free delivery for their next purchase (60% chance of winning), $5 off their next purchase (80% chance of winning), $10 off their next purchase (50% chance of winning), and $20 off their next purchase (30% chance of winning).

Finally, respondents are asked to indicate which delivery service applications they believe are most suitable for service robots. They are presented with several options, including food delivery, package delivery, prescription delivery, mail delivery, and laundry delivery. Respondents can choose one or more options from the list or indicate "All of the above" or "None of the above."

The results found that 72% of respondents expressed a preference for delivery robots with a chance to win a reward for each delivery made, with the delivery robot announcing it upon delivery. This indicates a strong inclination toward this option. On the other hand, 27% of respondents stated a preference for the traditional postal service with no reward.

In terms of the reward options, the results indicate that 32% of respondents showed a preference for the option that offered a chance to win a free delivery for their next purchase, with a 60% chance of winning. This suggests that the attraction of a completely free delivery resonated with a considerable portion of the participants. In addition, 27% of respondents selected the option of $5 off their next purchase, with an 80% chance of winning, which indicates that a tangible monetary discount was appealing to them. Furthermore, 23% of respondents selected the option of $10 off their next purchase with a 50% chance of winning, while 16% chose the option of $20 off their next purchase with a 30% chance of winning. These findings suggest that different levels of discounts influenced participants' preferences in which varying levels of probability affect their choice.

The results show that participants had different preferences for the reward options (Fig. 6). A significant portion preferred the chance to win a free delivery (32%), while others preferred monetary discounts of $5 (27%), $10 (23%), or $20 (16%) off their next purchase. The findings suggest that participants were motivated by the attraction of a completely free delivery and immediate savings. The different levels of probability associated with the discounts influenced participants' decision-making, with some valuing higher probabilities for smaller discounts and others being interested in lower probabilities for larger discounts. These results emphasize

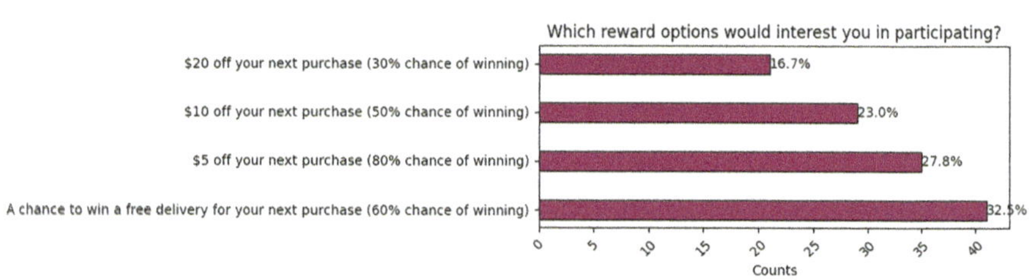

Fig. 6 The preference toward different reward options

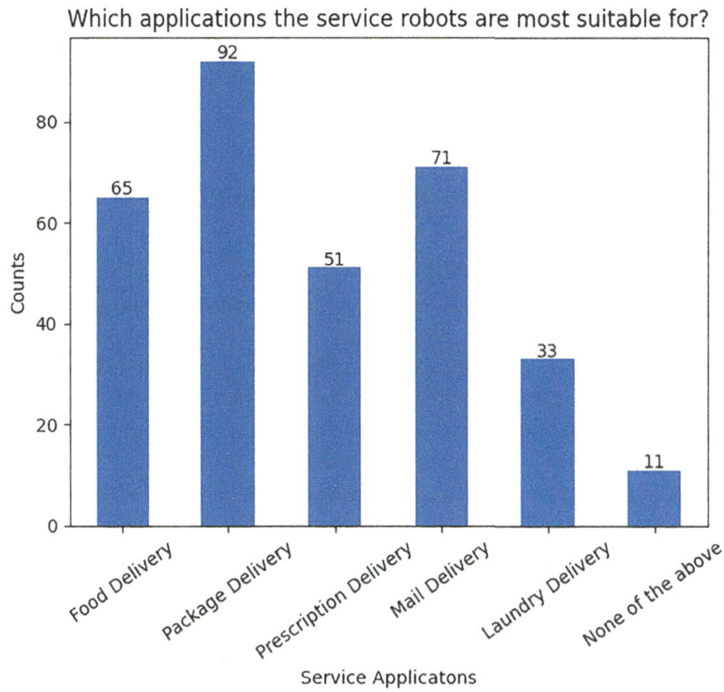

Fig. 7 The type of applications the service robots would be suitable for

the importance of considering a range of reward options and the corresponding probabilities when designing incentives.

Finally, respondents were asked about the service applications they consider most suitable for delivery robots. The results revealed that package and mail delivery were among the top choices, followed by food delivery in third place (Fig. 7).

Limitations of the Survey

Despite the insights gained from this study, several limitations should be acknowledged. The study relied on a relatively small sample size of 126 participants, which primarily consisted of students from a specific demographic (Generation Z). While this sample size provided the opportunity for focused analysis, it may not fully represent the diverse perspectives and preferences of the general population. Further, there is a potential bias in the data. The study focused on students who are potentially more inclined to adopt new technologies. This limits the generalizability of the findings to other demographic individuals with different technological backgrounds. In addition, the study relied on self-reported data, which may be subject to response bias or inaccuracies. Participants' responses may be influenced by social desirability bias or may not fully reflect their actual behavior. Moreover, we adopted a cross-sectional design to capture participants' opinions at a specific point in time. A longitudinal analysis that tracks participants' attitudes over an extended period is needed.

6 Blockchain for Implementing Marketing Practices

In this section, we briefly review the critical factors that matter to users based on the survey findings, and we further discuss how blockchain can play a role in implementing the identified marketing strategies.

Concerning strategies for enhancing acceptance (Hypothesis 1), offering additional services and discounts was found to increase the likelihood of using delivery robots. Same-day or express delivery was the most preferred additional service, and environmental impact was considered important by a majority of participants. In addition, the study examined the role of testimonials and case studies (Hypothesis 2) in building trust. Initially, participants felt somewhat comfortable with the idea of receiving packages from service robots. However, after learning about successful user experiences, their comfort levels increased significantly, which shows the positive impact of testimonials and case studies. In terms of a gamified rewards system (Hypothesis 3), participants showed a strong preference for delivery robots offering a chance to win rewards with each delivery. Free delivery and monetary discounts were attractive options with different levels of probability influencing participants' preferences. Package and mail delivery were considered suitable applications for delivery robots.

We will discuss the critical factors important to users under five main categories and elaborate on how distributed network platforms such as blockchain can complement a fleet of delivery robots. The categories include (1) same-day delivery, (2) personalization, (3) reduction of environmental impacts, (4) increasing trust and successful testimonials, and (5) gamified reward systems.

6.1 Same-Day Delivery

Coordination among robots plays a crucial role in achieving same-day delivery in practice. Blockchain can facilitate this coordination in several ways, ranging from optimized routing to dynamic reassignments, traffic and weather updates, and collaborative efforts. When multiple robots are involved in the delivery process, they can share information about their current locations, routes, and delivery schedules. Blockchain can then calculate and propose optimized delivery routes for each robot to minimize transit times. In cases where a robot encounters unexpected obstacles or requires maintenance, blockchain can quickly reassign its deliveries to nearby available robots. In addition, blockchain can be integrated with external data sources to provide robots with real-time traffic and weather updates. Furthermore, the transparency and product tracking capabilities of blockchain make collaborative efforts easier. In scenarios where a package needs to pass through multiple robots before reaching its final destination (e.g., in a relay-style delivery), blockchain provides smooth coordination.

6.2 Personalization

Information networks can securely store user preferences, such as delivery time windows, delivery locations, and package handling instructions. When a delivery robot is assigned to a user, it can access this information from the network to customize the delivery experience. For example, users can set predefined conditions for deliveries. This could include options such as leaving a package at a designated location or receiving it at a specific time. By analyzing real-time traffic data from the blockchain, delivery robots can optimize their routes to accommodate individual delivery schedules or even select more energy-efficient routes to delight green consumers. In addition, by accessing users' profiles and purchase histories, delivery robots can provide personalized humanlike emotions, product recommendations, or offers during the delivery process.

6.3 Environmental Impacts

Integrating robots with cloud-based networks can facilitate real-time data sharing among delivery robots toward selecting the most energy-efficient paths or selecting delivery time slots when robot delivery is available. The immutable ledgers allow for the tracking of carbon emissions and other environmental metrics. Robots equipped with sensors and data collection mechanisms can record the environmental footprint of each delivery, such as the distance traveled, energy consumed, and emissions generated. Blockchain can help with implementing token-based reward systems for eco-friendly actions. For instance, users may receive tokens for opting for eco-friendly packaging or selecting more efficient delivery routes despite delays, and delivery companies may earn tokens for using electric vehicles or delivery robots equipped with solar panels. Moreover, robots can be programmed to serve as agents for collecting recyclables and packages during deliveries.

6.4 Increase Trust (Testimonials)

Blockchain provides an immutable ledger that records all transactions involving delivery robots. Successful stories and testimonials from other users can be securely stored on the blockchain along with verification mechanisms. Users can access these testimonials and be confident that they are from real customers and that testimonials are not controlled by a single entity such as a delivery company. This decentralized verification adds credibility to customer reviews. Furthermore, blockchain can introduce incentive mechanisms where users are rewarded for sharing their stories. This encourages more users to contribute their experiences and create a self-sustaining cycle of trust-building.

6.5 Gamified Reward Systems

Smart contracts on the blockchain can automate the distribution of rewards based on predefined rules. For example, when a user completes a certain number of deliveries, the issuance of a reward can be triggered. Blockchain records all game-related data, including points, achievements, and rewards, in an immutable and transparent manner. This establishes the integrity of the game and prevents manipulation. Users can view all game-related transactions to see fairness in the reward distributions. The governance of the gamified reward system can be decentralized on the blockchain. This allows for community-driven decision-making on game updates and reward structures. Moreover, users' data generated during robot deliveries can be tokenized on the blockchain. Such blockchain-based incentives can motivate both users and robots to actively participate in federated learning by contributing data. Users can grant temporary access to their data for federated learning purposes through smart contracts.

The abovementioned points were examples of the capabilities of integrating robotic fleets with distributed networks to facilitate the flow of information between physical and cyber infrastructure. Table 3 presents a summary of adoption strategies and the specific characteristics of blockchain technology necessary for their implementation. While several characteristics are essential for executing these strategies, we have emphasized the significant features.

Table 3 The main characteristics of blockchain technology needed for implementing marketing strategies in delivery robots

		The characteristics of blockchain					
		Decentralization	Immutability	Transparency	Security	Consensus Mechanisms	Smart Contract
Marketing and services	Same-day delivery	X			X	X	X
	Personalization						X
	Reduction of environmental impacts	X		X			
	Increase trust (testimonials)		X	X			
	Reward systems						X

7 Conclusion

The use of delivery robots for last-mile logistics has gained attention in recent years. This study aimed to capture the opinions of future users regarding the marketing strategies that influence their acceptance and comfort levels. Furthermore, the study discusses how the capabilities of distributed network technologies such as blockchain can be employed to assist with implementing innovative marketing strategies. A questionnaire consisting of 16 questions was designed, and the opinions of over 120 respondents, primarily from the Generation Z group, were collected.

Offering discounts or additional services through delivery robots, providing testimonials from other users, and implementing gamified rewards systems were found to positively influence consumer acceptance. Based on the survey results, we discussed five factors critical to users that ease the adoption of delivery robots, including same-day delivery, personalization, reduction of environmental impacts, increasing trust through testimonials, and gamified reward systems. Furthermore, we explained how blockchain, as a distributed network platform, can increase the performance of delivery robot fleets.

The study can be extended in several ways. First, a larger sample size with participants from different age groups, cultural backgrounds, and professional settings would provide a broader perspective. Second, the survey can be extended to capture participants' and expert opinions on blockchain capabilities integrated with robotic infrastructure. Third, the results of the quantitative survey can be complemented with qualitative methods such as in-depth interviews or focus groups to provide richer insights. Comparing different design features, marketing strategies, or user experiences across various delivery robot platforms or service providers is another direction of future work. Furthermore, conducting actual field experiments can help analyze real customer behavior.

References

Abrams, A. M. H., Dautzenberg, P. S. C., Jakobowsky, C., Ladwig, S., & Rosenthal-von der Pütten, A. M. (2021). A theoretical and empirical reflection on technology acceptance models for autonomous delivery robots. In *Proceedings of the 2021 ACM/IEEE International Conference on Human-Robot Interaction* (pp. 272–280).

Alam, T., Taylor, J., Taylor, J., Badsha, S., Shahid, A. Bin, R., & Kayes, A. S. M. (2020). Leveraging blockchain for spoof-resilient robot networks. *Intelligent Robotics and Applications: 13th International Conference, ICIRA 2020, proceedings* 13, 207–216.

Alfeo, A. L., Ferrer, E. C., Carrillo, Y. L., Grignard, A., Pastor, L. A., Sleeper, D. T., Cimino, M. G. C. A., Lepri, B., Vaglini, G., & Larson, K. (2019). Urban swarms: A new approach for autonomous waste management. *International Conference on Robotics and Automation (ICRA), 2019*, 4233–4240.

Alsamhi, S. H., & Lee, B. (2020). Blockchain-empowered multirobot collaboration to fight COVID-19 and future pandemics. *IEEE Access, 9*, 44173–44197.

Alsamhi, S. H., Lee, B., Guizani, M., Kumar, N., Qiao, Y., & Liu, X. (2021). Blockchain for decentralized multi-drone to combat COVID-19 and future pandemics: Framework and proposed solutions. *Transactions on Emerging Telecommunications Technologies, 32*(9), e4255.

Araki, B., Strang, J., Pohorecky, S., Qiu, C., Naegeli, T., & Rus, D. (2017). Multirobot path planning for a swarm of robots that can both fly and drive. *IEEE International Conference on Robotics and Automation (ICRA), 2017*, 5575–5582.

Bogue, R. (2016). Growth in e-commerce boosts innovation in the warehouse robot market. *Industrial Robot: An International Journal., 43*, 583.

Boos, A., Zimmermann, M., Zych, M., & Bengler, K. (2022). Polite and unambiguous requests facilitate willingness to help an autonomous delivery robot and favorable social attributions. In *2022 31st IEEE International Conference on Robot and Human Interactive Communication (RO-MAN)* (pp. 1620–1626).

Cheah, W. C., Watson, S. A., & Lennox, B. (2019). Limitations of wireless power transfer technologies for mobile robots. *Wireless Power Transfer, 6*(2), 175–189.

Chen, C., Leon, S., & Ractham, P. (2022). Will customers adopt last-mile drone delivery services? An analysis of drone delivery in the emerging market economy. *Cogent Business & Management, 9*(1), 2074340.

Chen, C., Nakayama, M., & Ractham, P. (2023). Increasing the intention of gen Zers to adopt drone delivery services based on a three-step decision-making process. *Cogent Business & Management, 10*(1), 2188987.

Chen, H., Hu, Z., & Solak, S. (2021a). Improved delivery policies for future drone-based delivery systems. *European Journal of Operational Research, 294*(3), 1181–1201.

Chen, Y., Chen, M., Chen, Z., Cheng, L., Yang, Y., & Li, H. (2021b). Delivery path planning of heterogeneous robot system under road network constraints. *Computers & Electrical Engineering, 92*, 107197.

Dobrosovestnova, A., Schwaninger, I., & Weiss, A. (2022). With a little help of humans. An exploratory study of delivery robots stuck in snow. In *2022 31st IEEE International Conference on Robot and Human Interactive Communication (RO-MAN)* (pp. 1023–1029).

Dowling, K. (1997). *Power sources for small robots*. Carnegie Mellon University, the Robotics Institute.

Edrisi, A., & Ganjipour, H. (2022). Factors affecting intention and attitude toward sidewalk autonomous delivery robots among online shoppers. *Transportation Planning and Technology, 45*(7), 588–609.

Figliozzi, M., & Jennings, D. (2020). Autonomous delivery robots and their potential impacts on urban freight energy consumption and emissions. *Transportation Research Procedia, 46*, 21–28.

Gasteiger, N., Ahn, H. S., Lee, C., Lim, J., MacDonald, B. A., Kim, G. H., & Broadbent, E. (2022). Participatory design, development, and testing of assistive health robots with older adults: An international four-year project. *ACM Transactions on Human-Robot Interaction (THRI), 11*(4), 1–19.

Gehrke, S. R., Phair, C. D., Russo, B. J., & Smaglik, E. J. (2023). Observed sidewalk autonomous delivery robot interactions with pedestrians and bicyclists. *Transportation Research Interdisciplinary Perspectives, 18*, 100789.

Green, A., Huttenrauch, H., Norman, M., Oestreicher, L., & Eklundh, K. S. (2000). User centered design for intelligent service robots. *Proceedings 9th IEEE International Workshop on Robot and Human Interactive Communication. IEEE RO-MAN 2000 (Cat. No. 00TH8499)*, 161–166.

Gray, J., Seneviratne, O., & Godage, I. (2021). *Blockchain-based mechanism for robotic cooperation through incentives: Prototype application in warehouse automation*. 2021 IEEE International Conference on Blockchain (Blockchain), 597–604.

Gupta, A., van der Schoor, M. J., Bräutigam, J., Justo, V. B., Umland, T. F., & Göhlich, D. (2022). Autonomous service robots for urban waste management-multiagent route planning and cooperative operation. *IEEE Robotics and Automation Letters, 7*(4), 8972–8979.

Hakli, R. (2022). *Helping-as-work and helping-as-care: Mapping ambiguities of helping commercial delivery robots*.
Hang, P., Lou, B., & Lv, C. (2022). Nonlinear predictive motion control for autonomous mobile robots considering active fault-tolerant control and regenerative braking. *Sensors, 22*(10), 3939.
Imad, M., Doukhi, O., Lee, D. J., Kim, J. C., & Kim, Y. J. (2022). Deep learning-based NMPC for local motion planning of last-mile delivery robot. *Sensors, 22*(21), 8101.
Javaid, M., Haleem, A., Singh, R. P., Rab, S., Suman, R., & Kumar, L. (2022). Utilization of robotics for healthcare: A scoping review. *Journal of Industrial Integration and Management.*
Jean, J.-H., Wei, C.-F., Lin, Z.-W., & Lian, K.-Y. (2012). Development of an office delivery robot with multimodal human-robot interactions. *Proceedings of SICE Annual Conference (SICE), 2012*, 1564–1567.
Jeong, H. Y., Song, B. D., & Lee, S. (2019). Truck-drone hybrid delivery routing: Payload-energy dependency and no-Fly zones. *International Journal of Production Economics, 214*, 220–233.
Kaiser, R., De Benedetto, S., Müller, P., & Planing, P. (n.d.). *What will autonomous delivery robots bring us tomorrow?–an empirical multi-method study on the acceptance of different delivery scenarios*. Available at SSRN 4207359.
Kannan, S. S., Lee, A., & Min, B.-C. (2021). External human–machine interface on delivery robots: Expression of navigation intent of the robot. In *2021 30th IEEE international conference on Robot & Human Interactive Communication (RO-MAN)* (pp. 1305–1312).
Koh, L. Y., & Yuen, K. F. (2023). Consumer adoption of autonomous delivery robots in cities: Implications on urban planning and design policies. *Cities, 133*, 104125.
Kulyukin, V. A. (2006). On natural language dialog with assistive robots. *Proceedings of the 1st ACM SIGCHI/SIGART Conference on Human-Robot Interaction*, 164–171.
Law, M., Ahn, H. S., Broadbent, E., Peri, K., Kerse, N., Topou, E., Gasteiger, N., & MacDonald, B. (2021). Case studies on the usability, acceptability and functionality of autonomous mobile delivery robots in real-world healthcare settings. *Intelligent Service Robotics, 14*(3), 387–398.
Law, W., Li, K., Fan, K., Mo, T., & Poon, C. (2022). Friendly elevator Corider: An HRI approach for robot-elevator interaction. In *2022 17th ACM/IEEE International Conference on Human-Robot Interaction (HRI)* (pp. 865–869).
Leon, S., Chen, C., & Ratcliffe, A. (2023). Consumers' perceptions of last mile drone delivery. *International Journal of Logistics Research and Applications, 26*(3), 345–364.
Mangiaracina, R., Perego, A., Seghezzi, A., & Tumino, A. (2019). Innovative solutions to increase last-mile delivery efficiency in B2C e-commerce: A literature review. *International Journal of Physical Distribution & Logistics Management., 49*, 901.
Mann, J. A., MacDonald, B. A., Kuo, I.-H., Li, X., & Broadbent, E. (2015). People respond better to robots than computer tablets delivering healthcare instructions. *Computers in Human Behavior, 43*, 112–117.
Martinez, J. E., VanLeeuwen, D., Stringam, B. B., & Fraune, M. R. (2023). Hey?! What did you think about that robot? Groups polarize users' acceptance and Trust of Food Delivery Robots. In *Proceedings of the 2023 ACM/IEEE International Conference on Human-Robot Interaction* (pp. 417–427).
Milford, M., & Wyeth, G. (2010a). Hybrid robot control and SLAM for persistent navigation and mapping. *Robotics and Autonomous Systems, 58*(9), 1096–1104.
Milford, M., & Wyeth, G. (2010b). Persistent navigation and mapping using a biologically inspired SLAM system. *The International Journal of Robotics Research, 29*(9), 1131–1153.
Neloy, A. A., Bindu, R. A., Alam, S., Haque, R., Khan, M. S. A., Mishu, N. M., & Siddique, S. (2020). Alpha-N-V2: Shortest path finder automated delivery robot with obstacle detection and avoiding system. *Vietnam Journal of Computer Science, 7*(04), 373–389.
Pani, A., Mishra, S., Golias, M., & Figliozzi, M. (2020). Evaluating public acceptance of autonomous delivery robots during COVID-19 pandemic. *Transportation Research Part D: Transport and Environment, 89*, 102600.
Protasov, S., Karpyshev, P., Kalinov, I., Kopanev, P., Mikhailovskiy, N., Sedunin, A., & Tsetserukou, D. (2021). Cnn-based omnidirectional object detection for hermesbot autonomous delivery robot with preliminary frame classification. In *2021 20th International Conference on Advanced Robotics (ICAR)* (pp. 517–522).

Queralta, J. P., Qingqing, L., Zou, Z., & Westerlund, T. (2020). Enhancing autonomy with blockchain and multiaccess edge computing in distributed robotic systems. *Fifth International Conference on Fog and Mobile Edge Computing (FMEC), 2020*, 180–187.

Rai, H. B., Touami, S., & Dablanc, L. (2022). Autonomous e-commerce delivery in ordinary and exceptional circumstances. The French case. *Research in Transportation Business & Management, 45*, 100774.

Raje, S., Reddy, N., Jerbi, H., Randhawa, P., Tsaramirsis, G., Shrivas, N. V., Pavlopoulou, A., Stojmenović, M., & Piromalis, D. (2021). Applications of healthcare robots in combating the COVID-19 pandemic. *Applied Bionics and Biomechanics, 2021*.

Ramadhan, S. F., Taufik, M., Novita, D., & Turnip, A. (2021). Design of 2D LiDar-based indoor SLAM for medical robot Covid-19. *International Conference on Artificial Intelligence and Mechatronics Systems (AIMS), 2021*, 1–5.

Romanjuk, M. (n.d.). *Delivery robots serving last mile B2C: An evaluation of Tallinn residents' incentives behind the usage of delivery robots in 2020 on the basis of starship technologies example*.

Ryumin, D., Kagirov, I., Axyonov, A., Pavlyuk, N., Saveliev, A., Kipyatkova, I., Zelezny, M., Mporas, I., & Karpov, A. (2020). A multimodal user interface for an assistive robotic shopping cart. *Electronics, 9*(12), 2093.

Saif, A.-W. A., Dhaifallah, M. A. L., Muhaya, T. B, & Majeed, O. (2021). Intelligent Robot Powered by Solar Energy. *2021 18th International Multi-Conference on Systems, Signals & Devices (SSD)*, 194–200.

Sayed, A. S., Ammar, H. H., & Shalaby, R. (2020). Centralized multiagent mobile robots SLAM and navigation for COVID-19 field hospitals. *2020 2nd Novel Intelligent and Leading Emerging Sciences Conference (NILES)*, 444–449.

Seo, S., & Jung, H. (2023). A robust collision prediction and detection method based on neural network for autonomous delivery robots. *ETRI Journal., 45*, 329.

Strobel, V., Castelló Ferrer, E., & Dorigo, M. (2018). *Managing byzantine robots via blockchain technology in a swarm robotics collective decision making scenario*.

Waris, I., Ali, R., Nayyar, A., Baz, M., Liu, R., & Hameed, I. (2022). An empirical evaluation of customers' adoption of drone food delivery services: An extended technology acceptance model. *Sustainability, 14*(5), 2922.

Xu, J. (2017). *Design perspectives on delivery drones*. RAND London.

Yang, R., & Cheng, L. (2019). Path planning of restaurant service robot based on a-star algorithms with updated weights. *2019 12th International Symposium on Computational Intelligence and Design (ISCID), 1*, 292–295.

Yu, X., Hoggenmueller, M., & Tomitsch, M. (2023). Your way or my way: Improving human-robot co-navigation through robot intent and pedestrian prediction visualizations. *Proceedings of the 2023 ACM/IEEE International Conference on Human-Robot Interaction*, 211–221.

Zhu, M., & Schmidt, O. G. (2021). Tiny robots and sensors need tiny batteries—Here's how to do it. *Nature, 589*(7841), 195–197.

Behzad Esmaeilian is an Assistant Professor within the Andrew Brimmer College of Business and Information Science at Tuskegee University. His educational background includes a Ph.D. in Industrial Engineering and Management Systems from the University of Central Florida, and a Master of Science degree in Industrial and Systems Engineering from the University of Florida.

Sara Behdad is an Associate Professor with the Engineering School of Sustainable Infrastructure & Environment at the University of Florida. Sara completed her Ph.D. in Industrial and Enterprise Systems Engineering at the University of Illinois at Urbana-Champaign and pursued a Master of Science degree in Industrial Engineering at Amirkabir University of Technology in Tehran.

Artificial Intelligence and the Future of Decentralized Finance

Sami Basly

1 Introduction

Decentralized finance, or DeFi, is an innovative financial architecture that operates without traditional intermediaries like banks or brokerages. Built on blockchain technology, DeFi platforms offer an array of financial services, from lending and borrowing to insurance and asset management, all in a transparent and permissionless environment. For its part, artificial intelligence (AI) represents the endeavor to create machines capable of mimicking human cognitive functions such as learning, reasoning, and problem-solving (Russell & Norvig, 2016). Its applications have infiltrated nearly every industry, from healthcare to transportation to finance. The fusion of AI and DeFi heralds a new era in financial innovation. By integrating AI's data processing and predictive capabilities with DeFi's decentralized and transparent financial services, a new landscape of AI-driven DeFi (DeFi Intelligence) is emerging. In this landscape, AI algorithms can improve decision-making processes in DeFi platforms, enhancing efficiency and risk management. For instance, by analyzing vast amounts of data in real-time, AI can help DeFi platforms assess risks better, leading to optimized lending and borrowing rates and improved trading strategies.

Integration of AI and DeFi is an emerging field with significant potential. However, there are currently a few examples of AI-powered projects that have the potential to impact the DeFi ecosystem. For example, Athena GPT is an AI-powered

S. Basly (✉)
University of Paris Nanterre, Paris, France
e-mail: sbasly@parisnanterre.fr

S. Basly (ed.), *Decentralized Finance*, Financial Innovation and Technology,
https://doi.org/10.1007/978-3-031-49515-1_10

DeFi trading platform developed by NFA Labs.[1] Athena GPT serves as an AI-driven DeFi trading platform. This ecosystem also encompasses Canis, a lending protocol, and Hecate, an insurance protocol. The platform features a user-friendly interface along with robust AI functionalities, such as a portfolio management service capable of managing more than 35 crypto pairs. This service analyzes and forecasts real-time prices and also autonomously takes long and short positions. Additionally, what sets it apart is its 24/7 capability to gauge market sentiment via major social networks like Twitter and Reddit, offering investors chances for profitable trading in various market conditions. Another stimulating development in the field of AI-DeFi is SingularityNET that has developed SingularityDAO, a DeFi project that uses AI to manage dynamic token sets and execute predictive market-making. Another significant example is Numerai which operates as a hedge fund network, allowing participants to execute equity trades on the Ethereum blockchain. According to its official website, the platform leverages artificial intelligence (AI) and machine learning technologies to invest in global stock markets.

However, the integration of AI and DeFi is still in its early stages. As the field continues to evolve, we can expect to see more innovative projects that leverage AI to enhance various aspects of DeFi, such as risk assessment, data analysis, automation, and personalized financial services. Entrepreneurs and developers are actively exploring the potential of AI in the DeFi space, and it is likely that more AI-powered DeFi projects will emerge in the future. These projects have the potential to revolutionize the way financial services are delivered, making them more efficient, inclusive, and intelligent.

The objective of this chapter is to explore the potential applications of AI in the field of decentralized finance and to demonstrate that this technology will contribute to enabling DeFi to achieve its ideal objectives of speed, efficiency, and inclusion. However, despite the potential benefits, the integration of DeFi and AI is not without its challenges.

2 What Is Artificial Intelligence (AI)?

Artificial intelligence (AI) refers to the simulation of human intelligence in machines that are programmed to think and learn like humans. It involves the development of algorithms that allow computers to perform tasks that typically require human intelligence (Kaplan & Haenlein, 2019). This includes machine learning, natural language processing, and computer vision (Goodfellow et al., 2016). AI can be categorized into two types: narrow AI and general AI. Narrow AI, also known as weak AI, is designed to perform specific tasks and is limited to those tasks. Voice assistants like Siri and Alexa, recommendation systems, and image recognition

[1] https://cointelegraph.com/news/defi-meets-ai-can-this-synergy-be-the-new-focus-of-tech-acquisitions

software illustrate the concept of narrow AI. General AI, on the other hand, refers to AI systems that have the ability to understand, learn, and apply knowledge across a wide range of tasks, similar to human intelligence. Yet, general AI is still largely a concept and has not been fully realized.

AI algorithms and models are trained using large amounts of data, allowing them to recognize patterns, make predictions, and generate insights. Machine learning, a subset of AI, involves training models on data and allowing them to learn and improve from experience without being explicitly programmed. Deep learning, a subfield of machine learning, uses artificial neural networks to simulate the structure and function of the human brain, enabling machines to learn and make decisions in a way that resembles human thinking. AI has numerous applications across various industries, including healthcare, finance, transportation, manufacturing, and entertainment. It has the potential to revolutionize these industries by automating tasks, improving efficiency, and enabling new capabilities. However, AI also raises ethical and societal concerns, such as privacy, bias, and job displacement, which need to be carefully addressed.

There are a number of academic debates about artificial intelligence particularly in the realms of business and management sciences. Notably, academic debates on whether AI will create new jobs or replace existing ones continue to be a significant concern (Frey & Osborne, 2017). The integration of AI in decision-making processes raises also questions about potential biases and ethical implications (Danks & London, 2017; Alibašić, 2023). Finally, the debate around governance structures for AI, including regulation, standards, and ethical guidelines, is a prominent topic (Jobin et al., 2019). However, there is limited research specifically focused on AI in DeFi. This suggests that the integration of AI into DeFi is still an emerging area with significant research opportunities. A number of studies have explored the utility of AI in DeFi and have identified potential research opportunities and benefits (Omohundro, 2014; de Souza et al., 2019; Raheman et al., 2021; Sadman et al., 2022).

3 The Integration of Artificial Intelligence (AI) in the Decentralized Finance (DeFi) Ecosystem

Despite the paucity of research on the subject, extant studies highlight the potential and importance of integrating AI into the DeFi ecosystem. Some studies emphasize the transformative potential of AI in DeFi, particularly in terms of efficiency, security, risk assessment, predictive analytics, automated trading, and user experience (Jiang & Liang, 2017; Sadman et al., 2022). The fusion of AI and DeFi heralds a new era in financial innovation. By integrating AI's data processing and predictive capabilities with DeFi's decentralized and transparent financial services, a new landscape of AI-driven DeFi (DeFi intelligence) is emerging. In this landscape, AI algorithms can improve decision-making processes in DeFi platforms, enhancing efficiency and risk management (Jiang & Liang, 2017).

At first glance, AI can automate various tasks traditionally performed by humans, such as administrative, managerial, and professional tasks (Sadman et al., 2022). By leveraging machine learning algorithms, AI can streamline operations, reduce costs, and improve efficiency in DeFi projects (Jiang & Liang, 2017; Sadman et al., 2022). Predictive analytics is one of the most promising applications of AI in DeFi (Raheman et al., 2021; McNally et al., 2018; de Souza et al., 2019). By analyzing large amounts of financial data, AI algorithms can make predictions about future market trends. AI techniques, such as machine learning, can analyze historical data and market trends to make predictions about asset prices, market movements, and investment opportunities. Thus, AI algorithms can identify patterns, anomalies, and correlations in financial data, enabling more accurate predictions and informed investment strategies (Blockchain Council, 2023).[2]This can benefit decentralized exchanges, lending platforms, and other DeFi applications that need to make informed decisions based on market conditions. Furthermore, AI has the potential to revolutionize the execution of smart contracts in DeFi (Liao et al., 2019; Zhuang et al., 2021), as it can enhance the capabilities of smart contracts by enabling them to analyze and respond to real-time data (Blockchain Magazine, 2023).[3] This can enable more dynamic and intelligent contract execution, improving efficiency and accuracy in DeFi applications. For instance, a lending protocol could use AI to continuously monitor a lender's collateral level and predict potential defaults before they happen. This proactive approach would not only protect lenders but also provide borrowers with more favorable terms.

The anonymity of DeFi services can make it difficult to detect fraudulent activity. However, AI's pattern recognition capabilities can help identify and prevent dishonest behavior. By analyzing user behavior and transaction patterns, AI can identify possible scams or hacks, enhancing the security of DeFi platforms. Therefore, DeFi platforms can leverage AI algorithms to detect and prevent fraudulent activities (Chen et al., 2018), identify security vulnerabilities (El-Dosuky & Eladl, 2019), and enhance cybersecurity measures.

AI can also revolutionize DeFi lending by enabling more accurate and efficient risk assessment (Dietzmann et al., 2020). In fact, one of the challenges in DeFi lending is accurately assessing a borrower's creditworthiness without relying on centralized financial institutions. AI can solve this problem by analyzing a borrower's transaction history and on-chain behavior to create a comprehensive credit profile. By analyzing factors such as collateralization levels, liquidation history, and transaction patterns, AI can develop a quantitative profile of borrowers and lenders. This information can then be used to offer loans with more favorable terms to borrowers with a good credit profile.

Automated market makers (AMMs) are a fundamental component of DeFi, facilitating the exchange of assets in a decentralized manner. By incorporating AI,

[2] https://www.blockchain-council.org/ai/the-transformative-influence-of-ai-on-decentralized-finance-exploring-the-impact/

[3] https://blockchainmagazine.net/everything-you-need-to-know-about-the-impact-of-ai-in-defi-space/

AMMs can become even more efficient. For example, AI-powered AMMs can learn from historical market performance to create an asset distribution function that accurately reflects current market conditions. Furthermore, by incorporating AI, DeFi insurance protocols can evaluate the risk of specific smart contracts and provide coverage accordingly thereby significantly enhancing the security of the DeFi ecosystem and attract more users. Interoperability, or the ability of different systems to work together, can further be enhanced by AI through automating the relocation of liquidity based on real-time analysis of market conditions. By allowing funds to flow freely across different blockchain platforms, interoperability generates liquidity and creates a more user-friendly environment. A last but not least aspect is about AI-powered chatbots and virtual assistants that can provide personalized assistance to users, answer their queries, and guide them through various DeFi processes. This can enhance the overall user experience and make DeFi more accessible to a wider audience.

Overall, AI has the potential to revolutionize various aspects of DeFi by improving efficiency, security, risk assessment, and user experience. Further research and development in this area can unlock new opportunities and advancements in the field of decentralized finance. However, the integration of AI in DeFi requires careful planning, testing, and monitoring to ensure its effectiveness, reliability, and compliance with regulatory requirements. As the field continues to evolve, it is expected that more examples of AI-powered DeFi platforms will emerge, offering innovative solutions and benefits to users in the decentralized finance ecosystem.

4 AI and DeFi: The Challenges to Overcome

Despite the potential benefits, the integration of AI and DeFi is not without its challenges such as transparency, explainability but also legal and regulatory challenges (Omohundro, 2014), data privacy concerns, ethical issues (Alibašić, 2023), and the potential for over-reliance on AI. Indeed, developers and entrepreneurs should focus on realistic applications of AI in DeFi and avoid unrealistic expectations or overreliance on AI for decision-making. It is essential to address these challenges to ensure the sustainable growth of the AI-DeFi ecosystem. One major concern is the potential for unintentional bias in the algorithms used by AI (Manyika et al., 2019). If the AI algorithms are trained on biased or incomplete data, it can perpetuate existing biases and inequalities in the financial system. Ensuring fairness and transparency in AI algorithms is crucial to avoid unintended discriminatory outcomes. The lack of transparency in how AI tools work can also be a concern. Understanding the inner workings of AI algorithms and the data they rely on is crucial for trust and accountability. Developers should strive for transparency and provide clear explanations of how AI is used in DeFi projects. Furthermore, introducing privately developed AI tools can bring decentralization risks. Lack of transparency and dependence on a single entity for AI development and support can undermine the decentralized nature of DeFi. Ensuring open-source development and community involvement can help mitigate these risks.

Importantly, security remains a persistent challenge in both DeFi and AI. Integrating AI into DeFi platforms introduces additional security risks, such as vulnerabilities in AI models, data privacy concerns, and potential exploitation of AI systems. Robust security measures need to be implemented to protect user data and prevent unauthorized access or manipulation of AI algorithms. To sum up, more substantiated experiments and research are needed to support the applicability of AI in financial institutions, including DeFi (Sadman et al., 2022). Conducting thorough testing and validation of AI models in real-world financial scenarios is essential to ensure their reliability and effectiveness. Addressing these challenges requires a combination of technical expertise, regulatory frameworks, and industry collaboration. By addressing these challenges, the integration of AI into DeFi has the potential to unlock new opportunities and enhance the efficiency, transparency, and inclusivity of decentralized financial services.

5 Epilogue: The Future of Decentralized Finance

As DeFi continues to grow, the integration of AI will likely take center stage. AI can unlock a new level of innovation in DeFi, powering a new generation of decentralized and intelligent financial services. However, the regulatory landscape surrounding DeFi is still evolving, and there are inconsistent regulations in different jurisdictions (Makarov & Schoar, 2022). This uncertainty poses challenges for DeFi adoption as it creates a lack of clarity for businesses and users. Notably, DeFi operates on a global scale, which makes it difficult to determine which jurisdiction's laws and regulations apply. Identifying the appropriate jurisdiction for regulatory purposes can be challenging and can lead to regulatory gaps and conflicts. Further, it can be difficult for tax authorities to track and collect taxes on decentralized transactions, which can create complexities in tax compliance and enforcement (Makarov & Schoar, 2022). DeFi platforms face also challenges in ensuring consumer protection. Issues such as anti-money laundering (AML), privacy concerns, and fraud prevention need to be addressed to build trust and protect users. In addition, some DeFi platforms are vulnerable to security risks, including vulnerabilities in smart contract code, hacking attempts, and malicious protocols. These risks, combined with the high volatility of the crypto market, can make it harder for DeFi to gain wide adoption with average users. Finally, DeFi adoption faces challenges in integrating with traditional financial systems, as financial institutions may be reluctant to use DeFi protocols without clear regulatory frameworks and protections in place to safeguard their funds.

Efforts are being made to address these challenges and pave the way for wider adoption and regulation of DeFi. Regulatory bodies are working to understand the DeFi space better and develop effective regulatory architectures suitable for decentralized finance.[4] Additionally, researchers and industry experts are exploring ways to regulate DeFi while preserving its innovative features and encouraging accountability and compliance.[5]

As DeFi continues to evolve, it's likely that the integration of AI will become more prevalent. The combination of these two movements seems inevitable and will unlock a new level of innovation in DeFi that powers a new generation of decentralized and intelligent financial services. The convergence of AI and DeFi represents a potential seminal moment in the evolution of finance. By leveraging the potential of both technologies, the financial landscape could be transformed in ways we can only begin to imagine.

Furthermore, as an integral part of the Web 3.0 ecosystem, decentralized finance (DeFi) presents a myriad of prospects and potential future developments that could transform the financial sector. Web 3.0, often termed as the "semantic web" is characterized by a more open, trustless, and permissionless nature, factors which are intrinsically aligned with the principles of DeFi. One of the primary limitations currently facing DeFi is the issue of scalability. Layer-2 solutions and other blockchain protocols are being extensively researched to alleviate this bottleneck (Mavridou et al., 2019). Further, in a Web 3.0 environment, the focus on interoperability will likely help to break down silos between different DeFi platforms and other web services, allowing for more complex financial activities.

Although DeFi platforms aim for decentralization, they cannot operate in complete isolation from existing financial systems and regulations. The implementation of decentralized governance models and compliance protocols, potentially facilitated through smart contracts, will be crucial (Zohar, 2015). In addition, Web 3.0 aims to create a more user-centric web, and DeFi will likely follow suit. Advanced AI algorithms and machine learning techniques may offer more personalized and efficient services (Ferragina & Scaiella, 2010) thereby making DeFi platforms more accessible and appealing to mainstream users, thereby increasing adoption rates. Advanced algorithms and decentralized oracles could also be employed to improve risk assessment and management in DeFi platforms (Adadi & Berrada, 2018). These improvements could lead to more robust financial products that are still aligned with the decentralized ethos of Web 3.0.

Overall, decentralized finance and artificial intelligence are revolutionizing various sectors, and entrepreneurship is no exception. As explained in this book, these technologies offer a range of solutions that mitigate traditional barriers to entry, improve decision-making, and unlock new avenues for value creation in entrepreneurial ventures. Both AI and DeFi can automate labor-intensive processes. DeFi and Smart contracts can eliminate the need for legal intermediaries, thereby reducing costs and time (Maurer et al., 2013). On the other hand, AI can automate customer service, data analysis, and even some aspects of product development, which allows entrepreneurs to focus more on strategic aspects of the business. AI

[4] https://www.sec.gov/news/statement/crenshaw-defi-20211109

[5] https://mitsloan.mit.edu/ideas-made-to-matter/decentralized-finance-4-challenges-to-consider

algorithms can also help identify underserved market niches or even personalize products and services to meet individual customer needs, thereby offering avenues for market expansion (Li and al., 2018). DeFi expands this by facilitating cross-border transactions without the usual costs or complications, making international expansion more accessible for startups. The integration of DeFi and AI in entrepreneurship is not merely an additive but a synergistic relationship that has the potential to significantly enhance entrepreneurial capabilities and outcomes. By democratizing access to financial resources, enhancing decision-making, improving operational efficiency, and enabling market expansion, these technologies make a compelling case for their role in catalyzing entrepreneurship. However, while the promise is great, the journey is still in its early stages. The integration of AI and DeFi will undoubtedly face challenges and hurdles. But with continued innovation and collaboration, the dawn of a new financial era—the era of DeFi intelligence—is within reach.

References

Adadi, A., & Berrada, M. (2018). Peering into the mist: A survey of the decentralized internet's functionalities, limitations, and upcoming challenges. *Journal of Network and Computer Applications, 114*, 24–46.

Alibašić, H. (2023). Developing an ethical framework for responsible artificial intelligence (AI) and machine learning (ML) applications in cryptocurrency trading: A consequentialism ethics analysis. *FinTech, 2*(3), 430–443.

Blockchain Council. (2023). Web page accessible at: https://www.blockchain-council.org/ai/the-transformativeinfluence-of-ai-on-decentralized-finance-exploring-the-impact/

Blockchain Magazine. (2023). Web page accessible at: https://blockchainmagazine.net/everything-you-need-toknow-about-the-impact-of-ai-in-defi-space/

Chen, W., Zheng, Z., Cui, J., Ngai, E., Zheng, P., & Zhou, Y. (2018, April). Detecting ponzi schemes on ethereum: Towards healthier blockchain technology. In *Proceedings of the 2018 world wide web conference* (pp. 1409–1418).

Danks, D., & London, A. J. (2017, August). Algorithmic bias in autonomous systems. In Ijcai (Vol. 17, No. 2017, pp. 4691-4697).

de Souza, M. J. S., Almudhaf, F. W., Henrique, B. M., Negredo, A. B. S., Ramos, D. G. F., Sobreiro, V. A., & Kimura, H. (2019). Can artificial intelligence enhance the bitcoin bonanza. *The Journal of Finance and Data Science, 5*(2), 83–98.

Dietzmann, C., Heines, R., & Alt, R. (2020). The convergence of distributed ledger technology and artificial intelligence: An end-to-end reference lending process for financial services. In *Proceedings: Twenty-eighth European conference on information systems (ECIS2020)*. Association for Information Systems.

El-Dosuky, M. A., & Eladl, G. H. (2019). DOORchain: Deep ontology-based operation research to detect malicious smart contracts. In *New knowledge in information systems and technologies* (Vol. 1, pp. 538–545). Springer International Publishing.

Ferragina, P., & Scaiella, U. (2010). TAGME: On-the-fly annotation of short text fragments (by Wikipedia entities). In *Proceedings of the 19th ACM international conference on information and knowledge management* (pp. 1625–1628).

Frey, C. B., & Osborne, M. A. (2017). The future of employment: How susceptible are jobs to computerisation? *Technological Forecasting and Social Change, 114*, 254–280.

Goodfellow, I., Bengio, Y., & Courville, A. (2016). *Deep learning*. MIT press.

Jiang, Z., & Liang, J. (2017, September). Cryptocurrency portfolio management with deep reinforcement learning. In *2017 Intelligent systems conference (IntelliSys)* (pp. 905–913). IEEE.
Jobin, A., Ienca, M., & Vayena, E. (2019). The global landscape of AI ethics guidelines. *Nature Machine Intelligence, 1*(9), 389–399.
Kaplan, A., & Haenlein, M. (2019). Siri, Siri, in my hand: Who's the fairest in the land? On the interpretations, illustrations, and implications of artificial intelligence. *Business Horizons, 62*(1), 15–25.
Liao, J. W., Tsai, T. T., He, C. K., & Tien, C. W. (2019, October). Soliaudit: Smart contract vulnerability assessment based on machine learning and fuzz testing. In *2019 Sixth International Conference on Internet of Things: Systems, Management and Security (IOTSMS)* (pp. 458–465). IEEE.
Makarov, I., & Schoar, A. (2022). *Cryptocurrencies and decentralized finance (DeFi) (No. w30006)*. National Bureau of Economic Research.
Manyika, J., Silberg, J., & Presten, B. (2019). What do we do about the biases in AI. *Harvard Business Review, 25*.
Maurer, B., Nelms, T. C., & Swartz, L. (2013). "when perhaps the real problem is money itself!" the practical materiality of bitcoin. *Social Semiotics, 23*(2), 261–277.
Mavridou, A., Laszka, A., Stachtiari, E., & Dubey, A. (2019). VeriSolid: Correct-by-design smart contracts for Ethereum. In *Proceedings of the 22nd International Conference on Financial Cryptography and Data Security* (FC).
McNally, S., Roche, J., & Caton, S. (2018, March). Predicting the price of bitcoin using machine learning. In *2018 26th euromicro international conference on parallel, distributed and network-based processing (PDP)* (pp. 339–343). IEEE.
Omohundro, S. (2014). Cryptocurrencies, smart contracts, and artificial intelligence. *AI matters, 1*(2), 19–21.
Raheman, A., Kolonin, A., Goertzel, B., Hegyközi, G., & Ansari, I. (2021, December). Architecture of automated crypto-finance agent. In *2021 International Symposium on Knowledge, Ontology, and Theory (KNOTH)* (pp. 10–14). IEEE.
Russell, S., & Norvig, P. (2016). *Artificial intelligence: A modern approach*. Pearson.
Sadman, N., Ahsan, M. M., Rahman, A., Siddique, Z., & Gupta, K. (2022). Promise of AI in DeFi, a systematic review. *Digital, 2*, 88.
Zhuang, Y., Liu, Z., Qian, P., Liu, Q., Wang, X., & He, Q. (2021, January). Smart contract vulnerability detection using graph neural networks. In *Proceedings of the Twenty-Ninth International Conference on International Joint Conferences on Artificial Intelligence* (pp. 3283-3290).
Zohar, A. (2015). Bitcoin: Under the hood. *Communications of the ACM, 58*(9), 104–113.

Sami Basly holds a Ph.D. in Management Sciences (University of Bordeaux) and is authorized to supervise Doctoral research (University Paris Nanterre). Before joining the University Paris Nanterre, he was a lecturer at the University of Bordeaux. He is interested in family businesses, digital entrepreneurship, and digital technologies. He has conducted research on family businesses, internationalization, and digital transformation, and has published his findings in many national and international journals (Management International, Review of Entrepreneurship, Journal of Entrepreneurship, etc.).

SPRINGER NATURE

GPSR Compliance

The European Union's (EU) General Product Safety Regulation (GPSR) is a set of rules that requires consumer products to be safe and our obligations to ensure this.

If you have any concerns about our products, you can contact us on ProductSafety@springernature.com

In case Publisher is established outside the EU, the EU authorized representative is:

Springer Nature Customer Service Center GmbH
Europaplatz 3
69115 Heidelberg, Germany

The manufacturer's authorised representative in the EU is Springer Nature Customer Service Centre GmbH, Europaplatz 3, 69115 Heidelberg, Germany. If you have any concerns regarding our products, please contact ProductSafety@springernature.com

Printed and bound by CPI Group (UK) Ltd, Croydon, CR0 4YY
28/09/2026
02224074-0011